COAST and COUNTRY

Geology Walks in and around Dorset
(including excursions within the World Heritage Site)

compiled by members of the
Dorset Geologists' Association Group
to celebrate 10 years of their existence
1993 - 2003

This book is dedicated to the memory of
Michael House
eminent geologist and true friend
1930 - 2002

Published by the Dorset Geologists' Association Group
© Dorset Geologists' Association Group 2003
ISBN   0-9544354-0-0

CONTENTS

Excursions

Note: Sectioned geological logs, chapters 7, Culverhole and 14, Kimmeridge Bay, should be read from left to right and from bottom to top

ILLUSTRATIONS **Front cover**: *(top left clockwise)*
photographs by *Adrian Brokenshire, John Chaffey,*
Richard Edmonds, George Raggett, Doreen Smith, Jo Thomas
Kimmeridge Bay
Melbury Bottom
Lyme Regis
Compton Bottom
Osmington Bay
Old Bell, Cerne Abbas
Fossil Forest, Lulworth
Lano's Arch, Portland

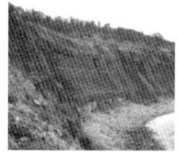

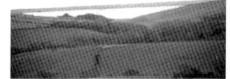

Title page:
photographs by *Margaret Dyos, Doreen Smith*
Weymouth Anticline and Portland
Millennium Celebrations: Michael House and a
Field Trip around Sutton Poyntz *(see chapter 25)*
Evidence for Milankovitch Cycles at Burton Bradstock

This page:
photographs by *Ray Chapman, John Patrick,*
Doreen Smith, Martin Vine
Pinhay Bay
The Fleet and Chesil Beach
The Hardy Monument
Bran Point from Ringstead Bay
Fountain Rock, White Nothe
Ammonite, Kimmeridge Bay

Back cover:
Swyre Head and Bat's Head from the Durdle promontory
(with permission from the Weld Estate) The spectacular
chalk cliffs from White Nothe to the eastern end of the
World Heritage Site are, of course, Cretaceous.
photograph: *John Chaffey*

Page 17
Michael House at White Nothe, photograph: *Ray Chapman*
Chairman's Field Trip and DGAG picnic 2002
photographs: *Cathy Race*

Chapter illustrations are by the authors unless indicated otherwise. Some of
the maps are derived from Ordnance Survey mapping, some from Dorset. A
Photographic Atlas, others are computer line drawings *(see page 197)*.
Fossil drawings, apart from chapter 19, figure 4 are © *Ray Chapman*

FOREWORD

This book is a remarkable combination of geology and people. First, the geology: the coast of Dorset, and adjacent east Devon, was given World Heritage status by the United Nations Educational, Scientific and Cultural Organisation (UNESCO) in December 2001. It ranks, therefore, with other natural World Heritage sites such as the Grand Canyon and the Great Barrier Reef. This new status was granted because the coast is recognised as having global significance in displaying a record of past environmental change in a rock record commencing some 250 million years ago and spanning 185 million years. But geology and beautiful landscapes are not confined to the coast - there is much to see inland as well as in Dorset towns, the character of which owes much to the use of local building stones and in some cases exotic imports. This book gives insights into all these facets of Dorset geology.

People have been investigating Dorset geology for more than two centuries, with early workers contributing much to the development of the science of geology *(see pages 9-10)*. Today the county provides a wonderful resource for visitors, researchers, and students of all ages. This resource needs to be conserved and explained so that visitors will continue to enjoy and learn from it. Members of the Dorset Geologists' Association Group (DGAG) have contributed to conservation work through their involvement with Dorset's Important Geological Sites Group (DIGS). The publication of this guide book is a wonderful extension of their work. In 2001 John Chaffey, Chairman of DGAG, suggested that a celebratory guide book be compiled to be published to coincide with DGAG's Tenth Anniversary. Since then the various authors have walked many miles and laboured over successive drafts.

As someone who became hooked on Dorset geology as a 16 year old A-level student, I look forward to using the book to explore parts of the county I have yet to visit and to see some old haunts with new eyes.

Chris Wilson
Department of Earth Sciences
The Open University
November 2002

PREFACE

This book has been written by members of the Dorset Geologists' Association Group which was formed in 1993. It is an easy-to-follow guide to a wide range of geological walks and car excursions in Dorset and neighbouring parts of adjoining counties. Many of the walks are half-day excursions although there are some longer ones. A location map is included with each excursion to be used with the appropriate Ordnance Survey map and, if available, the relevant British Geological Survey map.

By way of an introduction there is an overview of the geology of Dorset and the surrounding areas which sets the scene for the excursions. The majority of the excursions are coastal and inland Dorset. East Devon, Somerset, Wiltshire and Hampshire also feature in various chapters. Each excursion is presented in a similar format: a purpose is identified and practical details on parking and other facilities are given if available. The geological setting then outlines the excursion's place in the broader scene and details follow of the main localities to be visited. At the end of the book *(pages 206-208)* a glossary explains some of the less familiar geological terms *(indicated by slightly darker print)*. A brief list on page 16 gives suggestions for further general reading and a bibliography of more specific information is on pages 200 and 201.

The Dorset Group of the Geologists' Association includes both professional and amateur geologists, some working in the county, some now retired but maintaining a very active interest in the discipline. The principal aim of the Association is to promote interest in the fascinating geology of Dorset and areas adjoining the County. Field excursions are held most months and many of the itineraries have found their way into this book. A newsletter is published every two months and a Mineral and Fossil Fair is organised every August in the market town of Wimborne. Members' evenings are held to discuss newly acquired specimens and to share geological experiences. There is also a DGAG web site.

Dorset's Important Geological Sites Group (DIGS) has the conservation of valued geological sites within the County as its principal aim. Over sixty sites of geological and geomorphological importance have been identified and designated in Dorset, each with the owner's permission where appropriate. The sites are inland throughout the County ranging from individual quarries to the high valleys of Cranborne Chase, to sites along the Purbeck Chalk ridge and the whole of the Isle of Portland. Maintenance of the sites is carried out from time to time and interpretive boards are in position at some of them. Leaflets on some of the sites are available from the DIGS web site and are also published when funding can be obtained.

Many DGAG members are also members of the Open University Geological Society and both groups form work parties for RIGS maintenance as well as sharing some of the field trip expeditions. Many of the original DGAG Committee were graduates of OU geology courses.

The Dorset and East Devon Coast has been recognised by UNESCO as a World Heritage Site because the cliffs and foreshore, between Exmouth in east Devon and Old Harry Rocks in east Dorset, display 185 million years of the Earth's history in just 152km of coastline. The rocks record a virtually complete succession through the Triassic, Jurassic and Cretaceous periods of geological time, a feature unique to this coast. In addition to the geology, the coast contains a number of superb fossil localities. Put together, the rocks and fossils reveal a fascinating story of ancient Triassic deserts, tropical Jurassic seas, fossil forests and Cretaceous swamps complete with dinosaurs.

Along the length of the World Heritage Site the overall dip of the rocks is gently to the east. The oldest rocks therefore, are to be found in the west with younger rocks forming the cliffs to the east. The relationship between the Upper Cretaceous strata and the underlying rocks is slightly more complex and represents a spectacular example of an unconformity.

The coast also demonstrates ongoing geomorphological processes which include landslides, Chesil Beach and the 'classic' Purbeck coastline. The diversity of the geology gives rise to the beautiful and varied coastline and landscape but it is also responsible for the distribution of building stones, the use of which has created the character of local towns and villages.

Not surprisingly, this coast has been the subject of extensive research over the last two hundred and fifty years, the list of researchers reading like a 'Who's Who' of the earth sciences. New discoveries are made virtually every year while the application of modern research techniques leads to the development of new thinking about this coast and the story that it has to tell. The World Heritage Site extends from the cliff tops to the low tide mark and lies entirely within a number of Sites of Special Scientific Interest (SSSI), the designation that provides protection.

The coastal exposures of the World Heritage Site reflect the geology and geomorphology of the whole of the County of Dorset.

Please treat all sites visited, coastal or inland, with respect and read the useful and sensible guide lines offered on pages 198/199.

John Chaffey Chairman: Dorset Geologists' Association Group

useful contact details are available at
www.dorsetgeologistsassocation.com   details of Dorset geology maps can
www.dorsetrigs.com   be obtained from www.bgs.ac.uk
www.ougs.org.uk   Keyworth Nottingham NG12 5GG
www.jurassiccoast.com   Tel: 0115-936 3241

ACKNOWLEDGEMENTS

John Chaffey, Ray Chapman, Ron Hammock, Alan Holiday, George Raggett and Doreen Smith are the members of the Dorset GA Group responsible for the production of this book. A special word of thanks must go to Doreen Smith who has co-ordinated contributions from authors and prepared the text for printing and publication. We are also much indebted to Professor Michael House, who wrote the Introduction, and to Professor Chris Wilson of the Open University, who kindly contributed a Foreword. Officers of the British Geological Survey, Exeter readily helped us over technical matters and members of the World Heritage Team provided the liaison with Dorset and Devon County Councils.

The Dorset Geologists' Association Group wishes to acknowledge financial support from the Curry Fund of the Geologists' Association, Dorset and Devon County Councils and the Dorset Coast Forum, English Nature, the Environment Agency, Wessex Water, West Dorset District Council and Weymouth and Portland Borough Council. The British Geological Survey generously waived copyright fees for the several maps labelled *"by permission of the British Geological Survey, IPR/34-11C"*. Dorset County Council gave permission for the use of aerial photographs from: Dorset. A Photographic Atlas ©2000. Mrs Francesca Radcliffe also allowed us to make use of aerial photographs and Ms Semi Vine kindly drew location sketches.

We also would like to thank all members of the Dorset Geologists' Association Group and the Open University Geological Society and others who generously took out pre-publication subscriptions to the book. Finally we extend our gratitude to all the members and friends of the Association who volunteered to walk, drive or read the routes to check them for accuracy.

Note: Routes given in this guide do not necessarily imply a right of way. Where necessary, readers should seek permission to use footpaths and to gain access to exposures. Notes on safety have been included on pages 200 -1 but readers are reminded that the Dorset Geologists' Association Group cannot take responsibility for accident or injury which may occur on the excursion routes. Several of the excursions involve walking along exposed clifftops and proper care should be taken at all times. Where a route is tide-dependent, the appropriate tide-tables should be consulted before setting out and range walks also need to be checked as to when they are open.

The Association has done its utmost to ensure that the contents of this book are accurate and up-to-date. Change along the coast, and in some interior locations, is inevitable. If you find any modifications at the localities, then the Association would be very interested to hear from you.

Contacts: telephone 01300 320811 e mail Heldon47@breathemail.net
web site: www.dorsetgeologistsassociation.com

AUTHORS

Adrian Brokenshire   Past Chairman, Dorset Geologists' Association

John Chaffey   Chairman, Dorset Geologists' Association

Robert Chandler   Geologist, Shirley High School, Surrey

Ray Chapman   Secretary, Dorset Geologists' Association

Mike Cosgrove   Dr. Mike Cosgrove

Volker Dietze   Geologist, Riesburg, Germany

Richard Edmonds   Earth Science Manager, World Heritage Site Team

Paul Ensom   Head of Curation, Natural History Museum, London

Steve Etches   Dorset Geologists' Association

Ramues Gallois   Geological Consultant

Jake Hancock   Senior Research Fellow, Imperial College London

Alan Holiday   Lecturer in Geology, Weymouth College
Chairman, Dorset's Important Geological Sites

Michael House   Emeritus Professor of Geology,
University of Southampton

Hugh Prudden   Secretary, Somerset Geology Group
(Somerset Wildlife Trust)

George Raggett   Branch Organiser, Wessex Branch of the
Open University Geological Society

Doreen Smith   Events, web site and Newsletter Editor
Dorset Geologists' Association

Jo Thomas   Dorset Geologists' Association

Map showing main road and rail connections of the area with numbers showing approximate locations of the excursions in the book. Reproduced, in part, from OS maps. on behalf of the Controller of HMSO © Crown Copyright Licence Number 100039946.

INTRODUCTION Professor Michael House

The diverse scenery of Dorset, from the coastal cliffs and beaches to the inland hills and valleys, reflects the variations of Dorset rocks and their structural pattern. Dorset demonstrates well how the landscape and scenery of an area depend on the underlying geology. The vegetation and potential cultivation vary because of the nature of the bedrock which provides the character and nutrients for natural and human development. The landscape changes with the long-continued processes of climate and weathering. These processes have developed the variations of softness, hardness and chemical features of the rocks and produced the distinctive topography and vegetation. The Dorset rock succession comprises lithified sediments belonging to the Jurassic, Cretaceous and Tertiary *(youngest)* divisions. These three units form the most distinctive landscapes areas of Dorset (*Figure 1*).

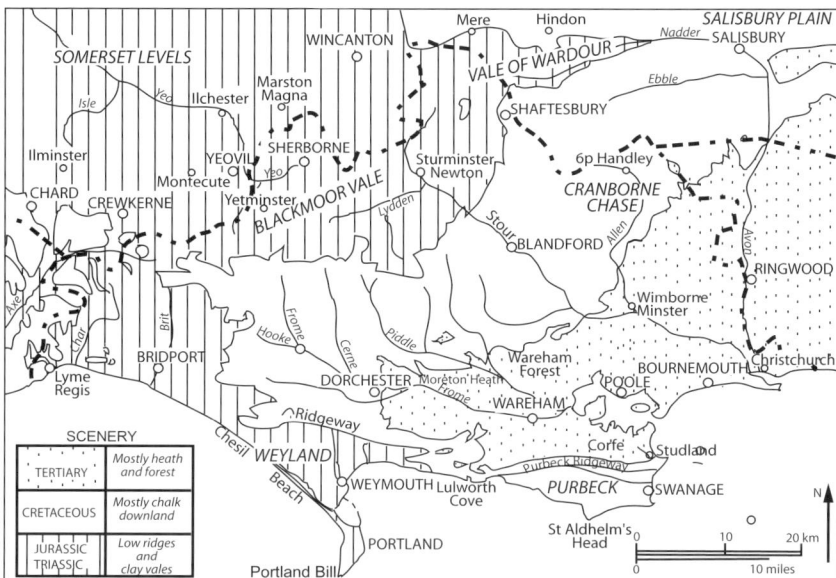

Figure 1 Map showing the three main scenic and physiographical areas of Dorset and adjacent areas. Based in part on BGS maps by permission of the British Geological Survey, IPR/34-11C

The Jurassic rocks comprise a variety of formations of clay, sand and limestone deposited under marine conditions, which are generally low-lying as they are relatively soft. These rocks contain lush areas of woodland with grassland for dairy cattle. They form the northern to western swathe of low-lying ground of the Vale of Wardour, Vale of Blackmoor and the Marshwood Vale, and this pattern repeats to the south in the Weymouth lowlands or Weyland. Notice how these form an arcuate curve reflecting a depression, along the line of the main Stour Valley to the east, which is dependent on a downsagging of that area along the Frome Syncline or Basin.

The Cretaceous rocks are dominated by the Chalk, a unit up to 400 metres thick, which mostly forms the highest hills of inland Dorset and the vertical coastal chalk cliffs. It is the most highly cultivated area. In Mediaeval times it was a major sheep-rearing area but is now mainly used for arable crops of barley, wheat and rape. These downs form the broad outcrop which forms Salisbury Plain to the north-east, Cranborne Chase and the central North Dorset Heights. They then curve to the south and east forming the narrow South Dorset Ridgeway which continues into the Purbeck Ridgeway to Ballard Down, north of Swanage. The narrowness of the southern outcrop is due to the fact that there the Chalk is turned to dip almost vertically, hence the outcrop width is scarcely more than the thickness of the Chalk. Again the outcrop shape reflects the geological structure around the Frome Syncline. The northern margin of the outcrop forms high, bold scarps overlooking the Jurassic vales. Beneath the Chalk are the Gault and Greensand which led to settlement of the many spring-line villages at the scarp foot. There are excellent panoramas over the Jurassic areas particularly at Gold Hill, Shaftesbury (ST 861228), Lewesdon Hill (ST 436013) and Pilsdon Pen (ST 413013) which are all Upper Greensand, Bulbarrow (SU 783059) and Gore Hill (ST 635039) both Chalk and the Hardy Monument (SY 613876) Tertiary remnants over Chalk.

The Tertiary rocks occur mainly in the east. They comprise sands and clays which, with the overlying Quaternary gravels, form extensive low-lying heathland and forested areas, naturally covered in silica-tolerating plants. This geology extends to the east into the larger New Forest area of Hampshire. Only the Lower Tertiary (Palaeogene) rocks are represented. After their deposition there was folding along the Frome Syncline which occurred in mid-Tertiary *(probably Miocene)* times.

More recent deposits occur as alluvium and gravel terraces along the river valleys, residual gravels on the downs and spreads of high level gravel material resulting from mid-Tertiary high sea levels in excess of 200 metres. Sea level fluctuated, during the Quaternary ice ages, with ice cap formation or melting. Some 18,000 years ago sea level was 100 metres lower than at present thus most of the beaches and superficial deposits have a complex history which is still poorly understood.

History of the Development of Geology and Palaeontology in Dorset
Following a tour with two friends in 1797, W. G. Maton in 1797 published

a map of the geology of south-west England at a scale of 17 miles to an inch, the first geological map known to cover Dorset although discrimination was hardly more than shown on *Figure 1*. William Smith (1769-1839) the 'Father of English Geology' had, by the early 1790s, established the detailed succession of Jurassic rocks around Bath and, probably in 1795, had mapped the Charmouth coast. Soon after that he had covered many other parts of the country so that he published a geological map of the whole of England and Wales in 1815. In addition to this his major contribution was the recognition that particular strata carried distinctive fossils. This recognition formed the subject of a book *"Strata Identified by Organized Fossils'* published 1816-1819. By then he had been freely giving his ideas to others for over twenty years.

A group developed around Lyme Regis and Charmouth which was to have fundamental repercussions on the development of geology internationally. William Buckland (1784-1856) was born in Axminster and knew the Lyme Regis coast well as a boy. He was destined to become, in 1813, Reader in Mineralogy at Oxford University where his vigorous teaching did much to ensure national interest. The role, around this time, of the brothers J. J. Conybeare (1779-1824) and W. D. Conybeare (1797-1857) is significant. The latter, with W. Phillips in 1822, published the first book on *'Outlines of the Geology of England and Wales'* including much work on Dorset. Henry de la Beche (1796-1855), destined to become the first Director of the Geological Survey, settled in Dawlish, Charmouth and then Lyme Regis (1811) where he lived in the present Lloyds Bank building. In 1822 he published an account of the geology of the coast between Bridport and Babbacombe, Devon. Buckland and de la Beche, in 1830 and 1836, published geological maps east to Portland. By then Thomas Webster (1773-1844) had reported in detail on the rocks of eastern Dorset and the Isle of Wight, together with a geological map, in Englefield's *'Picturesque Beauties of the Isle of Wight'* (1816). With the establishment, under De la Beche, of the Geological Survey of the United Kingdom 1835, geological maps have regularly been revised to the present day.

The fossils of Dorset are famous world wide. In 1668 Robert Hooke referred to the ammonites *(Snakestones)* of Portland as being of a "prodigeous bigness". Undoubtedly the most remarkable period of discovery was that of the marine reptiles particularly of plesiosaurs, ichthyosaurs and pterodactyls. That period will always be associated with the collector Mary Anning (1799-1847) "the greatest fossilist the world ever knew" who lived in Lyme Regis and who is buried in the churchyard there. *Plesiosaurus* and *Ichthyosaurus* were originally described by W.D. Conybeare (1824-26) with illustrations drawn by de la Beche. Buckland, in 1829, described a pterodactyl. All this led to a reconstruction of 'More Ancient Dorset' *(Durior Antiquior)* the first palaeoecological reconstruction, drawn by De la Beche, about 1830, to raise money for Mary Anning when she fell on poor times. The Lulworth 'Fossil Forest' was described and illustrated by Webster (1816) and the remarkable fossil cycadeoids of Portland were described by Buckland in 1829. Hundreds of palaeontologists have contributed to knowledge of Dorset fossils since those pioneer days. Good displays of fossils are to be found in the Dorset County Museum Dorchester, The Philpot Museum Lyme Regis, The Heritage Centre Charmouth and in Dorset fossil shops, especially in Lyme Regis.

Rock Succession

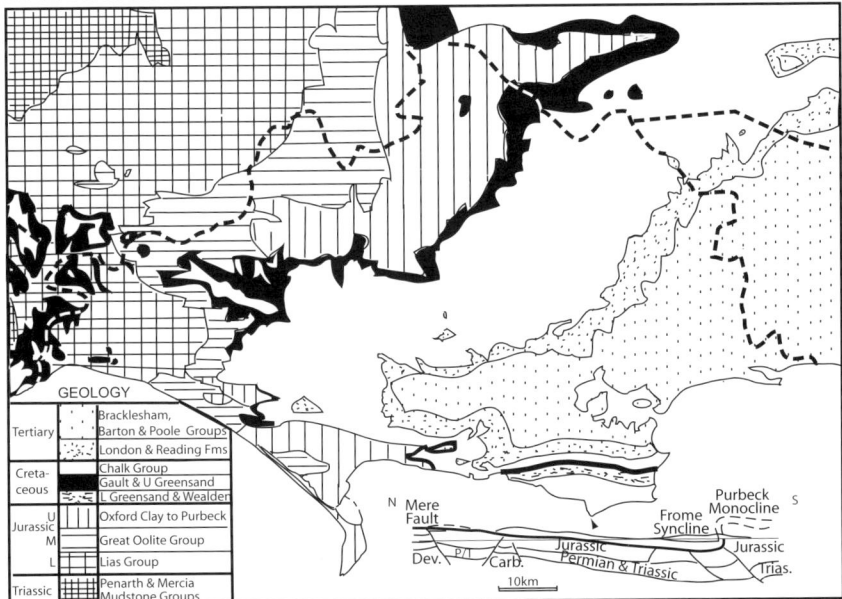

Figure 2 Map showing the distribution of geological units in Dorset. Based in part on BGS maps by permission of the British Geological Survey, IPR/34-11C

The distribution and succession of sedimentary rocks of Dorset and adjacent areas is shown in *Figures 2 and 3*. The succession includes a full section of the Mesozoic Era, perhaps the most spectacular anywhere in the world, which justifies its inclusion as a World Heritage Site. Most units thicken towards the east and southeast towards what is thought to be an area of regular deepening or down-sagging of the sea floor called the Wessex Basin, centred on the Solent area near Southampton.

Figure 3 Main geological divisions and successions of strata in the Dorset area

ERA	PERIOD		DIVISION	STAGE
	QUATERNARY		River alluvium, raised beaches, gravel spreads	
CAINOZOIC	LOWER TERTIARY (Paleogene)	U. EOCENE	Barton Beds Group (c.67.5m)	BARTONIAN
		M. EOCENE	Bracklesham Formation (180m)	LUTETIAN
		L. EOCENE	London Clay (110m)	YPRESIAN
		PALAEOCENE	West Park Farm Member (0-30m)	PALAEOCENE
MESOZOIC	CRETACEOUS	UPPER	Upper Chalk (250m)	(Maastrichtian) SENONIAN
			Middle Chalk (41m)	TURONIAN
			Lower Chalk (57m)	CENOMANIAN
		LOWER	Upper Greensand (60m) Gault Clay (12m)	ALBIAN
			Lower Greensand (0-60m)	APTIAN
			Unconformity	
			Wealden Group (up to 716m) Purbeck Beds (119m)	NEOCOMIAN
	JURASSIC	UPPER	Portland Limestone (73m)	PORTLANDIAN
			Kimmeridge Clay (532m)	KIMMERIDGIAN
		MIDDLE or GREAT OOLITE GROUP	Corallian (60m) Oxford Clay (230m)	OXFORDIAN
			Kellaways Beds (20 m) Cornbrash (7.1m)	CALLOVIAN
			Forest Marble (75m) Frome Clay (38m) Wattonensis Beds (7.6m) Fuller's Earth Rock (0-12m) Fuller's Earth Clay (250m)	BATHONIAN
			Inferior Oolite (9m)	BAJOCIAN
				AALENIAN
		UPPER LIAS	Bridport Sands (43m) Down Cliff Clay (21m) Junction Bed (4m)	TOARCIAN
		MIDDLE LIAS	Marlstone Rock Band (0.6m) Thorncombe Sands (27m) Margaritatus Beds (23m) Eype Clay (68m) Three Tiers (10m)	PLIENSBACHIAN
		LOWER LIAS	Green Ammonite Beds (34m) Belemnite Stone (0.15m) Belemnite Marls (23m)	
			Black Ven Marls (46m) Shales with Beef (25m)	SINEMURIAN
			Blue Lias (32m)	HETTANGIAN
	TRIASSIC		White Lias (Penarth Group) (c.18m) Mercia Mudstone Group (? 440m) Otter Sandstone Formation (80m) Budleigh Salterton Pebble Beds (68m) Aylesbeare Mudstone Group (c. 530m)	

The Triassic System. Triassic rocks of the early Mesozoic are well developed in Devon especially along the cliffs from west of Lyme Regis, at Axmouth and Sidmouth to Orcombe Rocks west of Budleigh Salterton. From west of Lyme Regis they dip eastward underneath the Dorset succession and both Triassic and Permian rocks are well known from deep boreholes in most parts of Dorset. The Permian and Triassic rocks (*New Red Sandstone)* were formed under terrestrial conditions of stony and sandy desert, dune and playa lake conditions. These rocks lie with a marked unconformity on intensively folded and thrust Devonian and Carboniferous rocks. Their deformation resulted from the Hercynian or Variscan Orogeny, the later stages of which were associated with the granite intrusions of Dartmoor and Bodmin Moor. Although altered Carboniferous and Devonian rocks are known from deep boreholes below Dorset, no evidence for granites has been found. The Triassic succession appears along the east Devon coast. At Budleigh Salterton there is a remarkable pebble bed of derived ovate and well-rounded Ordovician quartzite pebbles. These pebbles were later distributed, in low level gravel spreads at times of higher and lower sea level, into the south Dorset area. Above this bed is the Otter Sandstone, part of the Sherwood Sandstone Group which underground in east Dorset, forms part of the oil reservoir for the Wytch Farm field, the largest onshore oilfield in Europe. The whole Triassic section is terrestrial in nature until the very end when marine incursions over the desert areas occurred with the White Lias or Penarth Group, seen in Pinhay Bay just west of Lyme Regis.

The Jurassic System. Dorset is particularly famous for its Jurassic rocks. They are almost completely composed of shallow-marine sedimentary rocks, deposited as the proto-Atlantic formed and extended between the separating European and North American areas. The succession shows several shallowing-upward sequences. The Lower and Middle Lias represent the first major cycle with initial shales and limestones (*Blue Lias)* followed by deeper-water shales which then shallow to sands, then limestones in the upper part of the Middle Lias. The best record of marine reptiles is from the Blue Lias and Shales-with-Beef. The next cycle starts with the Down Cliff Clay which passes to the shallower water Bridport Sands and the limestones of the Inferior Oolite. A third deepening results in the Fuller's Earth Clay with eventual shallowing in the Forest Marble and the terminating Cornbrash limestone. Deepening resumes with the Kellaways Beds and Oxford Clay, passes through sands of the early Corallian, to the limestones of the bulk of the Corallian. The Kimmeridge Clay represents a major deepening with shallower water

Portland Sand following and the shallowest, purest water limestones of the Portland Freestone above. At the top of the Portland Beds marine conditions cease. The overlying Purbeck Beds are fresh water in origin, the lowest beds with tufas and fossil forests (*best seen east of Lulworth Cove*). The Jurassic/Cretaceous boundary is probably to be drawn a little above the base of the Purbeck Beds. In detail, the succession shows an incredible range of sedimentary environments and an enormous diversity in the fossil remains of the original fauna. Ammonites, in the marine sediments, bivalves and gastropods are common throughout.

Lower Cretaceous System. The lower Cretaceous follows in natural sequence with the bulk of the Purbeck Beds of limestones worked for stone especially in Purbeck. These beds carry an incredible fauna of insects, fish, turtles, dinosaurs and famous early mammal remains. The Wealden, humid conditions and mostly alluvial deposits, represents a return towards New Red Sandstone arid desert terrestrial deposits.

Mid-Cretaceous Tectonic Events. After the deposition of the Wealden Group there was a widespread period of east-west normal faulting in the area. This probably marked a major phase in the break up of margins to the proto-Atlantic. In the south Dorset area these show as east-west faults with down-throw to the south. The dating is probably pre-Aptian in age but as the Lower Greensand is absent west of Lulworth, the faulting is usually referred to as pre-Albian. A major period of marine erosion and peneplanation then took place so that the Gault and Upper Greensand, which are marine deposits, rest with marked unconformity on the older faulted rocks. A transect is illustrated here (*Figure 4*) showing this relationship between Swanage and Lyme Regis.

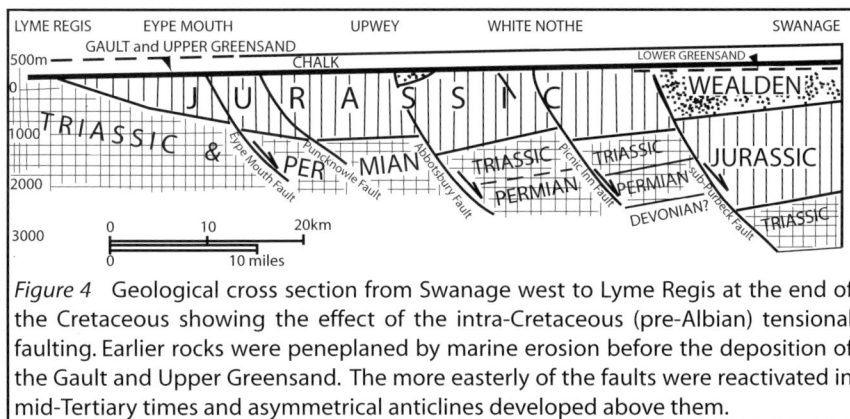

Figure 4 Geological cross section from Swanage west to Lyme Regis at the end of the Cretaceous showing the effect of the intra-Cretaceous (pre-Albian) tensional faulting. Earlier rocks were peneplaned by marine erosion before the deposition of the Gault and Upper Greensand. The more easterly of the faults were reactivated in mid-Tertiary times and asymmetrical anticlines developed above them.

As a result of the pre-Albian erosion, there is a complete succession of the Jurassic and early Cretaceous in east Dorset with the Gault and

Upper Greensand cutting down onto older and older rocks westward. By Lyme Regis the Gault and Upper Greensand rest on Lower Lias, in east Devon on Triassic and south of Exeter, on the Palaeozoic basement.

Middle and Upper Cretaceous System. The transgressive Lower Greensand and Gault reintroduced marine conditions into the area. The Upper Greensand, rich in the mineral glauconite which gives the rock its colour, is very siliceous in the upper part where cherts were formed. A sharp break, which is also slightly unconformable, introduces the great Chalk Group. At the base is the Cenomanian Basement Bed, rich in ammonites in many areas. The Chalk is thought to have formed under moderately deep waters in which calcareous algae, known as coccospheres, lived in the upper layers. Their remains, after passing through the gut of marine plankton, formed coccolith oozes now calcified as the Chalk. Levels of harder chalk, the 'Chalk Rock' horizons, are thought to represent shallowing events. The older classification in which a Lower Chalk without flints, a Middle Chalk with few flints and an Upper Chalk with many flints is now superseded but still provides a key to level in this thick division. Clay-with-Flints, often found on top of the Chalk, is a residuum of flints and clay material, probably resulting from *in-situ* rotting of a higher, more argillaceous chalk.

Lower Cainozoic or Palaeogene. At the close of the Cretaceous there was a period of regression and sea-level fall. There was also modest folding so that the age of the topmost Chalk varies from place to place. The very youngest Maastrichtian Chalk is not known to outcrop in Dorset. The Tertiary introduces alluvial and estuarine conditions but the London Clay is marine. In general the Tertiary sediments are thought to have been derived from land areas to the west. Sands and gravels are mostly derived from Cretaceous rocks to the west and sand and chert gravels predominate with plant remains. Several marine levels occur, the greatest of which is the extremely fossiliferous Barton Clay.

Mid-Tertiary Tectonic Events. Following the deposition of the early Tertiary deposits, and probably associated with the regional effects of the Alpine Orogeny, was a period of compression which produced asymmetric folds. The greatest of these is the Purbeck Monocline (*Figure 2, inset section*), another is the Wardour Anticline; all have steeper dips to the north. These two examples give an indication that earlier mid-Cretaceous normal faults were re-activated as reversed faults by regional pressures from the south. Between these is the broad basinal structure of the Frome Syncline, the western extension of the Hampshire Basin. Following these movements there appears to have been a marine erosion level at about 200m and more above present sea-level.

Superficial Deposits. Western hills of Dorset, in particular, are capped with some residual Tertiary deposits but also with chert and flint gravels thought to be derived from Cretaceous rocks in the west. In periglacial times these spread over a wide area, as over the Weymouth lowlands, to be etched in turn, by descending sea-level stands. Raised beaches at Portland Bill are dated at 125,000 and 210,000 years before the present. In glacial times, sea-level reached 200m below the present day datum. As the seas have risen, with the Flandrian transgression, coastal gravels will have been moved landward. The Chesil Beach, a spectacular storm beach (*with a fetch at right angles to the centre running past the Lizard and Finistere to the Caribbean*) is moving landward with storm activity. A good vantage point is from near the Fleet Nature Reserve, on the crossing to Portland (SY 669754).

River Systems. The mid-Tertiary folding and subsequent peneplanation had a fundamental role in establishing the drainage pattern of Dorset. The main rivers flow into the Frome Syncline (*Figure 1*) in a system concordant with the dips of the Chalk. The combined Frome, Piddle, Stour and Avon Rivers are thought to have passed eastwards as the Solent River surged between the Isle of Wight and the mainland. In the Blackmoor Vale, however, the down cutting Stour has successfully captured drainage which originally crossed the Somerset Levels to the Severn Estuary. The Axe has similarly captured water from north of the Marshwood Anticline. On the southern side the streams at Corfe Castle have cut down from the 200m level, giving an example of superimposed drainage.

Economic Resources

Sarsens, silicified conglomerates from the base of the Tertiary, were used in Bronze Age times for the local stone circles. Kimmeridge Clay Oil Shale was used to make a sceptre, decorated with gold studs, found at Clandon Barrow near Maiden Castle. The Romans exploited the Portland and Purbeck stones extensively including the Purbeck Marble which was also widely used in churches and cathedrals in Mediaeval times, mainly decoratively. Currently stone from both areas is used, the Portland Stone being a favoured freestone in London as well as internationally. Brick making, using the local Jurassic clays especially the Oxford and Kimmeridge Clays, continued from the 18th century but is almost defunct now. The Tertiary pipe (*ball*) clays have been utilised for several centuries and are still important. Oil has been produced at the Kimmeridge oilfield since 1959. The major discovery has been the oilfield under Poole Harbour which stretches eastward under Poole Bay.

Development began in 1973 from a reservoir in the Jurassic Bridport Sands. Some time later the effect of the pre-Albian faulting was cleverly recognised. That had led to oil migration from matured Kimmeridge Clay source rocks into the Sherwood Sandstone of Triassic age. A third reservoir in oyster beds of the Frome Clay was subsequently found. Tapping of the field under Poole Bay has been by novel extended reach drilling (ERD) techniques.

The Chalk is the aquifer which produces virtually all the water resources of the county.

Geological Maps

The maps of the British Geological Survey (BGS) covering Dorset and adjacent areas at a scale of 1:50,000, are: Sheets 326/340 Sidmouth (1974); Sheet 327 Bridport (1970); Sheet 328 Dorchester (1981); Sheet 312 Yeovil (1946); Sheet 341 and part 342 West Fleet and Weymouth (2000); Sheet 297 Wincanton (1996); Sheet 313 Shaftesbury (1994); Sheet 298 Salisbury; Sheet 342 and part 343 Swanage (2000); Sheet 329 Bournemouth (1991).

Geological Literature

Geology of the Dorset Coast (M R House, 1993, Geologists' Association Guide No. 22)

Geology and Scenery of Dorset (E. Bird, 1995, Ex Libris Press)

Geology (P Ensom, 1998), *Fossils* (R Edmonds, 1999), and *Stone Quarrying* (J Thomas, 1998) The Dovecote Press, Discover Dorset Series

Bibliography and Index of Dorset Geology (J Thomas, P Ensom, 1989 Dorset Natural History & Archaeological Society)

Classic Landforms of the West Dorset Coast (D Brunsden, A Goudie. The Geographical Association 1997)

Classic Landforms of the East Dorset Coast (A Goudie, D Brunsden. The Geographical Association 1997)

Regionally Important Geological/Geomorphological Sites in Dorset (Dorset RIGS, available from Dorset Environmental Records Centre)

Coastal Landforms of West Dorset (R J Allison, 1992, Geologists' Association Guide No. 72)

Inshore Along the Dorset Coast (P Bruce, 2001, Boldre Marine, Lymington)

Geology of Devon (Eds. E M Durrance & D J C Laming, University of Exeter 1993)

Fossil Identification

British Mesozoic Fossils (British Museum Natural History 6th Ed.)

British Cenozoic Fossils (British Museum Natural History 5th Ed.)

Fossils of the Oxford Clay (Eds. D M Martill, J D Hudson: Field Guide to Fossils No 4 The Palaeontological Association 1991)

Fossils of the Chalk 2nd edition (Eds. A B Smith & D J Batten: Field Guide to Fossils No 2 The Palaeontological Association 2002)

THE DORSET GEOLOGISTS' ASSOCIATION GROUP

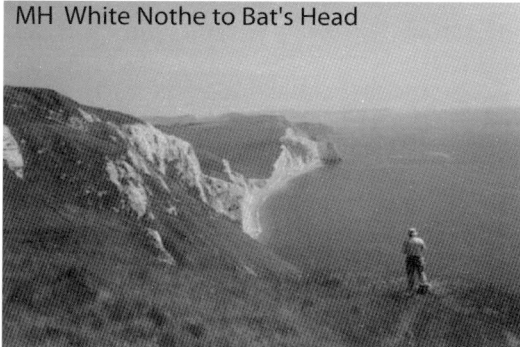

MH White Nothe to Bat's Head

"In February 2000 I visited Michael to return some borrowed books and happened to mention that three of us were proposing to walk the Dorset coast using his book as our guide. 'Can I come as well?' was the immediate response turning a reasonable idea into a series of unforgettable field trips - the most important day of the week - starting at Pinhay Bay on the 3rd of March 2000 and finishing at Barton-on-Sea in 2002."   *Robert Christian*

Thus was born the 'Geogeriatrics', also known as the 'Friday Fogies', a group of DGAG members who followed Professor Michael House's GA published best seller 'Geology of the Dorset Coast' from beginning to end.

A Chairman's Field Trip was launched in 1999. The field trip soon had the DGAG annual picnic attached to it. The tables have since been set up at Beer Head, Win Green, Ringstead and at Ulwell. The photos were taken in 2002 along the Purbeck Chalk ridge and at Ulwell. The day was a particularly special one as it also celebrated John Chaffey's 50 years of leading field trips. The original trip he led was from Corfe Castle to Studland and the 2002 Field Trip followed some of the same route.

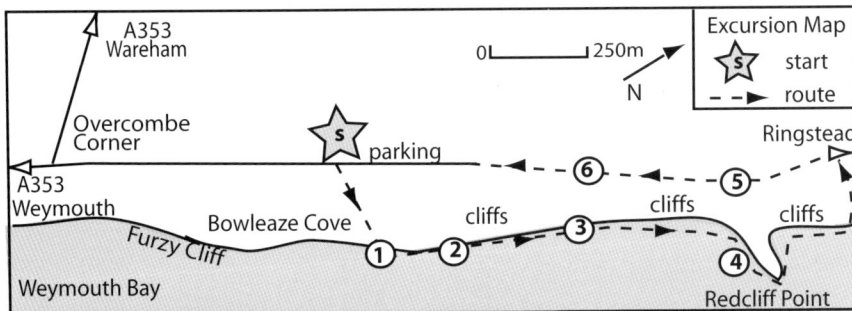

PURPOSE: To study the Corallian succession exposed, along the beach and in the cliffs above, from Bowleaze Cove to Redcliff Point. The geological interest is largely in the form of a variety of sediments and sedimentary structures but more especially, in a wealth of **trace fossils** all of which can be used to interpret the sedimentary environment. Impressive examples of mass-movement processes can also be seen.

PRACTICAL DETAILS: Approach the section from Weymouth via the A353 or, from the east, via Wareham and Wool. At the end of Preston Beach Road (SY 696816), follow Bowleaze Cove Way north-east until you reach the Waterside Holiday Park on the left (north). You can park anywhere on the road beyond this point (SY 703822). You can then walk down to the beach through the amusement park area or follow the coast path through a gate at the eastern end of Bowleaze Cove Way (SY 705811). The beach section is quite rough with fallen blocks and it is recommended that stout footwear be worn. The original path up from the beach at Redcliff Point is no longer viable because of recent landslips (Figure 9, page 23). A circular walk can be followed either by walking further along the beach to a 2nd World War pill box where a footpath can be followed up to the coast path then back to Bowleaze Cove or the reverse, according to tide conditions. Another alternative is to walk along the beach and then back again followed by a walk along the coast path. The length of the walk is approximately 2km and can be reasonably accomplished in half a day. Refreshments and toilets are available at Overcombe Corner.

Safety: This section of coastline is quite dynamic and mass movement events are frequent with rock falls and rotational slip movements as well as clay flows. Recent movements have been considerable because of the wet winter in 2000/2001 and the cliff path has been redirected between Bowleaze and Redcliff Point. As a result of mass-movement activity, the cliffs are nearly vertical in places and may give way. At high tide, it is now difficult to get along the beach between Bowleaze and Redcliff Point, the upper part of the beach being covered by mass-movement debris.

GEOLOGICAL SETTING: The cliff section between Bowleaze Cove and Redcliff Point exposes the Corallian succession, from the Nothe Grit to the Trigonia Beds. **Competent** sandstone and limestone units inter-bedded with less competent clay units provide an ideal geological environment for mass movement. The more competent beds form steeper cliffs, *e.g.* the Preston Grits and Osmington Oolite Series, while the less competent beds, such as the Nothe Clay, develop inclined cliffs. The beds can be readily recognised by lithology and fossil content. The succession *(Figure 1)* continues up from the Oxford Clay.

Figure 1		
Upper Jurassic	Corallian	*Myophorella (Trigonia) clavellata* Beds
		Osmington Oolite Series
		Bencliff Grit
		Nothe Clay
		Myophorella (Trigonia) hudlestoni Beds
		Preston Grit
		Nothe Grit
	Oxford Clay	Red Nodule Bed
		Jordan Cliff Clay

Looking west towards Furzy Cliff the beginning of the Corallian succession is the orange sandstone capping the eastern part of Furzy Cliff. This part of the Upper Jurassic succession is approximately 155-160 million years old.

Structure: As result of the plunging Weymouth **Anticline** the rocks **dip** gently to the east and north along most of the section. In places the rocks are dipping into the cliff so that they appear horizontal. The succession is exposed on the north side of the Weymouth Anticline which **plunges** east *(Figure 2)*. An east-west trending **fault** brings Oxford Clay back to the surface at Redcliff Point.

Figure 2
The rocks dip to the east with the plunge, but also to the north. The Bowleaze Cove - Redcliff section is parallel to the axis of the fold on the north side

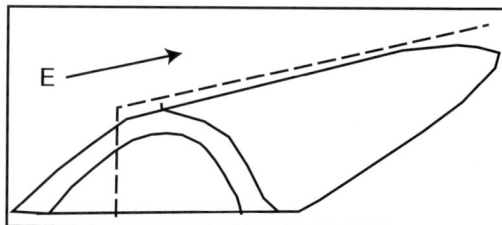

EXCURSION DETAILS

Follow the path through the amusement park area and walk along the cliff path past the Riviera Hotel. After a few metres make your way down onto the boulder-covered beach.

Location 1 *(SY 706817)* Bowleaze Cove

The loose material is of interest and shows a variety of sedimentary features as there are **trace fossils** as well as body fossils such as bivalves. Evidence for potential mass-movement is apparent with attempts made to stop this taking place in the form of gabions *(stone filled wire bags put in place in 1978/1979 at the south western end of the Riviera Hotel).* Some of the material on the beach was put in place in 1979 to allow heavy plant to move along the beach but all of it appears to be of local provenance. The dark patches in some of the paler coloured sandstone *(Nothe Grit)* is evidence of **bioturbation** *(reworking of sediment by organisms).* In other blocks single vertical tubes *(burrows)* can be seen which appear as circular indentations in plan. They stand out because the burrows are slightly harder than the sediment surrounding the burrow. The tubes are called *Skolithos.*

Figure 3

There are some large irregular tube-like trace fossils *(Thalassinoides)* weathered out on the upper surface of sandstone blocks. They probably represent the burrows of crustaceans, small lobsters or similar *(Figure 3).* Further information on these and other trace fossils can be found in the DIGS Group leaflet on trace fossils *(bibliography page 198).* In these same rocks, the bivalve *Pleuromya alduini* can be found although it is not particularly well preserved and is, almost invariably, found as an external mould.

Figure 4
Myophorella 0.25%

©RJC

Location 2 Approximately 100m further along large blocks of Preston Grit can be seen as fallen blocks on the beach itself and in the low cliff above. The coarse gritty sandstone contains numerous specimens of *Pecten* sp. but these are poorly preserved being rather fragile for the high-energy environment in which the sands were deposited. Another very common fossil is the distinctive bivalve *Myophorella (Trigonia),* with its ornamentation of rows of pustules or nodes *(Figure 4).* Unfortunately, it is difficult to collect well-preserved specimens here as the

fossils have a similar strength to the rock in which they are preserved, the two wearing away at a similar rate. The occasional ammonite can also be found - ?*Cardioceras* sp. - with some seen in section. The ammonites tend to lie flat on bedding surfaces so the orientation of the fallen blocks can be determined. The 'way up' of the blocks can also be determined from the trace fossils as the opening of the burrows always open onto what was the sea floor. 'U' shaped burrows of *Arenicolites* and *Diplocraterion parallelum* are common along this section and they are ideal for determining the 'way up' of the beds. The multiple burrows of *Diplocraterion* are sometimes seen in section and sometimes in plan. Occasionally the flower-like trace fossil *Gyrophyllites* *(Figure 5)* can be found with what appear to be petal like structures which were formed when sediment was systematically expelled from a central burrow.

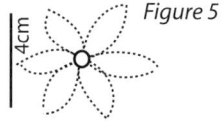

Figure 5

Location 3 *(SY 708817)* Further east large rounded boulders showing **cross-bedding** become apparent. These concretions, or doggers, are very well cemented sandstones *(with calcium carbonate)* and, because they are relatively hard, they have been preserved on the beach. The surrounding rock was less well cemented and has been eroded away. The cross-bedding developed where water currents carried sediment from shallow to deeper water *(as in a delta but these are not deltaic deposits)* and the beds were deposited on a sloping surface. Subsequent erosion partly cut through the beds before a later sequence was deposited on top *(see illustration in Chapter 8 Dorchester, page 64)*. Such features can also be used to determine the 'way up' of the beds as the upper unit always cuts across a lower unit. In this way we know that some of the boulders are upside down, being inverted as they tumbled onto the beach. Blocks on the beach also show **ripple marks** with symmetric ripples as well as ripple nets *(Figure 6)*. Some of these are rather worn now but they indicate the shallow water nature of the sedimentary environment, probably in a tidal or wave controlled situation.

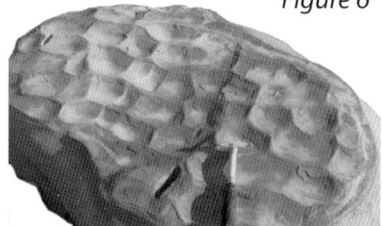

Figure 6

There are a number of large masses of pyrite or fool's gold *(iron sulphide)* on the beach. This mineral normally develops in an oxygen deficient environment *(anaerobic)* but much of the sedimentary evidence suggests a shallow water marine environment. The pyrite is often associated with fossil wood *(lignite)*. The oxygen deficient conditions probably developed locally where bacterial action was taking place on the organic material soon after it was deposited. The woody material probably floated into the Jurassic sea from land away to the west.

Location 4   As you approach Redcliff Point your way becomes more difficult because of the rock material transported, from higher up the cliffs, by mass-movement. Abundant **oolitic** limestone is apparent which has been derived from the Osmington Oolite at the top of the inland cliff. Similar oolitic limestone is now forming in tropical shallow water environments such as the Bahama Banks in the Caribbean. Geologists assume that ancient examples were formed in similar conditions. The round grains are formed from shell fragments being coated in layers of calcium carbonate mud. The high-energy conditions in the shallow water cause the grains to roll and they pick up concentric layers of the mud. The Oxford Clay is exposed at Redcliff Point having been brought to the surface by an east-west trending fault with the up-thrown side to the south. The change to a grey clay is very apparent and the abundant fossils, especially the large oyster *Gryphaea*, are a good indicator of the Oxford Clay. You can also find red nodules from the Red Nodule Bed, a useful marker horizon at the top of the Oxford Clay. At this point either make your way back along the beach or continue until you reach the footpath near the pillbox.

Location 5 *(SY 712817)* Redcliff Point

Figure 7

From the grassy area above Redcliff Point there is a good view westward, across the landslip area, to the east of Bowleaze Cove (*Figure 7*). The steep upper cliff is of the Osmington Oolite which is a distinctive pale creamy colour. Below this is an extensive slipped area with rotational slip blocks. As they break off the cliff top, the blocks slide down preferentially and the grassy surface tilts towards the cliff. Over a period of months they continue to move down, still tilting back, gradually disintegrating. The relatively level section, in the middle of the whole cliff profile, is developed on the Nothe Clay which, when wet, flows over the lower cliff, destabilises the upper cliff and causes mass-movement to occur. The combination of

Figure 8

more competent Osmington Oolite and less competent Nothe Clay is ideal for the initiation of the rotational slip area. As you walk back towards Bowleaze Cove you will get a good view of the rotational slip blocks, a classic example of the process *(Figure 8 photo: Bob Alderman)*.

Location 6 *(SY 707818)* At the time of writing a new fracture is starting to develop 20-30 metres back from the cliff edge. A scarp is developing on the cliff path that leads to the cliff edge west of Pontin's Riviera Hotel. This is almost certainly the next rotational slip area to develop, over the coming year or so.

The area immediately east of the Riviera Hotel has been very active over the past 20 years but appears to be less so at present. The section of cliff immediately east of here would now seem to be trying to catch up. The earlier movement could have been linked to work done to stabilise the cliff below the Riviera Hotel, in 1978-9, which destabilised the land just to the east. Currently further work is being done on the Riviera Hotel just inland from the cliff at Bowleaze Cove. It will be interesting to observe if this has any impact on the coastline.

Make your way back to the road either via the path on the seaward side of the Riviera Hotel, or via the footpath further inland, to the end of Bowleaze Cove Way.

Redcliff Point
The much-slipped Oxford Clay has removed the once well-used path to the shore. The off-shore reef is in the hard bands of the Corallian and provides a sheltered anchorage for small boats when the wind and tide are right (information from Inshore along the Dorset Coast, see bibliography page 16).

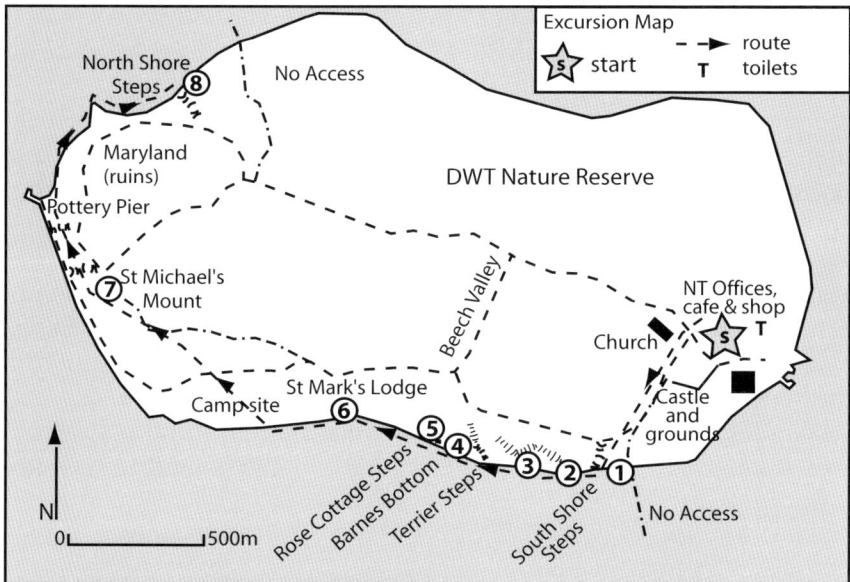

PURPOSE: To examine the Bracklesham sediments *(Palaeogene)* that are particularly well exposed in the southern and north-western cliffs of Brownsea: to study their mineralogy and the sedimentary structures they display: to consider the role played by the sediments in the establishment of the past industry of the island.

PRACTICAL DETAILS: This must be regarded as a whole day excursion even though the visit to the localities could be achieved in a half day. There are several factors to bear in mind when arranging a visit to Brownsea. Firstly, the island is owned by the National Trust and is only open to the general public from Easter to October. Secondly, access to the island is by ferry from Poole or Sandbanks with a fixed timetable. Thirdly, the exposures are not readily accessible at high tide so a visit is recommended commencing with a morning ferry and a falling tide.

Once on the island where a landing fee is payable in addition to the ferry fare, the walk is easy. There are steps and a fairly steep climb up from beach level at the western end of the island. Toilet facilities, a shop and restaurant are available near the landing quay at the National Trust Offices.

GEOLOGICAL SETTING: Brownsea Island sits almost centrally on the axis of the Hampshire Basin towards its western end. The Bracklesham Group *(Poole Formation)* sediments *(Branksome Sands above Parkstone*

Clay) dip gently eastwards. The boundary between the two units is high in the western cliffs near Pottery Pier and drops below sea level close to the castle in the east. The names of the stratigraphic units are confusing as the Branksome Sands can be quite clay-rich and the Parkstone Clay contains sandy horizons. Being near the western end of the Hampshire Basin both units are dominantly **fluviatile**. Marine horizons have been identified within the sediments by studying micro-fossil assemblages *(dinoflagellates in particular)* as macrofossils are rare.

The environment at the time of deposition *(some 40 million years ago)* was near a sea margin with shifting lagoons and sandbars and with wide rivers feeding in sediment from the west. Occasional rises in sea level, creating deeper water, favoured clay deposition.

Capping these sediments, and of much later development, are the gravel remnants of river terraces associated with an ancient Solent River flowing eastwards during warm phases of the Pleistocene. At the end of the last Ice Age, with a significant rise in sea level, the lower parts of the Solent River valley were drowned to form Poole Harbour, The Solent, Spithead and Southampton Water.

EXCURSION DETAILS

From the National Trust Offices follow the footpath west and then south-west to South Shore Steps. The localities should be identifiable from posts carrying a red-backed number.

Location 1 *(SZ 026874)* South Shore Steps *(east)*

These are Branksome Sands with several metres of medium-grained, yellow-brown sand and a few thin clay layers, strongly **cross-bedded,** in sets of up to one metre thick. At the base of this unit is a **lignite** and clay conglomerate which cuts into *(across the bedding)* the underlying bed of fine-grained, buff coloured sand.

Location 2 *(SZ 025874)* South Shore Steps *(west)*

Parkstone Clay emerges from beneath the overlying Branksome Sands. This boundary between the two units rises gently westwards until it appears well up the cliffs in the west of the island. A dark-brown clay occurs, at the base of the shallow cliff, whose colour is due to the inclusion of carbonaceous material and finely disseminated pyrite. These materials reflect the **reducing conditions** prevalent when the clays were deposited in relatively stagnant waters at the bottom of lagoons. Dissolved oxygen in the waters became quickly excluded from the newly deposited clay particles allowing only partial decay of organic matter *(hence the occurrence of carbonaceous material)* and the reduction of sulphate ions to sulphides. The brown clay weathers to a greyish colour and shows prominent displays of greenish-yellow jarosite - an oxidation product of the sulphide-rich clays. Jarosite is often mistakenly identified as sulphur but actually is a hydrated potassium iron sulphate. There is a distinct bed of lignite at the top of the clay. Towards the next locality to the west a buff-coloured sand appears at the base of the cliff with an irregular band of red-brown iron oxide-cemented sand at the clay - sand interface.

Location 3 *(SZ 024874)* Terrier Steps *(35 metres east)*   *Figure 1*

Protruding onto the shore is a very prominent outcrop of ferruginous sandstone and pebble conglomerate *(Figure 1)*. The sands and pebbles have been cemented together by iron oxides, such as hematite and goethite deposited from percolating groundwater over a long period of time, after the deposition of the original sands and clays. The groundwater is mildly acidic and can easily take iron into solution in its reduced *(ferrous)* form. The iron-rich waters would tend to be concentrated in the sands immediately overlying impervious clays and, on exposure to the atmosphere, the now oxidised iron *(ferric)* would precipitate out. These are the types of rocks that could have been used in the copperas industry *(see italics Location 6)* which was well established on Brownsea in the 17th century. Similar sandstones were used in the Poole Harbour area as building stones.

Location 4 *(SZ 022875)* Barnes Bottom   *Figure 2*

The cliff line recedes inland here due to the removal of clay for use in local pottery and brick making. The excavated face has since been heavily weathered so that now a prominent fan *(Figure 2)*, spreads out towards the shore. Immediately above the fan dark brown clay, laminated with fine-grained sand layers, can be seen. Above this very coarse sand *(grit)* occurs, becoming progressively finer upwards, which in turn is followed by a thin bed of silty clay. All of this succession is part of the Parkstone Clay. The overlying Branksome Sand is less well exposed towards the cliff top and is coarse and cross-bedded at the bottom, with clay clasts. A thin white **pipe-clay** seam occurs very near the top.

Location 5 *(SZ 020875)* Rose Cottage Steps
Just to the east of these steps is a microcosm of Brownsea's sedimentary history. Dark brown, weathered clay occurs at the base of the cliff which is cut into by a channel fill of cross-bedded ochrous sands containing **clasts** of clay and lignite.

Location 6 *(SZ 019875)* St. Marks Lodge
A 5m or so cliff shows 1.5m of ochrous sand overlying 3.5m of dark grey clay. The beach area is usually very wet. Water issuing from the base of the sand stains the clay red-brown with iron oxides, floods over the beach and causes frequent slumping of the cliff. A short walk westward along the beach from location 6 reaches the end of the south shore exposures. Cut inland across the campsite to pick up the footpath, tracking north-westwards, to location 7.

> *Note that the campsite (the site of Baden Powell's experimental camp in 1907) was the locality where the copperas works were established in the 16th century to be followed in the 19th century by a pottery that produced sanitary stoneware. Copperas is iron sulphate, a pale green salt, produced from the sulphide-rich sediments by encouraging natural oxidation, speeding up the process by a boiling operation. Copperas was used as a mordant (colour fixer) in the dyeing industry, for tanning and in the production of ink and the pigment Prussian Blue.*

Location 7 *(SZ 010879)* St. Michael's Mount
Two hundred metres or so south of Pottery Pier the shore is protected with metal piles supporting a coastal path. On the land side of the path a cliff, which rises to the highest point on the island, exposes the most complete succession of Brownsea's sediments. At the base of the cliff brown silty clays *(Parkstone Clay)* are frequently exposed with lenses of fine sand. The clays become finely laminated towards the top where the marked colour change to yellow-brown indicates the beginning of the overlying sands *(Branksome Sands)*. The sands are more resistant to erosion than the clays and tend to form a steeper, sometimes vertical, cliff. Very pale coloured gravels, from the overlying Solent River terrace, spill over the cliff onto the sands and clays. A little further south from this exposure there were extensive workings for the clay and sand for the manufacture of bricks and drainpipe stoneware.
If tides permit follow the beach north-east of Pottery Pier.

Location 8 *(SZ 014884)* A high cliff, of clays and overlying pale brown and orange sands, shows spectacular **cross** and **convolute bedding**. Beware of fallen trees at this fast-eroding corner of the island. A stepped path takes you up to the top of the island in the vicinity of Maryland *(clay workers' cottages, now ruins)*. Turn left *(east)* to walk back to the National Trust Offices and the ferry.

Alternatively location 8 can be omitted, in which case, take the stepped path up from Pottery Pier to the top of the island. There are a variety of pathways back to the ferry, the distance being about 2km.

A composite aerial view of Brownsea Island from

Dorset. a Photographic Atlas. ©Dorset County Council 2000

The geology trail is along the southern edge of the Island

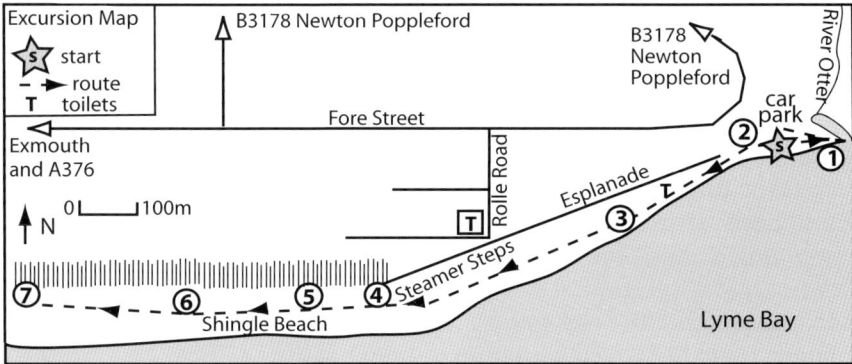

PURPOSE: To study the Triassic succession to the west of the River Otter at Budleigh Salterton and to interpret the environment of deposition of the sedimentary rocks. There are also interesting weathering patterns, evidence of faulting and significant cliff falls *(mass-movement)* as well as modern marine processes and industrial archaeology.

PRACTICAL DETAILS: Approach the section via the A3052 Lyme Regis to the M5-Jct30 and then the B3178 from Newton Poppleford. There is a convenient car park *(Lyme! Kiln Car Park)* at the eastern end of the esplanade in Budleigh Salterton *(SY 073820)*. Toilets are available at two locations along the seafront but not at the car park and there are also refreshments conveniently available on the esplanade and in the town. 0.5km west of Steamer Steps the beach can be used by naturists.

Safety: This section of coastline is affected by rock falls because the sandstone that forms the cliffs is not very well cemented. There are warning signs about the rock falls at intervals along the first 0.5km of the beach. A hard hat is recommended but obviously won't protect the visitor from a major fall! It is also clear that erosion of the **debris fans** from some of the larger falls has occurred during storms. Unless conditions are extreme, there should not be any difficulty walking along the beach to observe the features identified in this excursion.

GEOLOGICAL SETTING: The cliff section west of Budleigh Salterton exposes part of the Triassic succession which is outlined in *Figure 1*.

Period	Lithological Units	
Triassic	Mercia Mudstone	
	Sherwood Sandstone	Otter Sandstone
		Budleigh Salterton Pebble Bed
	Aylesbeare Mudstone	

Figure 1

Looking west from the esplanade *(Figure 2)* the strata can be seen dipping towards you so the rocks are getting progressively older as you walk along the beach to the west. The bright orange-red colour is a result of the rocks being deposited in a continental arid or semi-arid environment.

Figure 2

In Triassic times Britain was at the latitude of current day North Africa. Conditions were quite arid during the preceding late Carboniferous *(Stephanian)* and Permian periods but became less extreme in the Triassic and a sub-humid environment developed. With a hand lens it can be seen that the red colour is due to the presence of the iron oxide mineral hematite which is coating the sand grains.

EXCURSION DETAILS:

Location 1 *(SY 077819)* Walk along the footpath east from the car park to the end of the shingle spit. Note the size of the pebbles, which are generally smaller than those forming the main beach further to the west. Long shore drift has carried the smaller pebbles east and partially blocked off the estuary of the River Otter and the old port of Budleigh, causing the development of the marsh behind the spit.

Location 2 *(SY 073820)* If you retrace your steps to the car park you will be able to see evidence of a former lime kiln facing you as you look west. Devonian limestone from further west in Devon and Welsh coal were imported to make agricultural lime. Some of the limestone can still be seen in the wall to the right of the kilns. This is a pale grey finely crystalline limestone very typical of the Devonian limestone seen at Torquay and Plymouth.

Location 3 *(SY 068819)* Just to the west of the toilets, a red coloured sandstone *(Otter Sandstone)* can be seen which can be studied more easily further to the west. However, here there appears to be a fault emphasised by mineralisation that is harder than the surrounding sandstone. The fault and mineralisation cross the face going down from left to right *(west to east)*. It is possibly a **reverse fault** shown by the relative displacement of a slightly harder bed of rock. Just east of this and west of the first bench, there is evidence of both vertical and horizontal harder bands which are possibly **calcrete** mineralisation from the evaporation of water in the semi-arid conditions. These bands stand out because they are better cemented and harder than the surrounding sandstone.

Location 4 The start of the main outcrop is just west of Steamer Steps, a sequence of Otter Sandstone approximately 15m thick. The cliffs are vertical suggesting a reasonably **competent** rock. However it is not well cemented as can be seen with very cursory observation, as the sandstone can be rubbed away with the fingers. Trails can be seen where rainwater has eroded the surface of the rock. The upper part of the cliff has hollows which are probably the result of abrasion by sand grains carried by the wind *(Figure 3)*. The grains are whirled round dislodging other grains which

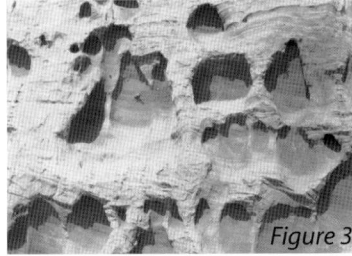

Figure 3

adds to the abrasive process although it has been suggested that the cavities are also related to a salt weathering process. These hollows are less well developed in the lower part of the cliff which could be the result of wave erosion of the hollows during occasional storm events. Standing back from the cliff the general **dip** of the strata is apparent but there is also **cross-bedding** where minor units of sandstone dip differently to the main bedding. Such cross-bedding is the result of the sand being deposited from suspension either in water or air. In this case it is likely that the sands were deposited in water. The dip direction of the cross-bedding is not uniform and suggests that this was a river, perhaps a **braided** channel system associated with an **alluvial fan**. The channels were orientated in different directions, at different times, although the flow is generally from west to east. These sands are part of the Sherwood Sandstone Group, one of the reservoir rocks for the Wytch Farm Oilfield in Dorset. Careful study of the sand under a microscope shows significant amounts of rounded grains typical of sands formed in desert conditions *(aeolian dunes)*. However there is also a large component of finer material and it is possible that a river reworked sand dune material from a nearby source.

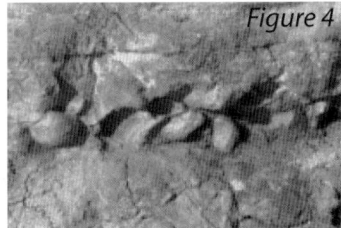

Figure 4

Location 5 A bright yellow band can be seen in the cliff approximately 100m west of Steamer Steps. This band follows the bedding and could be related to the hydration of hematite *(ferric oxide)* above an impermeable layer. This layer *(Figure 4)* is made of pebbles coated in hematite with hematite cement in the surrounding sands. The layer is very hard and it is quite difficult to remove the coated pebbles. This pebbly clay is one of the more unusual rocks in the area and is a fossil soil with wind-faceted pebbles *(dreikanter)*. It represents an erosional break between the Pebble Beds and the Otter Sandstone. The yellow band is very persistent and apparently occurs in sediments of the same age associated with the Wytch Farm Oilfield, 90 kilometres to the east.

Immediately below the impermeable pebble layer is the Budleigh Salterton Pebble Bed which is approximately 30 metres thick. The Pebble Bed is a conglomerate; a coarse clastic sediment made up of rounded clasts *(pebbles)* larger than 2mm in diameter. The pebbles in this case are very large, up to 20cm across, suggesting that significant flows of water would be needed to carry them. They are also well rounded, suggesting long distance transport. The only process that could transport and round such material is water. The pebbles were rounded by attrition *(banging together)* as they were transported. The relatively **poorly sorted** nature of the sediment also suggests fluvial transport by occasional torrential storms in the source area. The pebbles were eventually deposited because friction over the surface of the riverbed resulted in a loss of energy. Finer sediments, such as sand, were then trapped in between the pebbles which indicates variable amounts of energy in the river channel. There is also evidence of cross-bedding in the pebbles with clear alignment in places. The dip of the cross-bedding is to the east. The conglomerate is described as polymictic because the pebbles are of diverse rock types. Many of them can be seen to be white, milky quartz probably from quartz veins cutting the rocks in the source area. The pebbles are derived from rocks of Ordovician-Devonian age *(their age being based on their fossil content)* and may be from Devon and Cornwall but also from Brittany.

There are pebbles of great variety on the beach including some of black chert and others of conglomerate. There are also pebbles derived from the cliffs which are worth investigating. **Note that there is a £1000 fine for removing pebbles from the beach.** Such coarse, clastic sediments are typical of those formed from the erosion of a mountain chain following a mountain building event *(orogeny)* and are called molasse sediments. The rapid weathering and erosion of the mountains produces the sediment and the pebbles are rounded during subsequent transport. The south west of England and Brittany were affected by the **Hercynian/Variscan Orogeny** 285 million years ago. The Triassic sediments at Budleigh Salterton were deposited around 250 million years ago when the mountains were still being eroded.

Location 6 Approximately 300m from Steamer Steps, two faults can be seen in the cliff where the boundary, between the Otter Sandstone and the Budleigh Salterton Pebble Beds, is displaced. They appear to be normal faults with the downthrow side to the west: such faults develop when the crust is under tension. They formed after the Triassic sediments had been deposited. They are perhaps linked to earth-movements which relate to the 'relaxing' of the crust following a period of compression *(the Hercynian Orogeny)*. Both faults are associated with areas of current mass-movement including major cliff falls. The fault furthest west has a large debris fan which has largely been eroded on the seaward side *(but which may return this winter!)*. A stream, trickling down the cliff and possibly linked to the fault, may exacerbate the mass-movement processes.

The debris fans have a mixture of material in them including river terrace material from the River Otter. These were probably deposited by torrential streams linked to melt water flows during the Pleistocene glaciation. If you stand back you can see the paler-coloured material capping the cliff. Study of this, in the debris fan, shows it to be very different to the pebbles of the Pebble Beds. During the Pleistocene, when conditions were similar to the present-day tundra area of the Arctic, water from the melting snow in summer flowed across the area transporting material weathered by freeze-thaw processes. The recent cliff falls have brought it down to beach level. The large clasts are much more angular than the rounded pebbles described earlier. The locally derived flint and chert clasts come from the erosion of Greensand and Chalk inland from the coast *(seen around Beer, see Chapter 22)*. Other material in the debris fans includes well-cemented sandstone. Most of the Otter Sandstone is poorly cemented but occasionally areas can be found where hematite occurs in zones, which produce well-cemented material.

Below the Pebble Beds the exposure is less good with mass-movement bringing down material from above which hides the lower part of the cliff. Where exposure of fresh material does occur the rock can be seen to be a red mudstone. This is a silty clay of the Aylesbeare Mudstone Group.

Location 7 *(SY 060815)* The rock exposed here, about 500m west of Steamer Steps, is orange red with pale green mottling. This is the result of localised **reducing conditions** after the sediments were deposited. The mudstone was possibly deposited in a playa lake environment. The fine-grained muddy sediments were deposited towards the centre and, in the middle of the basin *(not seen as it is under Lyme Bay)*, the minerals gypsum and halite *(rock salt)* would have been formed. Such situations exist now in arid regions where water flows into basins but is lost through evaporation.

Thanks are due to Ramues Gallois for helpful information on this location

Chapter 4 Robert Chandler and Volker Dietze   **BURTON BRADSTOCK**

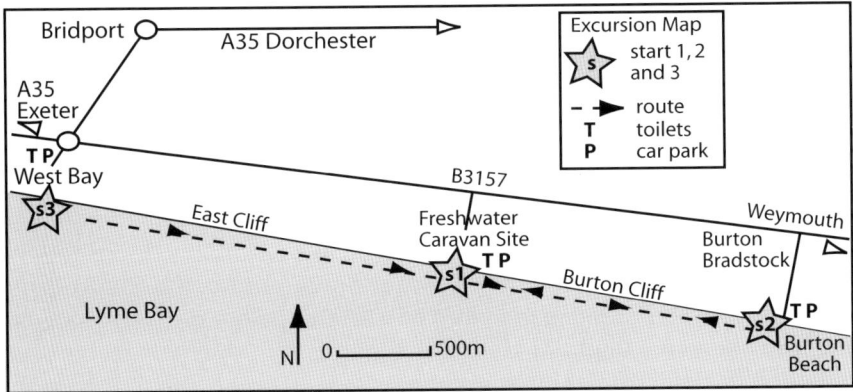

PURPOSE: To examine rocks *(Figure 1)* of the Lower Jurassic, Toarcian, Bridport Sands, Middle Jurassic Inferior Oolite *(Aalenian-Bathonian)* and the overlying Fuller's Earth Clay, between East Cliff *(to the east of West Bay)* and Hive Beach near Burton Bradstock. Fossils are plentiful, along this dramatic and beautiful stretch of the coastline, in fallen blocks of Inferior Oolite. The locality provides the opportunity for the visitor to examine coastal landforms, stratigraphy, body and **trace fossils** and the depositional environment of these rocks.

PRACTICAL DETAILS: This stretch of the Dorset coast is a Site of Special Scientific Interest (SSSI) and hammering/collecting from the cliff is inadvisable. Abundant fossils can be found in fallen blocks. Extreme care should be taken as the cliff is liable to collapse without warning. Tides must be checked as it is possible to get cut off and large waves present a significant danger to the visitor. The beach is composed of small shingle and some may find walking the entire distance demanding.

Access can be gained from three positions along the coast. 1. Access to the beach midway along the exposure may be made at Burton Freshwater Caravan Park *(SY 478898)* on the B3157. Permission is required from the site owner *(Tel 01308 897317)* and a fee is chargeable for parking. At certain times of the year it is possible to wade across the river; alternatively one can follow the coast footpath, east to a bridge, then return on the coast side of the river *(distance about 800m)*. 2. From Burton Bradstock village travel south to the beach near the National Trust car park at the eastern end of Hive Beach *(SY 491887)* and walk northwest. 3. Finally the excursion can begin near the Bridport Arms Hotel on the east side of West Bay *(SY 465903)*. From here walk south-east

Figure 1 Burton Bradstock section

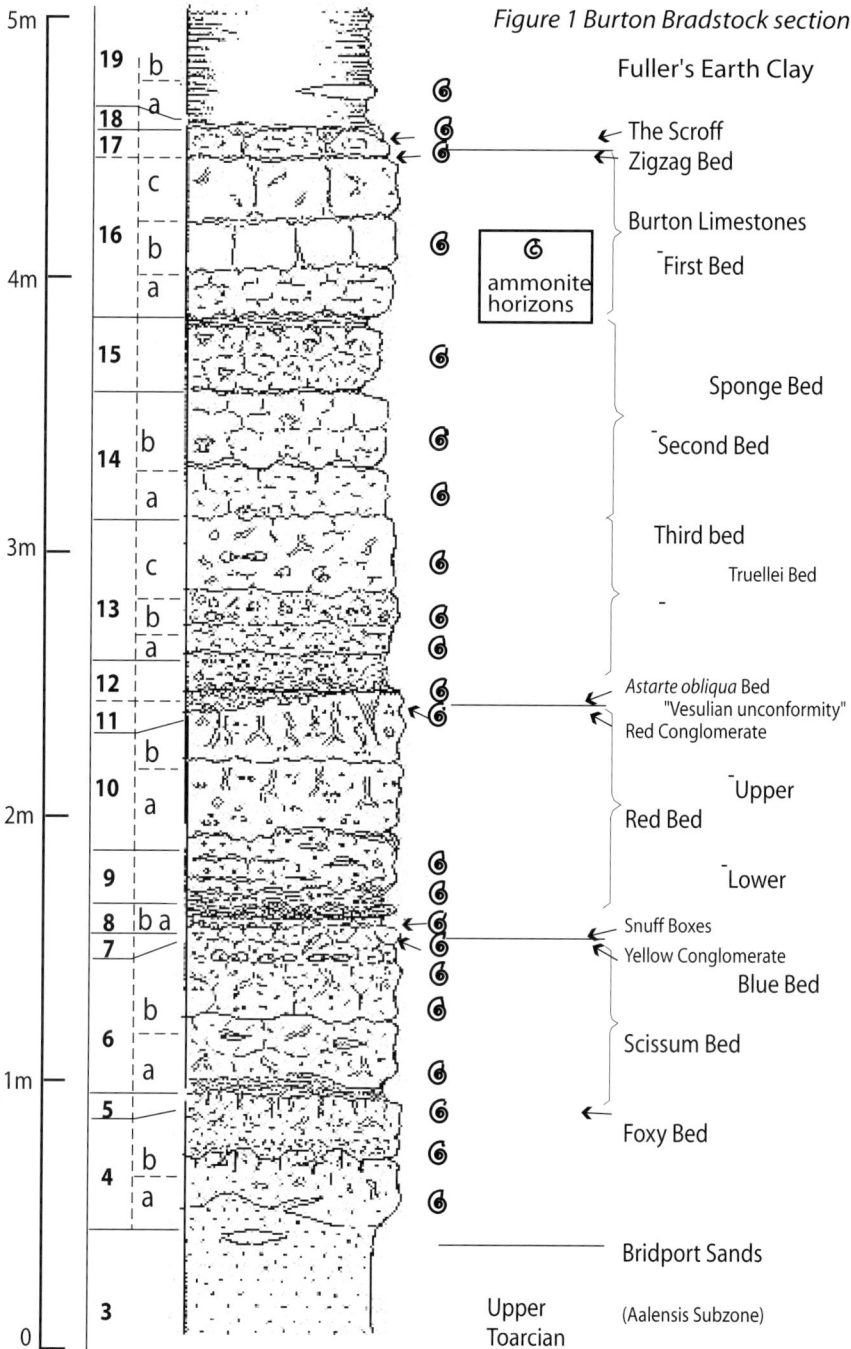

Fuller's Earth Clay

The Scroff
Zigzag Bed

Burton Limestones

First Bed

ammonite
horizons

Sponge Bed

Second Bed

Third bed

Truellei Bed

Astarte obliqua Bed
"Vesulian unconformity"
Red Conglomerate

Upper

Red Bed

Lower

Snuff Boxes
Yellow Conglomerate

Blue Bed

Scissum Bed

Foxy Bed

Bridport Sands

Upper
Toarcian   (Aalensis Subzone)

beneath East Cliff, past Freshwater Steps and on beneath Burton Cliff to the National Trust car park south of Burton Bradstock. At each starting location toilets and refreshments are available but opening times are subject to change in low season.

The geology of the area is the subject of a memoir, *Geology of the Country around Bridport and Yeovil*, HMSO 1958 and is accompanied by geological maps 327 and 312. The entire excursion from West Bay to Burton Bradstock is approximately 3km.

A hard hat is essential for those who intend to approach the cliff. A hammer and chisel, hand lens, collecting bags and newspaper are useful items to include on the trip.

Figure 2

GEOLOGICAL SETTING: Jurassic rocks outcrop along the length of the Dorset coast from east Devon to east Dorset. The rocks dip gently to the east, therefore a trip from west to east will traverse progressively younger rocks. Between West Bay and Burton Bradstock entirely marine rocks of Lower and Middle Jurassic age are exposed in high sea cliffs *(Figure 2)*. The Lower Jurassic is represented by the Bridport Sands of Upper Lias, Toarcian age and these rocks form most of the cliff apart from the top few metres. These strata are rather soft, feebly cemented sands with bands of harder calcium carbonate rich material that forms concretions or 'doggers' throughout the Group. These tall imposing cliffs of orange-yellow sand provide a spectacular aspect of the local scenery.

Towards the top of the sands the lime content increases, the nodular bands become more persistent and more closely spaced vertically. Within these upper beds lies the boundary of the Lower and Middle Jurassic that commences with the Inferior Oolite belonging to the Aalenian, Bajocian and lowest Bathonian stages. The Formation in total seldom exceeds 5m in the area and consists of thin limestone beds often separated by spectacular planed-off erosion surfaces. The lower part of the Inferior Oolite is variable, and often a deep rust red, while the upper part is more massive and of a generally paler colour. The top of the Inferior Oolite consists of a grey nodular layer, the Zigzag Bed of early Bathonian age. The top is sharply defined by a dead flat surface upon which the grey 'scroff' and Fuller's Earth Clay are deposited.

Each lithological unit in the cliff can be easily made out *in situ* from the beach by their resistance to erosion and by colour. The lower sands are soft and cut back easily leaving the hard resistant limestone overhanging the beach. The very soft clay cap is easily eroded to give a gentle slope back to the cliff edge.

The Bridport Sands consist of beds of rather fine quartz sand with small amounts of organic material and other minerals *e.g.* feldspar. At intervals in the cliff, levels of cemented sand burrs *(doggers)* are developed. Body fossils are rare but become more frequent towards the top, the most common occurrence being shells enclosed in the sand burrs. The sands display medium scale **cross-bedding** and any shell material within them is fragmentary. At Ham Hill, near Yeovil, the equivalent of the sand is so rich in detrital shell debris that it constitutes a bioclastic sandy limestone celebrated for its quality as a building stone. In some of the burrs, original stratification of the sand can be traced indicating their origin to be post-depositional to the sand. In these concretions it is possible to find well-preserved fossils including belemnites, bivalves and ammonites in an uncrushed state.

Near the top, the sands grade upwards in thin continuous beds of sandy limestone, intercalated with thin sands. These are the lowest beds with relatively rich fossil faunas. Above is the first persistent limestone that forms a prominent marker in the cliff. This is the Scissum Bed above which the succession is dominated by hard resistant limestones, beneath the recessive Fuller's Earth Clay.

Near West Bay the Inferior Oolite is much thinner and the Fuller's Earth Clay is often absent because of erosion. The Inferior Oolite only attains maximum thickness, on the coast, to the east of Freshwater at Burton Cliff. This section of coastline is the only natural exposure of the Inferior Oolite in the region; however, nearby road cuttings and old quarries provide splendid semi-permanent sections.

The very localized variations in thickness, of the Inferior Oolite, are the result of sedimentation accompanied by adjacent, contemporaneous local erosion. At West Bay, and north towards Bristol, relative elevation of the seabed inhibited the thicker accumulation of sediment. On the flanks to the west near Chideock and to the east at Burton Bradstock, in contrast, sagging allowed thicker sediments to gather. The topography of the sea bed at the time was probably rather flat, the differences in sedimentation being due to differential rates of sagging with sediment filling negative areas in pace with it. This pattern of sedimentation is further disturbed by the effects of local **faulting** so that in a very localised area considerable variation in the succession can be observed.

The Inferior Oolite can only be examined safely in the fallen blocks that litter the beach in some areas.

Many of the beds are oolitic or rich in lime-mud pellets. The origin of the ooids is a matter of continuing debate. It is likely that they are the product of biological activity, accumulations of limonite upon a gelatinous coat formed by bacteria or algae in water of moderate depth rather than resulting from precipitation around a nucleus in agitated water as in the Great Oolite Series around Oxford.

Certain features of the succession can be seen better at some locations than at others. *Figure 1 (page 35)* is a composite profile and can be referred to throughout.

EXCURSION 1: Freshwater to Burton Bradstock.

Starting from the beach just south of the caravan site, walk southeast. The river has cut down through the sands to expose the lower part of the Bridport Sands in a series of eroded platforms that pick-out the harder bands. There are occasional belemnite guards but few other intact fossils. The surfaces of the weathered concretions display some excellent trace fossils, mostly *Thalassinoides*. Proceeding along the beach some 400m you arrive at some scattered blocks from an old cliff fall. In many such blocks detachment has occurred along the weaker beds and it is common to find some blocks upside down. One enormous block of Inferior Oolite dwarfs the rest at this point. It rests on one side but is the correct way up and is known locally as the "House Block" and in it one can observe almost the entire succession of the Inferior Oolite.

The complete section in the cliff from the top downwards:

Lower Bathonian, Great Oolite Group:

Zigzag Zone, Yeovilensis Subzone

Bed 19: Lower Fuller's Earth Clay with *Oxycerites* sp.   max 0 .3m

Lower Bathonian, Upper Inferior Oolite:

Zigzag Zone, condensed interval Convergens-Yeovilensis Subzone

Bed 18: The Scroff: marl with poorly preserved ammonites from the Zigzag Bed

Bed 17: Zigzag Bed: nodular hard limestone with abundant ammonites: *Zigzagiceras* sp., *Morphoceras macrescens*, *Ebrayiceras* spp, *Oxycerites* spp., *Gonolkites* spp., *Parkinsonia pachypleura*, *Procerites* sp.   0.15m

Upper Bajocian, Upper Inferior Oolite:

Parkinsoni Zone, ?Bomfordi Subzone

Bed 16: First Bed: limestone with poorly preserved fossils.

Parkinsoni Zone, Bomfordi Subzone

Bed 15: The Sponge Bed: Pale yellow limestone, well bedded and separated by thin marly partings. Crowded with the moulds of sponges, occasional brachiopods (*Rugitela* spp.)., corals, echinoids (*Cidaris, Stomechinus*), bivalves, mostly disarticulated, and broken ammonites (*Parkinsonia* spp.). The matrix is almost entirely composed of finely broken shell and echinodermal debris. Trace fossils are abundant   0.40m

Bed 14: Harder more massive limestone than above and divisible into two courses by an indistinct parting. Fossils less common but including large intact ammonite moulds, *Parkinsonia bomfordi, Procerites costulatosus* 0.40m

Parkinsoni Zone, Truellei Subzone

Bed 13: The Truellei Bed, three courses of very hard limestone. The upper two parts are pale buff to grey with abundant scattered cream pellets. Very abundant small spherical brachiopods *Sphaeroidothyris sphaeroidalis* preserved in calcite, some hollow and filled by dogtooth sparite, occur throughout. At this point the bed attains a maximum thickness and the fossils are exquisitely preserved. Large ammonites occur in the middle of the bed: *Parkinsonia dorsetensis, P. parkinsoni, Cadomites* spp., *Polyplectites* spp., *Bigotites* spp., and *Strigoceras truellei*. Belemnites, bivalves and nautiloids are also common. The lowest bed is thinner and contains clouds of brown ooliths in the lower part. Again fossils are beautifully preserved and include fossil wood, echinoids (*Stomechinus*), ammonites (*Parkinsonia* spp.) and bivalves (*Coelastarte* spp.)   1.0m

Parkinsoni Zone, Acris Subzone

Bed 12: The *Astarte obliqua* Bed

The bed takes its name from the bivalve species that occurs so commonly within it, *Neocrassina modiolaris = A. oblique (olim)*. In any study of the bed and its lateral variation, it is important to understand that considerable changes occur in the succession over very short distances. The different sub-units come and go in an irregular fashion. At some locations the bed can be subdivided into two parts while at another nearby locality three distinct lithological sub-units can be identified with four horizons of fossils.

Brown to cream, fine grained, locally densely ironshot oolitic **wackestone** and **packstone**. Somewhat irony, with micrite clouds and much calcified shell material. Fossils include: *Parkinsonia rarecostata, P. bradstockensis, Garantiana longidoides, Bajocisphinctes curvatus, Prosisphinctes messeres,* and *Spiroceras* spp., *Neocrassina modiolaris, Pseudomelania procera, Discocyathus* spp.   0.1-0.3m

-----*marked erosion surface at which the entire succession often parts into two*-----

Lower Bajocian, Middle Inferior Oolite

Humphriesianum Zone

Bed 11: Red Conglomerate. A rust red limonitic conglomerate with reworked, corroded fossils. Most of the fossils are fragmentary or are planed through by erosion.   0-0.03m

Bed 10: The Red Bed. Near Freshwater the bed is clearly divisible into two rather massive courses of roughly equal thickness *(Figure 3)* but locally it thins dramatically or wedges out completely. When freshly broken the rock is pink and full of glistening particles. Examination with a hand lens shows it to consist of much

Figure 3

broken calcite shell debris, mostly echinodermal. The bed is intensely hard and **bioturbated** with the two courses cut across by vertical burrows. Intact fossils are scarce but those that do occur are often pebble like and coated in a red limonite crust   0.5m

Sauzei Zone

Bed 9: Dark, rust red and thinly bedded with much broken shell debris. Here the bed is thin and has yielded little intact fossil material. However during excavations at nearby Freshwater Caravan Park it was found that the bed thickens and is sub-divisible, with abundant fossils that are coated by an irony laminated crust.   0.10m

Discites Zone

Bed 8: Snuff-boxes. Limestone, bluish when fresh and containing clouds of large red ooliths. Many oval laminated structures resemble Victorian snuffboxes. They are deep rust red, probably of stromatolitic origin, and often enclose shell fragments. The structure of these bodies is similar to that of the iron ooliths but on a much larger scale. In places on the beach the blocks have split along this horizon to give an opportunity to view large areas of these curious structures *(Figure 4)*.

Figure 4

Lower Inferior Oolite

Aalenian

Murchisonae to Concavum zones

Bed 7: The Yellow Conglomerate. Thin yellow marl with pebbles of yellow limestone. Small, well preserved fossils, mostly ammonites, are abundant including *Graphoceras limitatum, decorum* and *stigmosum* indicating the upper part of the Concavum Zone. In places ammonites of the lowest Discites Zone, *Hyperlioceras politum* and aff. also occur at this level. At some parts of the beach the bed thickens to 0.15m and is divisible into two well-differentiated levels, the Bradfordensis Zone below and Concavum Zone above. Apart from these pockets of sediment, no record of this interval remains on the coast.   0.01m

- - - - - - - - - - - - - -*erosion surface*- - - - - - - - - - - - - -

Scissum Zone

Bed 6: Scissum Bed: A hard sandy limestone forming the first relatively thick and persistent limestone unit above the sands. The bed weathers pale yellow, but is bluish when fresh. It is often divisible into two courses, clearly seen in weathered section in the cliff. The top of the bed is covered in shell debris preserved in calcite. The surface is extensively bioturbated and bivalves are common including *Plagiostoma* spp. and *Ctenostreon* spp. Within the bed burrowing forms in life position can also be found including *Pleuromya* spp. Well preserved gastropods and small solitary corals, *Montlivaltia* sp. are also found. Ammonites are the most common fossil and include numerous compressed discoidal forms of the genus *Leioceras*. The small zonal index species *Tmetoceras scissum* with its **evolute** coiling and coarse spines is also relatively common here. Occasional giants of the genus *Megalytoceras* can be seen protruding from the bed and in places a slightly higher horizon preserves a fauna of the ammonite *Bredyia*, a form that takes its name from Port Bredy or Bridport. 0.20m

Below this level the beds are invariably broken away due to the difference in hardness between the limestone and sandy beds below. Scattered blocks of the sub-adjacent beds are present on the beach but they soon erode once fallen from the cliff.

EXCURSION 2: Hive Beach, Burton Bradstock.

From the National Trust car park at the eastern end of the cliff walk westwards towards Freshwater. In the cliff it is occasionally possible to see fractures in the Inferior Oolite filled with cream limestone. These structures are interpreted as neptunian dykes formed by slight Jurassic rifting of the seabed followed by sediment infilling. Records of fossils from the dykes include perfect gastropods with intact spines and ammonites of the Upper Bajocian, Subfurcatum Zone.

At certain points accumulations of fallen blocks can be examined. The upper part of the succession is similar to that seen in Excursion 1. Here, however, there is a much better chance of seeing the lower beds in a more intact state due to the way the material has gathered in a heap at the foot of the cliff. In May 2000 the following section was recorded from a fallen block.

From above:

- - - - - - - - - - - - - - ***erosion surface*** - - - - - - - - - - - - - -

Bed 11 - Red Conglomerate 0-0.02m
Bed 10 - Red Bed: Divisible into three parts:-
(i) Hard slightly pink stone, which splits into two equal parts. 0.15m
(ii) Hard, yellow echinodermal stone with pale pink patches. 0.20m
(iii) Pale yellow stone, softer and slightly echinodermal. 0.15m

- - - - - - - - - - - - - ***erosion surface*** - - - - - - - - - - - -

Bed 9: Divisible into three courses.
Bed 9c: Very hard, red, iron-stained stone with large echinoid spines and belemnites
~~~~~~~**very undulating sinuous parting**~~~~~~~
Bed 9b: Irony mud with laminated ironstones, mud and oncoliths *(small snuff boxes)* orientated with the long axis parallel to the undulations of the laminations. At the base a flat hardground level of *Ctenostrum* and *Plagistoma* spp
<div align="right">0.07m</div>

- - - - - - - - - - - - - - **erosion surface** - - - - - - - - - - - - - -
Bed 9a?: Hard, pale grey flinty limestone with sparse red rotted ooliths, heavily bioturbated. Ammonites include *Skirroceras* and *Emileia* sp.   0.20m
~~~~~~~very marked sinuous undulating parting~~~~~~~~
Bed 8a & b: snuff-boxes
0-0.5m
Bed 7 - Yellow conglomerate: pockets of coarse yellow to blue marly stone with red ooliths near base. *Brasilia, Graphoceras, Hyperlioceas [Darellia]* spp.
0.03m

-----------**flat encrusted surface**-----------
Scissum Bed that divides in two courses.
Bed 6b: Scissum Bed. Very reworked and full of debris including ammonites *Leioceras* spp., *Erycites* sp. and fine gastropods perfectly preserved. Near the base a laminated clay band, the lower part full of disarticulated bivalves *Astarte* spp.
0.13m
Bed 6a: Scissum Bed: Pale grey fine grained, slightly sandy stone. Echinodermal with abundant infaunal bivalves in life position. Ammonites previously listed, *Leioceras* spp.
0.20m

Opalinum Zone
Bed 5: Foxy Bed. Sandy with a knobbly texture. A few ammonites spread through the sand. *Leioceras opalinum, Leioceras costosum, Cylicoceras* sp., *Bredyia* spp.
0.20m

---------**parting**--------
Bed 4b: Hard, rust red, sandy stone with soft patches of sand. Ammonites mostly preserved as internal sandy moulds, *Leioceras aff. lineatum.*
Bed 4a: Hard yellow stone, sandier than above, fewer fossils. *Pleydellia buckmani, Leioceras opalinum.*   4a & b together 0.45m
~--~~~--~~**uneven surface**~~--~~--~
Bed 3: Bridport Sand, mostly unfossiliferous, a few poorly preserved ammonite body chambers. *Pleydellia buckmani, Leioceras opalinum.*   1.0m
Bed 2: yellow sandy stone band.
0.20m
Bed 1: Divisible into three parts based on the ammonite assemblage. The upper-most part is sand but contains progressively more small doggers towards the base
Bed1c: Sand with black ammonite moulds in it and a level of gritty blocks,

yellow and rather soft. The blocks are packed with ammonites preserved in white calcite with a fine gritty, yellow coating and include: *L. opalinum, Leioceras - Pleydellia* spp. *P.* cf. *buckmani, L.* cf. *opalinum, P. lotharingica, Pleydellia leura Pleydellia fluens, Cyphiolioceras* aff. *opaliniforme, Leioceras opalinium, Catulloceras dumortieri.*

Bed 1b: Iron-stained, red to brown sands with scattered, lightly cemented blocks full of ammonites, mostly body-chambers as sandy internal moulds. *Pleydellia* aff. *aalensis., P. misera, P. burtonensis, Canavarina folleata, Walkeria subglabra, Cyphiolioceras* aff. *opaliniforme, Leioceras* aff *opalinum.*

Bed 1a: Sands with occasional doggers.   total thickness 0.8-1.0m

<div align="center">~~~~<strong>wavy surface</strong>~~~~</div>

Below, ammonites are the only relatively common fossils to occur as poorly preserved **phragmocones** with better preserved examples in occasional nodules.

Upper Lias, Toarcian

Irregular bed of gritty yellow calcareous stone with fossils, almost exclusively ammonites at all angles. *Leioceras.* cf. *opalinium, Pleydellia buckmani, P. misera, P. declinans, P. pseudoradiosa, P. superba, P. aalensis, Pleydellia trans. L. opalinium, P. misera, P. folleata*   0.30m

Below - large burrs embedded in soft orange sands. Some doggers crammed with ammonites, *Grammoceras distans, Pleydellia aalensis.*   1.0m

EXCURSION 3: West Bay to Freshwater.

Looking east from West Bay it is possible to see a panoramic view of Chesil Beach, a shingle bank extending to the base of the Isle of Portland. The shingle is mostly flint, some of it translucent blue chalcedony derived from the Cretaceous rocks above a major **unconformity** to the west *(see the Introduction page 9 and Chapter 7 Culverhole Point page 60)).*

East Cliff has a much thinner capping of limestone and cliff falls are less frequent. The most interesting feature is the replacement of the yellow conglomerate in places, by typical 'iron-shot' oolite seen in abundance around Beaminster. Here the fossils indicate the Bradfordensis and Concavum zones and include ammonites, *Brasilia bradfordensis, Abbasites abbas* and gastropods including large *Pleurotomaria* spp.

Another important feature is the presence of small pockets of hard oolitic stone, beneath the Astarte Bed, containing well-preserved *Strenoceras* spp. indicating the preservation of the Upper Bajocian Subfurcatum Zone locally.

Thanks for advice and assistance in compiling this chapter are due to Rod Condliffe, David Sole and Tony Gill

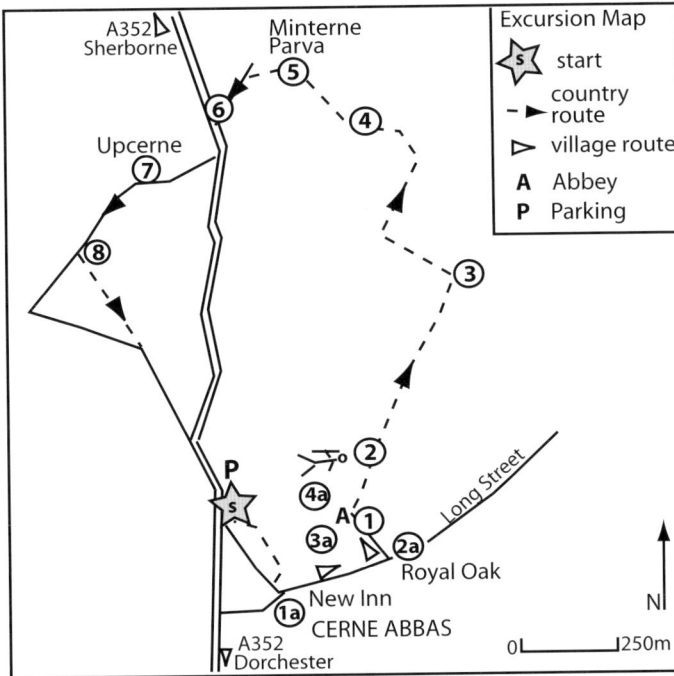

PURPOSE: To identify the building stones used in the village and to investigate the source of those obtained locally, by a walk over the hill.

PRACTICAL DETAILS: Picnic site near Giant View *(ST 663016)*, space for 12 cars or road parking in the village *(busy with visitors in summer)*.

Access: All on public footpaths, well signposted; small fee for entry to Abbey. Bus service from Sherborne and Dorchester - hourly in the morning, two hourly after lunch. Railway stations at Sherborne and Dorchester, from Waterloo.

Facilities: Three public houses, three cafes, public toilets.

Maps: OS Explorer 117, 1:25,000 Cerne Abbas and Bere Regis.

British Geological Survey sheet 328 Dorchester 2000.

Distance: Countryside walk of 6.25 km. Time about 2 hours. Village walk: 1 hour.

Clothing: Stout boots essential, very steep hills, often muddy and very slippery. Clothing according to weather.

GEOLOGICAL SETTING: *(Figure 1)* The village of Cerne Abbas is in a valley in the Chalk downland of central Dorset. The steep-sided valley has been cut through the Chalk into the Upper Greensand by the action of

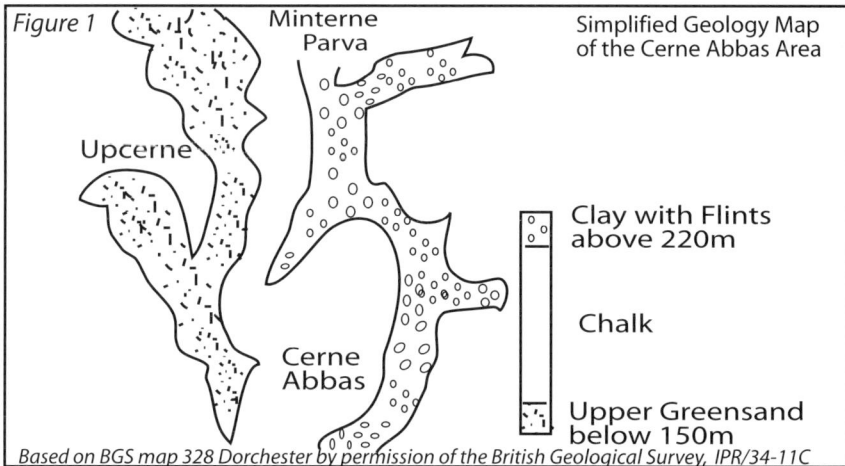

Figure 1 — Simplified Geology Map of the Cerne Abbas Area

Minterne Parva

Upcerne

Cerne Abbas

Clay with Flints above 220m

Chalk

Upper Greensand below 150m

Based on BGS map 328 Dorchester by permission of the British Geological Survey, IPR/34-11C

water. Initially the freeze-thaw action, under periglacial conditions in the Pleistocene period, would have broken up the Chalk, aiding later erosion. Springs issue from the Cann Sand *(Foxmould)* which overlies the Gault Clay. Around Minterne Magna and Parva, and Upcerne, the Cann Sand is overlain by a narrow outcrop of Shaftesbury Sandstone of the Upper Greensand.

Above the Greensand the steep hillsides show a succession through the Lower and Middle Chalk, in the Cenomanian and Turonian stages. The recently updated British Geological Survey map *(published 2000)* shows that the village has been built on the Cann Sand with the remains of the Abbey on the Zig-Zag Chalk *(Cenomanian, Grey Chalk subgroup, Lower Chalk)*. A narrow outcrop of the Holywell Nodular Chalk *(Turonian)* forms the base of the steep hill and the Giant is cut into the New Pit Chalk *(Turonian)*. Above these, as the slope lessens, is the Lewes Chalk *(Turonian)*. The top of the hill is covered with Clay-with-Flints, mostly angular flint gravel in a red-brown clay matrix. On the highest part of the hill the Clay-with-Flints covers the Seaford Chalk *(Coniacian)* which is low in the Upper Chalk.

EXCURSION DETAILS

Turn left out of the car park, right before Kettle Bridge and follow the stream into the village. Go past a mill building and an old barn. The walling stone includes Purbeck Limestone, Upper Greensand, Glauconitic Chalk, Upper Greensand chert, a Lower Chalk phosphatic nodule and both a *Sciponiceras* and a *Turrilites* ammonite. Turn left on reaching the street and left again into Long Street. In general the buildings are a mix of flint, stone, brick and render of different types. The public toilets are opposite the Royal Oak pub, near the Post Office.

THE COUNTRYSIDE WALK starts from the Royal Oak.

Take the road leading past the church *(Abbey Street)* to the pond and go through the right hand gate into the graveyard.

Location 1 *(ST 666014)* St Augustine's Well

St. Augustine's Well is below the level of the graveyard! Has the spring eroded to this level since the graveyard commenced, perhaps when the Abbey was founded in the 9th century? The rubble walls on the north and east sides are said to be mediaeval. Return and take the northern gate in the graveyard wall, then go diagonally right through grassy mounds covering the site of the Abbey, to meet a fence at the bottom of the wooded hill. Follow the fence, remaining in the field below the trees on the hillside behind the Giant and keeping the hill on your left, to a stile. Then look left for the remains of an old lime kiln.

Location 2 *(SY 668017)* A huge quarry has been cut into the side of the hill on the left. The quarry is in the Lower/Middle Chalk and is the probable source of the Chalk building stone in the village but no bare rock can be seen nowadays.

Location 3 *(SY 667028)* Follow the track to the top of the hill meeting a fence *(new in 2002)* and go straight ahead at the first fingerpost. Then go left at the second Wessex Ridgeway sign where the footpath goes across the Clay-with-Flints. Aim at the left side of the wood, go over the crest of the hill and down through a gate (Giant Walk). Follow the contour path towards Minterne Parva until you reach a bridle path marker on an isolated post. Almost immediately, in the bushes to the left, a gate opens downhill onto a farm track. Most of the field is on the Zig Zag Chalk but near the house the corner of the field is on the Upper Greensand *(Shaftesbury Sandstone)*.

Location 4 *(SY 666034)* A small excavation shows pale green rubbly Greensand, known as Shaftesbury Sandstone. The green colouration is because of the mineral glauconite in the rock. If you pick up a small handful you will find it has a hard, gritty texture.

Location 5 *(SY 665034)* Dower House, Minterne Parva

The house has been built of Upper Greensand rubble with Ham Hill Stone dressings. The outbuildings are of flint, sandstone rubble and some scattered pieces of Ham Hill Stone. The sandstone is not used as ashlar *(cut square)*, as it is in Shaftesbury, but as small roughly cut blocks. Where it can be seen *in situ* the sandstone has a rubbly appearance not the even texture that would be necessary for ashlar. Past the outbuildings, the stump of a parish cross is of Ham Hill Stone. Follow the sunken road towards the main road.

Location 6 *(SY 663033)* As the sides steepen badger holes show the

"Foxmould", renamed, by the British Geological Survey, as the Cann Sand. Cross the Cerne stream and turn left onto the main road - TAKE CARE! After about 100m turn right for Upcerne.

Location 7 *(SY 660029)* Chalk is visible on the brow of the hill. This is a small knoll of the Holywell Nodular Chalk over Zig Zag Chalk, visible on the right as you go downhill again. The first two cottages are late 17th and early 18th century respectively and are built of flint and chalk block, with strengthening courses of stone including some Ham Hill Stone rubble. The church and manor house are not accessible but they can be seen from the second gate. The manor house was built in the early 17th century by Sir Robert Mellor *(d. 1624)*. The front is of Ham Hill Stone and the north wing was built in the late 17th century of brick.

Location 8 *(SY 656027)* You can see the Upper Greensand *(Shaftesbury Sandstone)* in the field on the right of the road and as the footpath turns left into the next field. Lumps of the glauconitic, calcite cemented, fossiliferous sandstone are visible in the upper half of the field.

Walk diagonally right across the field towards the oak trees and rejoin the road. It may be possible to see the Cann Sand in the roadside. The Nursing Home was built as the Union Workhouse in 1836 and 1841. The Giant has been cut into the Middle Chalk. Continue along the road back to the car park.

THE VILLAGE WALK

Location 1a Walk back into the village either by the previous route or along the road and start from the terrace of chequered houses to the right when facing the New Inn. These were built in the late 19th century of knapped flint and chalk block walls on an ashlar plinth. Ham Hill Stone has been used for the quoins.

The front wall of the New Inn is a patchwork of brick and stone. At the right hand end, a mixture of material, including Ham Hill Stone *(orange/brown)*, Chalk *(white)*, Purbeck Stone *(small, light grey)* and flint goes up to the roof. Below the windows the stone is mainly small blocks of Purbeck with the mix as before between them. The window surrounds are of Ham Hill Stone. At the left hand end the striped appearance is created by using flint banded with Chalk. The Chalk has a greyish look and contains scattered crystals of glauconite *(dark green)*. On the left corner, above head height, a block of chalk has weathered so that a *Calycoceras* ammonite and a bivalve can be seen. Stone tiles on the roof are from Purbeck and weigh 230 tons. The barns have more Chalk and flint and a carving of Catherine wheels from the Abbey is leaning against the back wall of the Inn. A side wall of the next house has Greensand, Chalk, Ham Hill Stone and flint but the front is brick.

The next stone house is the Old Bell *(Figure 2)* where the lower wall is of thinly-bedded Purbeck Limestone. The bedding and weathering is characteristic of stone from the Lower Purbeck Ridgeway quarries. These quarries are found from Portesham to Poxwell and the limestone has been used around Weymouth and Dorchester and up the Frome, Piddle and Cerne valleys. In the Old Bell, from the lower windows upwards, flint is

Figure 2

banded with the greyish Lower Chalk. Glauconite crystals are visible with some phosphatic nodules and at least one specimen of *Turrilites acutus*. This identifies the rock as Cenomanian - the Zig Zag Chalk. The lower windows are built of Ham Hill Stone. The house next to the Old Bell has painted rubble walls at the side, and the rear range is of cob with an earth floor. "Earth" does not mean soil but that it is made of chalk, crushed and beaten smooth.

Location 2a The Royal Oak inn was built in the early 16th century while the Abbey was still standing. Its walls are of flint and rubble. St. Mary's church was started in 1300, the nave and south porch being 15th century and the west tower 1500. The tower and entrance porch are of Ham Hill Stone with the plinth of the nave being of Ham Hill Stone and Portland Limestone ashlar. The 19th century south wall of the nave is banded with small blocks of Purbeck Limestone, then ashlar blocks of Ham Hill Stone and Portland Limestone banded with flint.

Opposite the church the Pitchmarket, built in about 1500, has walls of flint banded with both Purbeck and Ham Hill Stone and timber frame above. The cobbles in front of this row of houses are flint. It is most likely that all the flint used in the village has come from the Clay-with-Flints as these are so easy to collect.

Location 3a Abbey Farm, at the end of the street, incorporates part of the Abbey buildings. The south wing with the buttresses, facing Abbey Street, is partly the 15th century Abbey gatehouse. The walls are of Purbeck Limestone and flint with some Ham Hill Stone. Much of this has been rebuilt after a fire. The gate into the graveyard is built of Ham Hill Stone *(fee to enter Abbey)*. The 15th century Hospice or lodging house, has walls of flint banded with Purbeck Limestone and some Ham Hill Stone windows and quoins. The oriel window at the side is mostly constructed of Portland Limestone. Inside, the walls are lined with chalk block. The Abbot's Porch, built 1497-1509, has walls of Ham Hill Stone and Portland Limestone. Return to the graveyard and the field beyond, this time moving northward at the rear of the Hospice and Porch, turning left to reach the Pottery and then right to the North Barn, now called Beauvoir Court *(Figure 3)*.

Location 4a This was originally built in the 15th century of very large chalk blocks with smaller pieces at the gable ends. The large chalk blocks are nodular in appearance, white with scattered flints. These blocks are so large that they must have come from the huge quarry seen at the beginning of the countryside walk.

Figure 3

The many blocks of chalk seen in various buildings are somewhat whiter than the grey, glauconitic chalk from the Zig Zag Chalk, particularly noted in the New Inn and the Old Bell. They may, therefore, come from the higher parts of the old quarry in the New Pit Chalk. The nodular chalk in the North Barn would be from the Holywell Nodular Chalk in the middle. The huge size of the quarry would suggest that far more chalk has been used in the village buildings than can be seen from the street. The Purbeck Limestone is recognisable by comparison with the limestones used from Weymouth northwards. It weathers in a totally different way from the Middle Purbeck Limestones quarried in the Isle of Purbeck. The Portland ashlar seen in the church, the Hospice *(Figure 4)* and the Abbot's Porch is similar in character to the Portland ashlar used for the Abbey at Abbotsbury, also a Benedictine foundation. At Abbotsbury this

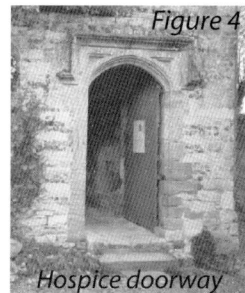
Figure 4
Hospice doorway

has been identified as coming from Portesham quarry, the westernmost quarry on the Ridgeway. However, there are other quarries on the Ridgeway where Portland Limestone of similar character is available. It is recorded that the original Anglo-Saxon Cerne Abbey owned Poxwell where the quarry is the easternmost of the Ridgeway series.

The footpath at the northern end of North Barn leads over Kettle bridge back to the picnic site car park.

CHARMINSTER to SHERBORNE
An Inland Traverse

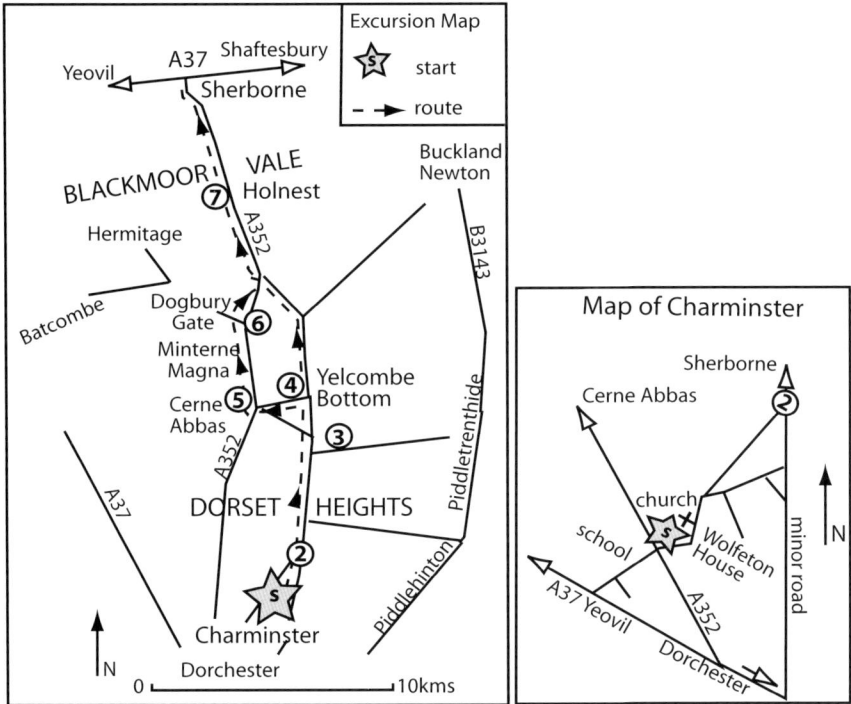

PURPOSE: This south to north traverse, undertaken by car, touches on the contrasted landforms, landscapes and soils of inland Dorset between Charminster and Sherborne.

PRACTICAL DETAILS: The following maps will enhance the visit: OS Explorer series 1:25,000 Cerne Abbas and Bere Regis (117); Yeovil and Sherborne (129). OS Landranger Series 1:50,000 Dorchester, Weymouth and surrounding area (194). BGS 1:50,000 England and Wales Series Dorchester (328) revised edition 2000; Shaftesbury (313) revised edition 1994; Yeovil and Bridport (312).

Charminster to Sherborne is 25km and needs a full day. There are pubs at Godmanstone, Cerne Abbas, Middlemarsh and Long Burton. Beware snowdrifts in winter!

GEOLOGICAL SETTING: The first half of the journey takes the visitor across some 13km of Chalk upland; the wide outcrop is due to the very low **dip** of the strata compared, for example, with that in the Isle of Purbeck. The underlying Cretaceous Upper Greensand appears from below the Chalk on the northern outcrop. Progressively older strata crop out toward Sherborne. Various Jurassic clay formations underlie Blackmoor Vale whilst a succession of tilted beds of mainly limestone *(Cornbrash, Forest Marble, Fuller's Earth Rock)* crop out to form escarpments and dip slopes immediately south of Sherborne.

Location 1 *(SY 679927)* Charminster
Park opposite Charminster Church. The colourful church is a mix of off-white Purbeck Limestone from the Ridgeway north of Weymouth, orange-brown Ham Hill Stone and flint. The Ham Hill Stone is a shelly, iron-stained limestone from near Yeovil, more often used for mouldings at this distance from the quarries, but also in the tower in this instance. A sarsen can be seen on a street corner some 150m west of the church.

Location 2 *(SY 684937)* Continue eastward along the lane, bearing to the left along Vicarage Road, and park near the junction with the secondary road that leads north to Sherborne *(see small map)*. You are standing on the feather-edge of one of the high-level gravel terraces of the Frome valley. The terrace marks the time when the valleys were choked with debris during tundra-like conditions in the last Ice Age. The river valleys were subsequently eroded to a lower level thus leaving the gravel patches perched on the valley sides.

Proceed northward *(left)* along the old Sherborne road. There are impressive views of the Chalk landscape; note the large, mainly arable fields with white and brown patches of soil. The brown patches are remnants of Clay-with-Flints whilst the white patches tend to be mainly accumulations of underlying flints with a white patina, or a chalky subsoil in some instances. These patterns reflect the serious soil erosion that the landscape has suffered plus the uneven thickness of the Clay-with-Flints.

Figure 1 illustrates Clay-with-Flints, deeply piped into the underlying Chalk, in an old pit at Buckland Newton now overgrown *(ST 704052)*. The photographs show angular, highly weathered flints in a reddish sandy matrix overlying dark, chocolate-coloured clays. These deposits have clearly been let down into pipes in the Chalk following solution of the latter. Note the steep sides of the pipe.

 *Figure 1*

Figure 2 shows how the escarpment cuts across these pipes; only the truncated lower parts of the pipes remain. This suggests that the pipes developed before the land surface was lowered. Indeed pipes are thought to be mainly a relic of sub-tropical weathering during the Tertiary Era before the last Ice Age. Shallow exposures of the Clay-with-Flints can be seen at the Batcombe Down Picnic Site *(SY 637039)*. These superficial deposits tend to be acidic unlike the calcareous soils usually associated with the Chalk.

The Chalk on the left in *Figure 2* is riven with joints and the old pit showed steeply dipping **slickensides**. The recently revised BGS 1:50,000 Sheet 313 (Shaftesbury) indicates a group of N-S *(approximately)* **wrench** *(dextral strike-slip)* **faults** which cut the Cretaceous rocks.

Figure 2

These strike-slip faults and associated joints are found extensively in Somerset, Hampshire and further west and are the result of a Tertiary compressive tectonics regime. Deep seismic investigations suggest that these faults overlie reactivated **Variscan** faults in the basement rocks. The resultant Chalk valleys and combes make a fascinating pattern. Continue along the ridge road to the cross roads above Cerne Abbas *(ST 683004)*.

Location 3 *(ST 682002)* Turn right into the road signposted to Piddletrenthide and park by the spinney to view the landscape. Note the general slope of the hilltops from north to south reflecting the dip of the Chalk *(dip slope)*. But there is more to this! The valleys of the Frome, Sydling Water, Cerne, Piddle, Devil's Brook and Winterbourne run southward in sub-parallel courses. This may be no accident. A Tertiary erosion surface extends across east Devon and west Dorset and there is evidence that earth movements have both faulted and tilted this surface. It would seem that major elements of the stream pattern were determined by these events including the location of the watershed separating streams draining to the English and Bristol Channels. Perhaps the wrench faulting mentioned above has also played a part. The Clay-with-Flints is associated with the Tertiary erosion surface.

Location 4 *(ST 680021)* Go back to the 'main' road and turn north *(right)* along the ridge for one and half kilometres to the next road junction on the left leading steeply downhill to Cerne Abbas. Park carefully near the top of the hill. Observe the steep slopes and shape of Yelcombe Bottom and note other similar combes shown on the topographic maps.

The revised Dorchester geological map shows the outcrop of the formations in the Chalk Group in ascending order as follows: off-white Zig Zag Chalk, hard Holywell Nodular Chalk, white firm New Pit Chalk, flinty, hard and nodular Lewes Chalk followed by white, flinty firm Seaford Chalk. These are the revised stratigraphic terms that demonstrate that the Chalk is far from being homogeneous. The combe is the result of hillslope recession processes, under periglacial conditions, removing the weaker lower beds. The harder Chalks maintain the steepest slopes. One has to visualise Arctic-like conditions with mass wasting and debris *(head)* accumulating in the valley bottoms. There is some evidence on the 1:50,000 geological maps that the shapes and alignments of these combes were partly determined by structural weaknesses *(joints in particular)*. Joints and faults may also have influenced the flow of ground water; saturated ground facilitates mass movements.

Location 5 *(ST 662016)* Cerne Abbas

Visitors can drop down into Cerne Abbas for refreshments and to see the Giant where there is a car park on the A352 with a picnic site nearby. Take the second turning to the right *(signposted)* in the village opposite the New Inn *(see map page 44)*. The Giant is cut into the Chalk and demonstrates the thinness of the soils on the steeper valley sides.

Location 6 *(ST 647056)* One can either return to the ridgetop road or make a detour northward on the A352, via Minterne Magna, through a more lush landscape underlain by the Upper Greensand. Turn west *(left)* on to a minor road signposted to Leigh at Dogbury Gate. One can park on a short open section of road about 1km along the road near the trig. point. This minor road traverses the face of the Chalk escarpment where the Chalk rests upon the underlying Greensand. There is an old limekiln *(ST 648056)* in a derelict state backed by steep-faced degraded Chalk workings. The Foxmould sands can be examined in the adjacent cuttings. The clay vale can be viewed from a nearby gateway.

> *'At Hermitage in Dorsetshire,'* says Stow in his Summary, January the thirteenth 1582, *'a piece of Ground of three Acres remov'd from its old place, and was carried over another Close where Alders and Willows grew, the space of forty Rods or Perches, and stopt up the high-way that led to Cerne, a Market-Town, and yet the Hedge, that it was inclosed with enclose it still, and the trees stand bolt upright and the place where the Ground was is left like great Pit.'*
>
> *(There are variations in the year according to different sources).*

This is a superb description of the features of a typical landslip. January is significant in that the ground would be saturated at that time of the year. The Shaftesbury geological map shows landslips on the north side of the road. The exact location is uncertain and challenges the visitor. The site is likely to be associated with a steep backscar, a low point along the road and a spring serving a stream. No doubt the landslips were facilitated by the presence of the clays of the Hazelbury Bryan Formation *(Lower Calcareous Grit)* at the base of the Corallian below the Greensand *(compare the cliffs of Black Ven page 126)*.

Return to the A352 and turn north toward Sherborne. The road descends over landslip country on to the clay vale-the Blackmoor Vale *(Corallian HBF)*. It is close, well-wooded country still embroidered with many hedges. The soils are heavy except where alleviated by valley gravels, head or alluvium. There is widespread pasture and a dispersed settlement pattern of scattered farms and hamlets. The clay vales are one of our major landforms and one needs to stand on a hilltop in order to visualise the vast amount of erosion that has removed so much rock. Where, when and how did it go? The answer must lie in the widespread mass wastage of hillslopes during periglacial episodes in the last Ice Age. The river system transported the fine waste to the sea but left some of it behind as clayey alluvium on the flood plains. The more resistant Chalk was less easily removed.

Location 7 *(ST 656098)* Holnest

Call in at the isolated church at Holnest and note the extensive use of the Jurassic Forest Marble shelly limestones from the Long Burton area. We have left behind the flints and Purbeck Limestone of the Cerne valley. The stone tiles are from the Forest Marble and are becoming a valuable resource. Forest Marble is still worked at Landshire Lane northeast of Stalbridge *(ST 717185)*. This is part of the great belt of Jurassic building stones that extends to Bath and the Cotswolds.

The road passes onto the Oxford Clay and then ascends the dip slope of the Forest Marble which was formerly quarried at Long Burton. Suddenly the road descends the fine escarpment that overlooks Sherborne. But note a second, smaller platform *(with playing fields)* and scarp formed by the Fuller's Earth Rock.

One can either retrace the route that has been followed or continue on the A352 to the traffic lights at the junction with the A30 on the west side of Sherborne. Turn left to Yeovil and follow signs for the Town Centre and the Swan Theatre; this will bring you to the Dorchester Road *(A37)*. Revisit the clay vale and enjoy the views of the remnants of the Tertiary erosion surface as you cross the Chalk upland back toward Dorchester.

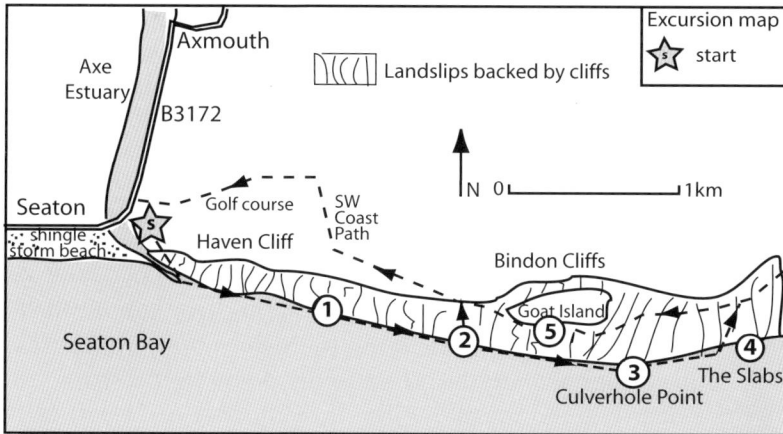

PURPOSE: to examine the transition from the terrestrial environments of the latest Triassic to the marine environments of the early Jurassic. The walk also includes the most accessible sections in the Upper Greensand in Devon, and traverses the spectacular 1839 Bindon Landslip.

PRACTICAL DETAILS: the complete walk is about 7km long and can be done in a brisk 3 hours, but there is enough to linger over to make it a good day out. Shorter variants are possible that can reduce the time to between 1½ and 3 hours. These include (i) returning via the beach from Locations 2 or 3 (ii) returning from Location 2 via a fisherman's path and the South West Coast Path; and (iii) reversing the walk and returning from Location 4 via the beach.

Park alongside the B3172 Seaton to Axmouth road *(SY 253901)* about 100m north of Axmouth Bridge. Additional parking is available in the roads immediately west of the bridge. A short *(800m)* level walk leads to Seaton bus station where there are connections to Sidmouth, Lyme Regis and the Exeter-Waterloo line station at Axminster. The usual precautions with respect to cliff falls, greasy boulders on the beach and incoming tides should be taken. Most of the walk can be done at most states of the tide in calm weather but Culverhole Point cannot be passed at high water. Low tide has the advantage that the rock structures in the cliff can be seen more clearly, that it avoids the possible danger from rock falls and that it provides easier walking conditions.

GEOLOGICAL SETTING: Continuous cliffs on the first part of the walk expose red and green mudstones that pass up into grey mudstones and white limestones, a succession of lithologies that represents the late Triassic change from hot desert to brackish marine environments. The later part of the walk includes foreshore exposures in fossiliferous, marine Jurassic mudstones and limestones and large collapsed masses of marine Cretaceous sandstones, **calcarenites** and Chalk. They are in the western part of the 7km-long Undercliff Landslip, the largest in England. The final part provides views of the well-documented Bindon Landslip and the extensive Eocene **planation** surface of east Devon.

EXCURSION DETAILS

Follow the path along the left bank of the River Axe to its outfall at SY 256897. The opposite bank of the river is a spit of storm beach gravels, composed almost entirely of chert and flint, derived by longshore drift from cliffs of Cretaceous rocks between Seaton and Sidmouth. The growth of the shingle bank has diverted the river mouth progressively eastwards over the last few hundred years. Prior to the early 16th century the river entered the sea at the thriving port of Seaton, at the western end of its wide floodplain.

Location 1 *(SY 255898-262898)* Haven Cliff

From the River Axe outfall walk eastwards along the beach to Culverhole. The coastline on this part of the walk consists of an upper cliff *(Haven Cliff)* of Upper Greensand and Chalk, separated from a lower cliff of Triassic rocks by a bench of jumbled Cretaceous rocks that have collapsed along slip planes in the Gault. The lower cliff provides continuous exposures in gently folded red and green silty mudstones of the late Triassic Seaton Mudstone Formation and in green and grey mudstones of the Blue Anchor Formation. Part of the succession is repeated by **faults** that run almost parallel to the cliff face and beneath the foreshore. These produce confusing cliff sections which give the false impression that there are large lateral variations within the Triassic succession. There are not.

The lowest beds exposed are in typical 'Keuper Marl' facies, reddish brown silty mudstones with lines of green blotches and a few thin green beds. These mudstones contain few sedimentary structures largely because they have been disturbed by insolation *(diurnal heating and cooling in a desert environment)* and the repeated crystallisation and dissolution of salt and gypsum. They contain no fossils other than a few concretions *(rhizocretions)* around poorly preserved rootlets. The red colouration, lithology and sedimentology are indicative of inland **sabkha** environments not dissimilar from those of the present-day Persian Gulf.

A prominent bed of coarse green siltstone *(0.8m thick)* marks an upward change to alternations of red (60%) and green (40%) silty mudstones. These mudstones were called the Variegated Marls by early geologists but are now the Haven Cliff Mudstone in modern terminology. These distinctively striped beds represent a regional change to a slightly wetter environment and can be traced in boreholes and sections via Devon and Somerset to the South Wales coast.

The base of the overlying Blue Anchor Formation, named after a pub on the Somerset coast, is taken at the base of a thin *(0.3m)* **dolomitic** limestone that forms the lower of two prominent limestone ribs in the cliffs. It marks the incoming of thin beds of limestone and dark grey mudstone which were deposited in **fluviatile** environments, probably in brackish water. Thin beds of red mudstone continue into the lower part of the Blue Anchor Formation but these die out upwards as the hot dry desert conditions were replaced by a wetter climate. The highest part of the formation contains gypsum nodules, possible algal structures and slump structures indicative of deposition in coastal sabkhas and on tidal flats.

NB a fisherman's path *i.e.* not a public right of way *(SY 272894)*, just east of the end of the main cliff, leads northwards to the SW Coast Path which can then be followed back to the start point *(see locations map)*. Details of the geology of this part of the route are given under Location 5.

Location 2 *(SY 273894)* Culverhole

The highest beds of the Blue Anchor Formation and the mudstones of the overlying Westbury Formation and Cotham Beds crop out on the foreshore in front of a low cliff of White Lias. Exposures in the lower beds vary considerably depending on the extent of the beach shingle. The complete succession is summarised in *Figure 1*. The dark grey pyritic mudstones of the Westbury Formation, with the famous Rhaetic Bone Bed at their base, rest with minor **unconformity** on the underlying beds throughout southern England. Mary Anning collected fish and marine reptile teeth and bones from the bone bed at this locality but it is now rarely well exposed. The mudstones contain an abundant, but low diversity, fauna dominated by bivalves (including *Rheatavicula contorta*) and gastropods that indicate deposition in brackish lagoons connected, from time to time, to a shallow sea. The overlying Cotham Beds consist of pale green mudstones with thin bone beds and **ripple trains**, composed of sand and limestone **ooliths**, with a similar fauna to that of the Westbury Formation. The highest bed, the distinctive algal limestone known as the Cotham *(Landscape)* Marble, has been recorded here, but only as loose blocks.

The low cliff of White Lias is composed almost entirely of fine-grained, white-weathering limestone, a distinctive lithology which prompted William Smith to use this quarrymen's name on his earliest geological

Figure 1 Generalised vertical section for the Triassic succession at Culverhole
(note the scale change for the lower half of the section)

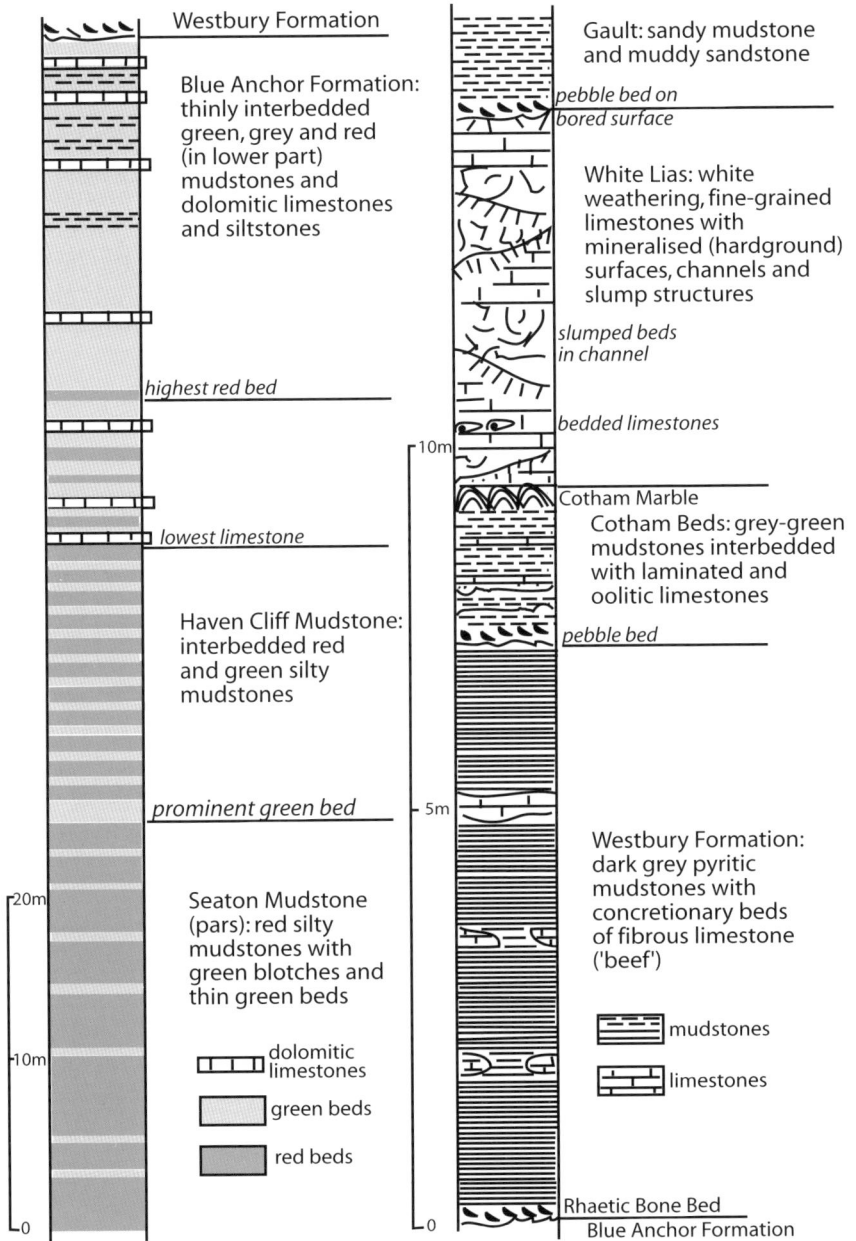

Westbury Formation

Blue Anchor Formation:
thinly interbedded
green, grey and red
(in lower part)
mudstones and
dolomitic limestones
and siltstones

highest red bed

lowest limestone

Haven Cliff Mudstone:
interbedded red
and green silty
mudstones

prominent green bed

Seaton Mudstone
(pars): red silty
mudstones with
green blotches and
thin green beds

dolomitic
limestones

green beds

red beds

Gault: sandy mudstone
and muddy sandstone

pebble bed on
bored surface

White Lias: white
weathering, fine-grained
limestones with
mineralised (hardground)
surfaces, channels and
slump structures

slumped beds
in channel

bedded limestones

Cotham Marble

Cotham Beds: grey-green
mudstones interbedded
with laminated and
oolitic limestones

pebble bed

Westbury Formation:
dark grey pyritic
mudstones with
concretionary beds
of fibrous limestone
('beef')

mudstones

limestones

Rhaetic Bone Bed
Blue Anchor Formation

Figure 2 Generalised vertical section for the
          Upper Greensand at Culverhole Point

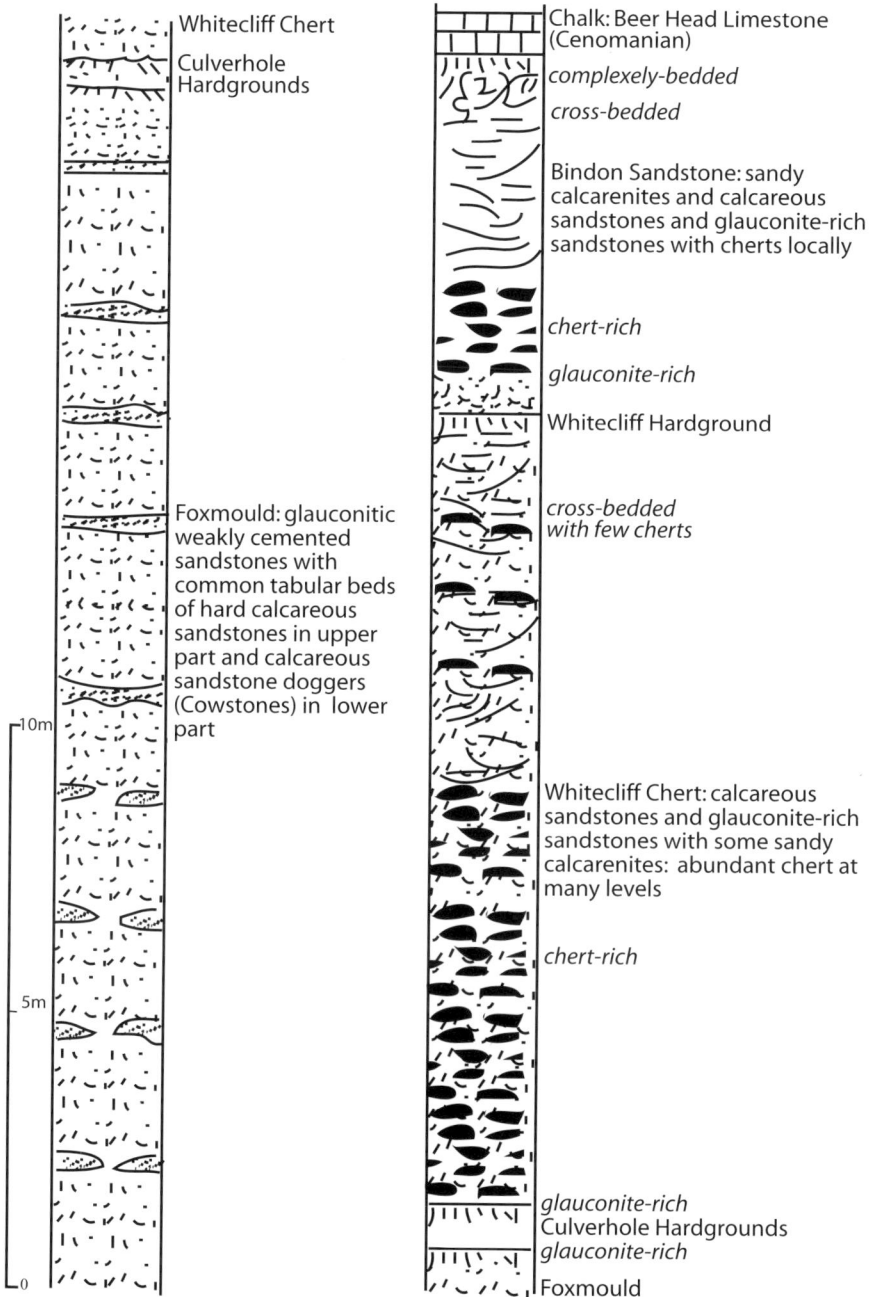

Whitecliff Chert

Culverhole
Hardgrounds

Foxmould: glauconitic
weakly cemented
sandstones with
common tabular beds
of hard calcareous
sandstones in upper
part and calcareous
sandstone doggers
(Cowstones) in lower
part

10m

5m

0

Chalk: Beer Head Limestone
(Cenomanian)

complexely-bedded

cross-bedded

Bindon Sandstone: sandy
calcarenites and calcareous
sandstones and glauconite-rich
sandstones with cherts locally

chert-rich

glauconite-rich

Whitecliff Hardground

*cross-bedded
with few cherts*

Whitecliff Chert: calcareous
sandstones and glauconite-rich
sandstones with some sandy
calcarenites: abundant chert at
many levels

chert-rich

glauconite-rich
Culverhole Hardgrounds
glauconite-rich
Foxmould

map. At Culverhole, and elsewhere on the east Devon coast, the White Lias consists of alternations of evenly bedded limestone and channels infilled by limestones with distorted (*slump*) bedding. The latter contain angular **clasts** of densely cemented limestone derived from mineralised **hardgound** surfaces that occur throughout the sequence. A low diversity fauna of bivalves and gastropods, combined with the slumping and hardgrounds, suggests deposition in very shallow seawater of almost normal salinity. At the top of the cliff an irregular bored surface in the limestones is **unconformably** overlain by grey pebbly, clayey sand, at the base of the Cretaceous Gault, an erosion surface that represents a gap of over 100 million years of Earth history. The unconformity has removed the upper part of the White Lias here. The remainder is overstepped by the Gault within 100m to the west.

Location 3 (*SY 279892*) Culverhole Point

The walk continues eastwards along the beach to Culverhole Point at the foot of the Bindon Landslip. The boulder-strewn beach here is composed of rounded **doggers** of calcareous sandstone derived from the lower (*Foxmould*) part of the Upper Greensand and larger blocks derived from the overlying Whitecliff Chert and Bindon Sandstone (*Figure 2*). These blocks contrast with published accounts of the Upper Greensand which commonly describe the formation as a glauconitic sand. When fresh, much of the upper part consists of tough calcareous sandstones and sandy **calcarenites** some of which were used (*under the name Salcombe Stone*) for the exterior of Exeter Cathedral and numerous local churches. The larger fallen blocks are the best place to examine the sedimentary structures and faunas at this stratigraphical level, the cliff sections being either mostly inaccessible or deeply weathered. The doggers that cover the beach here were likened by some mediaeval romanticist to a resting herd of cows and the name 'Cowstones' has continued as a geological term.

Culverhole Point is composed of a large mass of Upper Greensand and Chalk that remained largely intact when it slid down from its outcrop about 600m to the north. The Chalk section is high in the cliff but this is one of the few localities in Devon where almost the whole of the Upper Greensand can be accessed (*Figure 2*). The formation can be divided into three members in Devon, each of which is separated from its neighbour by one or more erosion surfaces. The lower of the two closely spaced Culverhole Hardgrounds is well exposed at beach level. It separates the weakly calcareous sandstones of the Foxmould Member, with its Cowstone doggers and tabular calcareously cemented beds, from the highly calcareous Whitecliff Chert Member with its abundant chert. The

Foxmould here has yielded *Hysteroceras* and other Albian ammonites, but they are extremely rare. The most common fossils are oysters, pectinids and serpulids.

The Whitecliff Chert also contains numerous oysters and other, commonly fragmentary, bivalves but has yielded fragments of only four ammonites (all *Mortoniceras*) after 200 years of searching. The overlying Bindon Sandstone has yielded six species of late Albian ammonite, including the zonal index *Stoliczkaia dispar* but all from a single inland locality.

NB Culverhole Point cannot be traversed at high sea states.

Location 4 *(SY 286894)* The Slabs

Continue eastwards along the beach to the series of seaward dipping limestone beds known locally as The Slabs, passing en route the skeleton of a dragline, all that remains of an abortive attempt to make an access road to the beach. The upper surface of the most prominent limestone bed is crowded with large specimens of the early Jurassic *(Sinemurian)* ammonite *Coroniceras*, which identifies it as the Grey Ledge of the Blue Lias. At Lyme Regis, 5km east-north-east of here, this limestone marks an upward change to mudstones with few limestone beds, the Shales-with-Beef, but at The Slabs there are several limestones above the Grey Ledge. This is an unusual example of lateral lithological variation in the Lias over a short distance. In addition to ammonites and bivalves, the site has yielded almost complete marine reptiles.

A path at the western end of The Slabs leads northwards in about 150m to the ruins of a cottage that was occupied until the 1940s and then to the SW Coastal Path.

Location 5 *(SY 274894)* Follow the path westwards for about 1km to a viewpoint where a cliff face of Upper Greensand and Chalk can be seen to the north. This is the southern face of Goat Island a 10 million ton mass which slid forward, about 150m over a period of several hours on Christmas Day 1839, as part of the Bindon Landslide. In addition to numerous eye-witness accounts and drawings, this was the first landslip in Britain to be geologically documented and analysed in detail *(by the Reverend William Conybeare and others)*. Continuing westwards the coastal path emerges from the wooded landslip area onto the Clay-with-Flints plateau, an early Tertiary feature that was tectonically modified in the Miocene and dissected in the Quaternary. The walk back to the start point via the golf course provides splendid views of the extent of the plateau in East Devon, and of the Upper Greensand and Chalk cliffs on the opposite side of Seaton Bay.

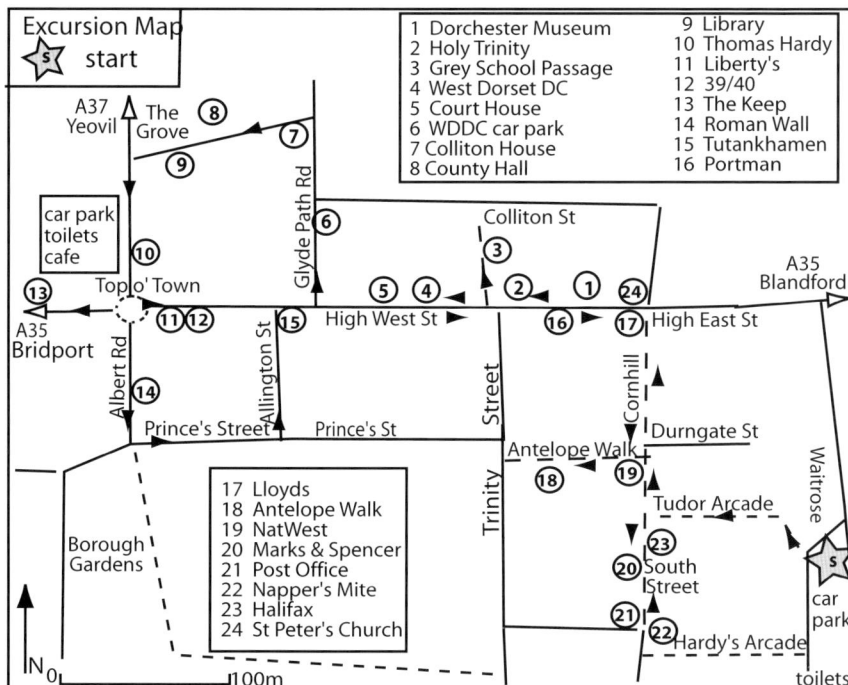

Excursion Map

☆ **start**

1 Dorchester Museum	9 Library
2 Holy Trinity	10 Thomas Hardy
3 Grey School Passage	11 Liberty's
4 West Dorset DC	12 39/40
5 Court House	13 The Keep
6 WDDC car park	14 Roman Wall
7 Colliton House	15 Tutankhamen
8 County Hall	16 Portman

17 Lloyds
18 Antelope Walk
19 NatWest
20 Marks & Spencer
21 Post Office
22 Napper's Mite
23 Halifax
24 St Peter's Church

PURPOSE: To study the building stones seen in the central part of Dorchester and to bring the variety of stones in use there to the attention of the interested observer. Over the past decade there has been a considerable increase of interest in the building stones within our towns. This is very much geology on our doorstep. Most towns have a great variety of geological interest within central business districts and Dorchester is no exception. It is intended to show how building stone can be recognised and how the evidence for the origin of the rocks can be interpreted. It should be remembered that, over a period of time, some features change especially stone used for shop fronts. A thin veneer is often used for such purposes and some of these can be quite exotic. A good example of this can be seen, in other places than Dorchester, at MacDonald fast food outlets which use travertine from Italy and black 'granite' from South Africa.

PRACTICAL DETAILS: There is parking in a number of locations in Dorchester having reached the town via the A35 from the east *(Bournemouth)* or the west *(Exeter)*, via the A37 from the north *(Bristol and Yeovil)* or the A354 from Weymouth. Probably the best car park for this walk is the one to the east of the main shopping centre. It is an easy walk through one of two shopping arcades to reach South Street and Cornhill though the Tudor Arcade is probably the most convenient.

Safety: You will be walking in the main streets of Dorchester, some with significant traffic. South Street, however, is pedestrianised and has several ancient alleys and lanes leading off it. The starting point of the walk is the County Museum with many interesting displays. There are also several other museums in the town.

EXCURSION DETAILS

Location 1 Dorset County Museum

This building *(Figure 1)* is made of white Purbeck *(Lower Cretaceous)* Limestone. This stone came from former quarries south of the Ridgeway at Upwey, north of Weymouth. Some concentric patterns can be seen in the limestone which are probably shell fragments from oysters *(bivalves)*. These fossils are emphasised by the effects of pollution on the surface of the stone. There is also evidence of varying degrees of weathering; the more thinly bedded limestone *(where the planes are closer together)* is more prone to weathering. This is seen particularly well on the east side of the Museum facing on to St Peter's Church. Some of the limestone blocks are cut by calcite veins formed from calcium carbonate deposited from ground water passing along cracks in the rock. An orange/brown limestone is also present in the Museum facade and is largely used for quoins *(corner stones)* and window surrounds. This is Ham Hill Stone from a quarry near Montacute in south Somerset, about 8km west of Yeovil.

Figure 1

Ham Hill Stone, which has been quarried since mediaeval times, is a renowned building stone. It is made up of large numbers of shell fragments so it is a bioclastic limestone, 'bio' from the shells and 'clastic' meaning broken fragments of rock or shell. The Ham Hill Stone contrasts with the unfossiliferous Yeovil Sand of which it is the lateral equivalent. There is some evidence of bedding in the limestone with the shell fragments lying parallel to the bedding. Some splitting off *(spalling)* of the stone is apparent probably due to changes in volume following chemical weathering. It is also possible that the stone has been laid with the bedding parallel to the building face and again spalling is likely.

Location 2 Holy Trinity Church

This church is built of Portland Limestone plus Bath Stone from the Great Oolite, a cream coloured Jurassic limestone. The limestone shows evidence of damage from pollution with calcite ($CaCO_3$) changing to gypsum ($CaSO_4$). There is also evidence of biotic weathering caused by lichens on the surface of the limestone. In the Portland Limestone there is evidence of single burrows *(Skolithos)* formed by organisms burrowing into the sediment while it was still on the sea floor. This is best seen to the right of, and slightly above, the seat in High West Street. Another feature in the Bath Stone is **cross-bedding**. This is best seen on the right hand side of the entrance to Grey School Passage. Cross-bedding forms where sediment is transported by water currents *(or by wind)* and then deposited as ripples *(or as dunes)*. The top of the first unit was cut across by erosion before another such unit was deposited producing the cross-bedding. Such structures are useful to show whether the stone is the right way up or inverted, and are called 'way up' structures *(Figure 2)*.

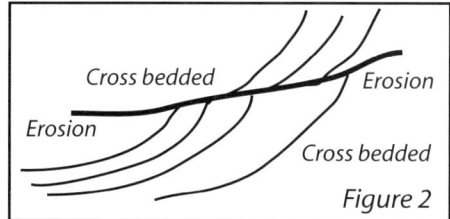

Figure 2

Location 3 Grey School Passage

Here there is evidence of the use of flint. Flint, a very hard siliceous rock, is present in Chalk and is used as a building material when other stone is less readily available. The Chalk around Dorchester would be the source of the flint as it can be picked up from field surfaces. It would be less expensive *(and probably free)* to use than the imported Portland, Purbeck, Ham Hill and Bath Stone and has been used for the garden wall on the right at the far end of Grey School Passage.

Location 4 West Dorset District Council *(Figure 3)*

Again Bath Stone has been used and here has good examples of cross-bedding in the shelly limestone. An oolitic texture is also obvious. Ooliths are small spherical grains that make up most of the limestone. These are currently forming in tropical marine shallow water conditions ($< 6\,m$) such as on the Great Bahama Bank. Geologists assume that fossil examples of oolitic sediment formed under similar conditions. Britain was in a sub-tropical latitude well to the south of its current location when these Jurassic rocks were being formed. The ooliths *(the individual grains)* are made of shell fragments, coated with concentric layers of calcium carbonate, which were rolled to form the round grains. Cross-bedding is again apparent especially to the left of the left-hand door.

Calcite *(crystalline $CaCO_3$)* veins cut across the limestone surface, the

Figure 3

calcium carbonate being derived from within the limestone and transported by ground water. The building has a very different rock for the nameplate. This is larvikite, a distinctive blue, feldspar rich igneous rock from Norway. Larvikite is frequently used as an ornamental stone in many town centre buildings, usually as a facing stone. This is the lighter variety. A darker one can be seen later in the walk, used as a facing stone for Marks and Spencer.

Location 5 Old Crown Court

The building is of Portland Stone, called a freestone because it can be cut in any direction. The stone is in large cut ashlar blocks, very common in Georgian and Regency buildings. The fossiliferous nature of the stone can be seen around the doors where oyster shells are particularly obvious below the Tolpuddle Martyrs' Plaque. Turn right along Glyde Path Road at the end of the building.

Location 6 West Dorset District Council car park

Portland Limestone has been used as cut blocks, a common use in the 1960s and 1970s. The next building also has Portland Limestone but here it has been crushed and used for pebble dash of the walls.

Location 7 Colliton House

Colliton House is an elegant Georgian building made of Purbeck Limestone from the Upwey Quarries mentioned earlier.

Location 8 County Hall

Across the road is County Hall, built of Portland Limestone and Swanage bricks. There were extensive brick making industries in Dorset especially at Gillingham, Broadmayne, Weymouth and Swanage. The Jurassic, Cretaceous and Tertiary clays of the County proved an ideal resource. With the increasing scale of brick making in England however, centralisation has occurred mainly in the Midlands (Bedfordshire, Northants). Only one brick making operation remains in Dorset, at Swanage. The last major brick works closed in Weymouth in 1969.

Location 9 County Library

Re-cross the road to the library which is mainly of Portland Limestone with rather crude dressing marks.

Location 10 The Thomas Hardy Statue

At Top o' Town, Thomas Hardy is probably made of Portland Stone Base Bed, a massive limestone which is the best Portland building stone.

Location 11 Liberty's Club

Liberty's has Purbeck Limestone forming the front of the building. Small oyster shells can be seen in the stone blocks if they are studied carefully.

Location 12 39/40 High West Street

This is of Portland Freestone used as ashlar; occasional shell fragments can be seen weathered out. There is also evidence of orientation of the blocks if you look at the lineation of the shell fragments.

Location 13 Castle Keep *(Devon and Dorset Military Museum)*

The Keep shows good examples of shelly, oolitic limestone forming the quoins around the gate and windows and more thinly-bedded limestone making up most of the walls. The stone again is from the Ridgeway quarries. Return to the Top o' Town roundabout and turn right into Albert Road.

Location 14 Roman wall

There are a variety of stones in the relic wall. They include flints, thinly-bedded Purbeck Limestone and some yellow coloured stone which could be Ham Hill Stone although it doesn't look shelly enough. As the wall is protected by fencing it is difficult to say. It is unlikely to come from too far afield to be used in a wall. A sand and lime mortar *(from the Chalk)* holds it all together. Turn left down Prince's Street, left again down Allington Street and you will see a redundant church on the right.

Location 15 Tutankhamun

The building is made of Bath Stone *(Jurassic Great Oolite)* and Doulting Stone *(Jurassic Inferior Oolite)*. Turn right into High West Street.

Location 16 Portman Building Society

This has a facade of both Portland and Bath Stone and illustrates a shelly, oolitic limestone which is particularly obvious next to the Judge Jeffrey's Restaurant. Continue down High West Street.

Location 17 Lloyds Bank

The bank is made of Portland Freestone with inclusions of pink/red granite around the doorways. This is probably a Scottish granite possibly Balmoral or similar. The pink/red mineral is orthoclase feldspar, a common mineral in granite although the feldspar can also be white. You should also be able to see grey glassy quartz. Quartz and feldspar are essential minerals in granite *i.e.* they have to be present for a rock to be termed granite. Black biotite mica is also present although this is rather weathered and not as shiny as it should be. There are dark grey patches in the granite which has been used for the entrance on the corner of High West Street and Cornhill. The patches are xenoliths and are fragments of rock taken into the granite when it was molten but were then not completely melted before the granite cooled. The wall just above pavement level is unpolished granite and, therefore, looks rather dull. Turn right into Cornhill where, above the modern facades at street level, interest can be found in both building materials and architectural features.

Location 18 Antelope Walk
Note the yellow bricks brought from Poole.

Location 19 National Westminster Bank
The bank is built of the orange/brown Ham Hill Stone seen at the Museum. The bedding is clearly picked out by differential weathering.

Location 20 Marks and Spencer
The store has dark larvikite as a facing stone. The blue feldspar crystals stand out, producing what is called the Schiller Effect where light is reflected because of the alignment of very small mineral grains within the feldspar. There is also some almost black stone which is called 'black granite' and comes from South Africa. It is actually gabbro, a coarse grained equivalent of basalt, in which the minerals reflect the light. It comes from an important gabbro structure called the Bushveld Complex in South Africa, which is important for platinum and chromium ores.

Location 21 Post Office
The steps are orthogneiss, a metamorphic rock formed from granite subjected to further pressure and heat. This is almost certainly derived from deep in a mountain belt such as the Alps.

Location 22 Napper's Mite
This ancient building shows badly weathered thinly-bedded limestone, again probably derived from the quarries at Upwey.

Location 23 Halifax
The facade again has granite facing stone but this time it is very pale with white feldspar and quartz plus black biotite and silvery muscovite mica. Mica is a common accessory mineral in granite; *i.e.* it is often present but doesn't have to be for the rock to be a granite.

Location 24 St Peter's Church
The church is built of Portland, Purbeck and Ham Hill Stone. There has been some recent replacement of the Ham Hill Stone with Guiting Stone from Gloucestershire. This stands out at present as it is rather a bright yellow/brown colour. The church has a feature not commented on so far in that it has stone 'slates' on the roof near the tower. They are thinly-bedded Purbeck Limestone which could have come from the Upwey quarries or from further afield on the Isle of Purbeck in east Dorset.

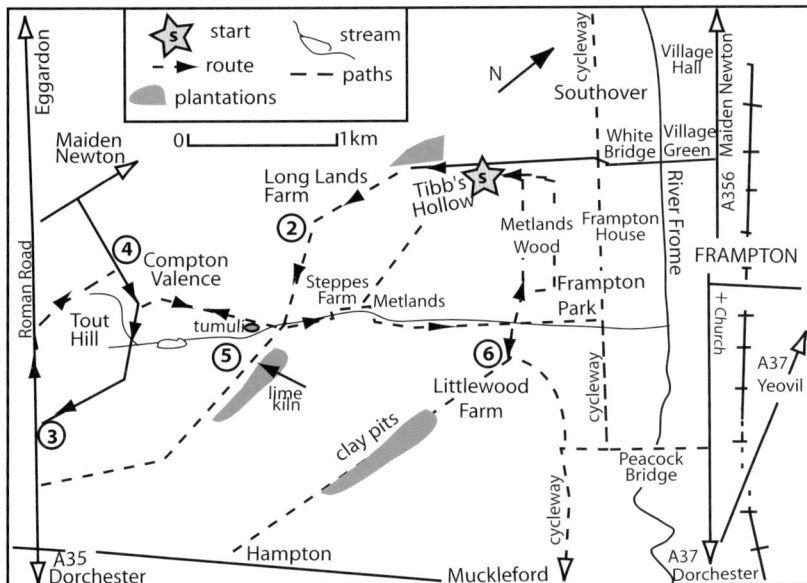

PURPOSE: To demonstrate the link between the agricultural activities of man over some 5000 years and the geology of the area. Geology, geomorphology, archaeology and history combine throughout this walk. Man's recorded use of these valleys, shaped by their geological formation and subsequent weathering patterns, can be plainly traced.

PRACTICAL DETAILS: The A356 runs between Frampton and Crewkerne joining the A37 at Grimstone. In Frampton turn south off the A356 into a lane signposted Southover and Tibb's Hollow. You then cross the flood plain of the Frome which, in a wet winter, can cause difficulties! Cross the White Bridge *(built in the 1790s, from Tertiary clay bricks fired in Southover)* to the crossroads. Swing slightly right and then left up a steep hill to a car park and picnic site *(SY 610945)*. OS Explorer Map 117 covers the whole walk. Distance is 8km with some moderate slopes.

Safety: The walk is on rights of way and country lanes. Cattle and sheep will be encountered so please keep dogs under control. There are no houses between Long Lands Farm and Compton Valence and none, on returning, until Steppes Farm. There is a public phone at Compton Valence but no other facilities. If there has been heavy rain, the trickle of water flowing from Compton Valence can quite quickly become a rushing torrent. Cream teas are served at Frampton Village Hall on Sunday afternoons in August.

GEOLOGICAL SETTING: The geology for much of the walk is Upper Chalk with Tertiary clays and gravels draped over the hillsides. At Compton Valence the geology is very different and much older but the events which changed the geomorphology there have had a direct influence on the rest of the valleys between Compton Valence and Frampton. Much more recent climatic changes have also played their part in making these valleys so favourable to man.

EXCURSION DETAILS

Location 1 *(SY 618944)* Tibb's Hollow, an Upper Chalk pit, was donated by the landowners and turned into a car park by local volunteers. From the entrance you are looking across the flood plain of the Frome which is flowing on the Middle/Upper Chalk boundary. A clump of trees, to the right across the field, hides a small chalk quarry and a chalk pit is visible in the hillside rising away from the A356, both are in Upper Chalk.

To the left is a wood planted on Tertiary material which slipped down over the Chalk slope because of the effects of **solifluction**, a pattern repeated throughout the area. Road and other workings frequently reveal the surface effects of this periglacial process as well as pipes of Tertiary material deposited by water scouring the chalk surface *(Figure 1)*.

Figure 1

Walk up the road toward Long Lands Farm noting the gorse patches which mark slips of Tertiary deposits onto the chalk of the valley sides. Follow the track straight on through the farmyard and start down the slope. Chalk is soon apparent in the sides of the track where, in the right season, the plants are full of butterflies.

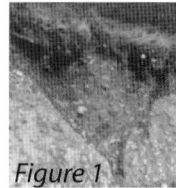

Location 2 *(SY 612940)* As you round a corner part way down *(Figure 2)* you will see that there are several valleys which join the one you are approaching. Three from the south meet the stream at right angles. To your right another valley sweeps round to the west. It seems likely that this valley, now dry, carried the main flow of water at one time. It is much wider than any of the others and cuts into Middle Chalk. The

Figure 2

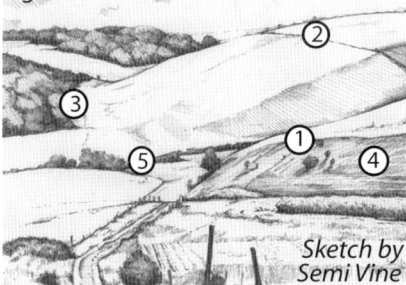

Sketch by Semi Vine

1. A Bronze Age barrow sits on a spur with two others along the ridge.
2. Across the stream, faintly outlined, are Iron Age field systems.
3. A lime kiln below the main wood.
4. Field systems and **terracettes**.
5. The stream from Compton Valence to Frampton. A sheep wash and two kinds of field systems are further up stream to the right.

other valleys and the present stream are mainly on Upper Chalk. There are several interesting features to be seen from the vantage point of the track, bearing in mind that chalk is not a good growing medium. Ahead there are planted woods and, high on the hill opposite, there are the shadows of Iron Age field systems. Such features indicate that there is, or was, Tertiary material on top of the chalk. Weathered chalk will grow crops using modern equipment and fertilisers whereas older cultures used the more fertile and easily worked Tertiary soils to grow their food. Nowadays, Early Purple Orchids and numerous interesting fungi are to be found in the many plantations.

Turn up the valley immediately to the right, called Compton Bottom. You are now walking on Middle Chalk, with the surrounding hillsides in Upper Chalk. It would be difficult to see the difference even if the hillsides were bare chalk instead of grass. Geologists use characteristic fossils *(zone fossils)* to identify different geological layers and echinoids *(sea urchins)* are used to identify some of the Chalk strata. If found *in situ*, the echinoid *Micraster cortestudinarium (Figure 3)* would indicate that the layer in in which it was found, is the Coniacian Stage of the Upper Chalk. Fossils are more likely to be found among the flints lying on the surface of the fields. The echinoid *Micraster* is probably the most recognisable with its heart shaped outline although the most frequently present, but often difficult to identify, are the porifera *(sponges)*.

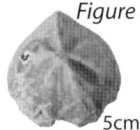

Figure 3

5cm

The valley floor is wide most of the way to Compton Valence and the incline is slight. The slopes, too steep for cultivation, grow natural grasses suitable for sheep and beef cattle, grazing which would also have been utilised by earlier farmers. The hilltops and valleys have been changed to some extent by agricultural use over several thousands of years. Early farmers lived on the hilltops and cleared the land downslope. They had no knowledge of replenishing the soils as they changed from hunter-gatherers to agriculturists. Constant use broke down the structure of the soil which was then subject to wind blown weathering and finished up in the valleys. The valleys were both wooded and swampy and some are still so today. Later communities lived further down in the valleys and cleared the slopes upwards.

On your left, eventually, there is a quarry in the Middle Chalk with interesting structures in the face but little in the way of fossils. To the right, valleys divide as T junctions similar to those seen earlier, rather than the usual V, cutting off a curious flat topped rise of ground. Most of the valleys have a sharp bend in them. Walk on, crossing Lower Chalk and Greensand *(older than the Chalk)* until you reach the road at

Compton Valence and then turn left. The hollow in which the village sits was once a dome of rocks pushed up by forces operating mainly from the south west some 25Ma. The events then, and others since, shattered the Chalk which subsequently weathered along lines of weakness. Erosion of the older rocks beneath the Chalk has produced the opposite effect, that of an empty 'bowl' *(Figure 4)*. The **dip**

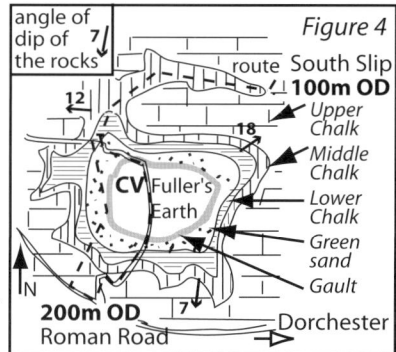

Figure 4

angle of dip of the rocks 7

route South Slip 100m OD

12

18

CV Fuller's Earth

Upper Chalk
Middle Chalk
Lower Chalk
Green sand
Gault

N

200m OD 7
Roman Road
Dorchester

of the pushed rocks is still in place. The oddly shaped valleys are also evidence of the enormous forces which, in the past, have operated over much of the now peaceful Dorset landscape.

The rocks in the 'bowl', and along the valley to Frampton, are all of marine origin with the layers being deposited horizontally. They became dry land as sea levels dropped at the end of the Cretaceous. The oldest layer in Compton Valence is the Fuller's Earth Clay which is Middle Jurassic and formed about 160Ma. The Tertiary material, on top of the Chalk, was deposited by terrestial river systems from 50Ma *(time gap!)*.

As you turn onto the road you are on the Gault Clay which, in this location, is the lowest layer of the Cretaceous. An outcrop of Upper Greensand, the layer between the Chalk and the Gault, is visible on the left in the road bank. A little further on the road is running through the Fuller's Earth, in the centre of the 'bowl'. Follow the lane up to the Roman Road, taking note of the valley above the field with the line of rushes and the fine set of mediaeval strip lynchets *(Figure 5)*. These particular strips also have terracettes running across them. The lynchets, once built, could be worked by early mould-board ploughs. There are hundreds of ancient fields along the Frome and its tributaries including the small square fields of the Iron Age and earlier. Much physical effort went into making them which indicates a large population needing to be fed. The bend in the lane above the lynchets marks the boundary between the Middle and Upper Chalk. You have recrossed the Gault, Greensand, Lower and Middle Chalk and some 75 million years of time.

Figure 5

Location 3 *(SY 592922)* At the top of the hill you are standing on a Roman road. The traffic climbing the A37 beyond Frampton is also travelling a Roman road and you can see field systems on both sides of the valley you walked up. The valley you are looking

along carries the stream to Frampton which must have had a constant flow, as we will see later, but now it is often dry in the summer. Turn right *(north-west)* along the Roman road. Traffic tends to speed along here but it is only a short distance to the double stile in the hedge on the right.   Look back and you will see the Hardy Monument in the distance, marking Tertiary gravel pits and heathlands *(see Chapter 10)*.

Note the *(Upper)* Chalk pit on the left as you enter the field then keep to the hedge on your right. You will cross the head of the oddly shaped valley you saw as you climbed the hill. What is slipping? At the field boundary follow the wide track downhill. You are walking along the top edge of the western rim of the steeply dipping Upper Greensand as you head back down to Compton Valence. The Eggardon Grit, the topmost layer of the Upper Greensand *(the 'bowl' is tilted to the north-east),* can be seen at a bend in the track where a stream emerges from the foot of a small cliff.   The track emerges onto the village road opposite the church which stands on a plateau of the Eggardon Grit.

Location 4 *(SY 591932)* St Thomas of Canterbury

The church *(rebuilt 19th century, tower 13th century)* is partly built of Upper Greensand *(a valuable building resource throughout the area)*; it has a stone tile roof and a fine Purbeck flagstone pathway leading to the main door. The tower is of flint and Purbeck Stone and there is Ham Hill Stone embellishment throughout and a number of Portland Stone monuments in the churchyard. Go down the lane and turn left back down the valley at Lower Dairy, crossing the eastern lower rim of the 'bowl'. The steep slopes on the right again show terracettes, a natural progression exacerbated by sheep and cattle using the ledges as an easy way across the slope.   Cross the stream *(if necessary, by a railway sleeper slightly to the left of the gateway)* and walk a short distance up the valley directly opposite and you will see a lime kiln in the wood.

Location 5 *(SY 613934)* The Bronze Age barrows can be seen clearly outlined on the ridge. Go back toward the stream, climb the slope to the left and you will see the mediaeval strip lynchets which run along the hillside and later furlong strips running vertically up the slope. Look along the other side of the hedge and you can see the remains of an old sheep wash in the stream. Further upstream the Foxlease Withy Beds are growing in the Upper Greensand. At South Slip you are on Upper Chalk as when you were 100m higher above Compton Valence because of the angle of the rocks *(Figure 6)*.

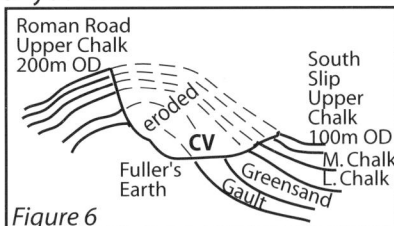

Figure 6

Follow down the west bank of the stream, through three way marked gates but look up the valley beyond the second plantation, North Slip. It too has a bend but it also has obvious ledges in its bed, possibly man-made. Note the busy badger setts and the terracettes. Cross the stream near the end of the third field and follow the east bank to a spinney where the footpath turns west *(right)*. You recross the stream, note the chalk in the fallen tree's roots, and turn north *(left)* onto a wide track. Behind Steppes Farm there is a *(private)* chalk pit with flint bands and hard chalk which is on the Middle/Upper Chalk boundary. At the next house, Metlands, archaeological work revealed a water channel constructed for the 14th century priory in Frampton Park. The line of it can be seen across the field to the west as you continue down the track to the cottages at Littlewood Farm. Pause here and look back because the valley you have just walked down from Steppes Farm was once a reservoir. The stream, running freely from Compton Valence, supplied Dorchester, 2000 years ago, with the Roman essential of clean water.

Location 6 *(SY 627944)* Walk up through the spinney to the east where, well up the path, was the first sluice gate which controlled the flow into the aqueduct. Continue up to the stile, turn right and lean on the gate. Look back up the valley and you will see that it held a very large body of water. An earth dam, with a puddled chalk core, held the water back. It was guarded by a small fort directly left of the gate. The track, used for at least 2000 years, continues up into a wood which conceals Tertiary clay pits that were, almost certainly, the source of the clay which lined the dam. There are furlong fields crossing the track where you stand *(only visible on aerial photographs)*. Go back to the stream and through the stile across the track. Walk uphill to the wood where you will find an information board on the Romans. The large house, below the wood, stands on the site of the priory. Follow either track through the wood and, at the end, walk up the field or the lane back to the car park.

Many kinds of people have lived, worked and left their mark in these valleys. They were all here because of the geology and subsequent weathering which produced the variable soils, the useful Greensand, Gault Clay and Chalk as well as the water. Figure 7

Nowadays the cry of the buzzard and the skylark's song mark a landscape essentially unchanged for thousands of years despite man's long term and continuing agricultural use *(Figure 7)*.

Thanks are due to Mr Bill Putnam and to Dr John Beavis of Bournemouth University for helpful information in compiling this chapter.

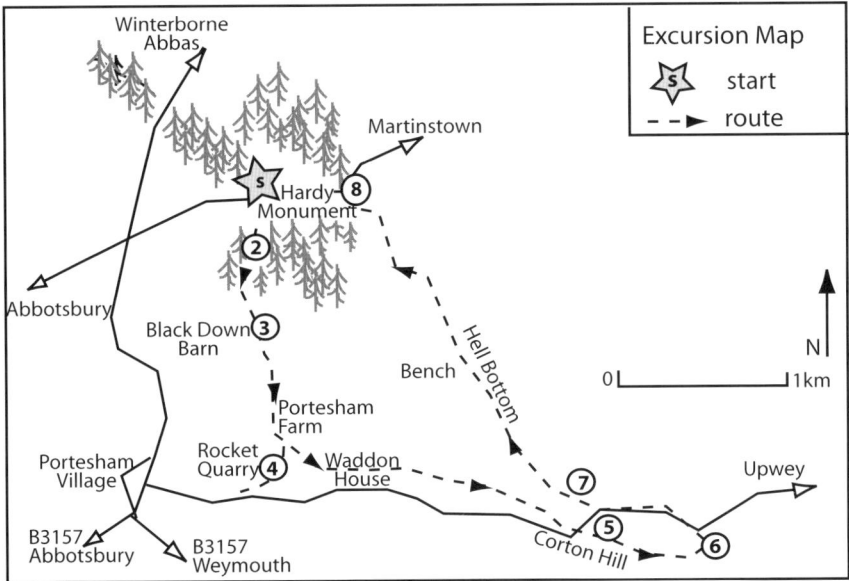

PURPOSE: To observe the effect of rock types (Tertiary sands and gravels, Chalk and Portland limestone) on landscape and land use.

PRACTICAL DETAILS: The walk takes about 3 hours and uses designated footpaths and minor roads. The start is from the Hardy Monument *(Figure 1)* SY 613876 Outdoor Leisure Map 15, Purbeck and South Dorset. The car park closes at 5.30 pm but there is room to park on the

Figure 1

roadside. You can also start from a gateway 100m to the west, signposted Black Down Barn, where there is room to park. The path will then take you to Location 2. The nearest facilities are in Portesham.

GEOLOGICAL SETTING: Around the Hardy Monument is some typical Poole Formation. These are of Eocene age, *i.e.* early Tertiary about 50 million years old. The beds around the Hardy Monument are dominated by clasts *(pebbles)* of chert and flint. These are to be seen in the pits to the south of the car park *(Figure 2)*.

Figure 2

The rock is described as a conglomerate as it is made of large *(>2mm)* rounded clasts in a finer groundmass. These sediments were deposited as an **alluvial fan** on the north side of the Ridgeway **Fault**, some 1.5km to the south, in Tertiary times. This is evidenced by the poorly sorted nature of these sediments, sorting in terms of size and shape being accomplished during transport. However some of the clasts are derived from further afield and have come from Devon or Cornwall, suggesting long distance **fluvial** transport. The rocks from which they are derived are of Devonian or Carboniferous age *(400-285 Ma)*. The British Geological Survey map suggests that these deposits are only 9m thick and yet they extend from the top of the hill at 237m down to below 152m in places. Assuming that the British Geological Survey map is accurate, then the gravels are a drape over the hill. They are likely to have moved down slope by solifluction after they were initially deposited. This is a gravity induced process often, but not exclusively, linked to winter freeze and summer thaw during the Pleistocene glacial episodes.

The sands and gravels produce acid soils which are favoured by the heathland plants such as bracken, gorse and heather. Conifer plantations are the only commercial use for this poor stony soil. Further information on this location can be found in 'A traverse across the Weymouth **Anticline'** published by Dorset's Important Geological/Geomorphological Sites Group (DIGS), *(see page 199)*.

EXCURSION DETAILS

Location 1 *(SY 613876)* The Hardy Monument *(see Geological Setting)*
A footpath leads south-west, from the south-west corner of the car park, towards some woodland. It soon links up with a path to the south which is signposted to West Bexington.

Location 2 *(SY 610873)* The coarse pebbly nature of the Poole Formation can be seen in the footpath and this continues on through the woodland. In the footpath, within the woodland, the remains of a Sarsen Stone can be seen. This is a rock made from flint and chert clasts, cemented with silica and produced, in early Tertiary times, from the weathering of Chalk and the underlying Upper Greensand. The rock is both physically and chemically strong. Large examples can be seen in the village of Portesham in the stream and in the foundations of some of the buildings.

Location 3 *(SY 610868)* Emerging from the woodland at the bottom of the hill turn east then south past Black Down barn. You have now left the sands and gravels and are on the Chalk. The sands and gravels form a capping resting **unconformably** on the Chalk. There is a time gap, in excess of 20 million years, between the formation of the Chalk and the deposition of the overlying sands and gravels, during which erosion occurred.   Exposures of the Chalk are few as it forms rolling downland used either for pasture or for crops *(Figure 3)* but any ploughed field will show the thin soils and abundant chalk fragments.

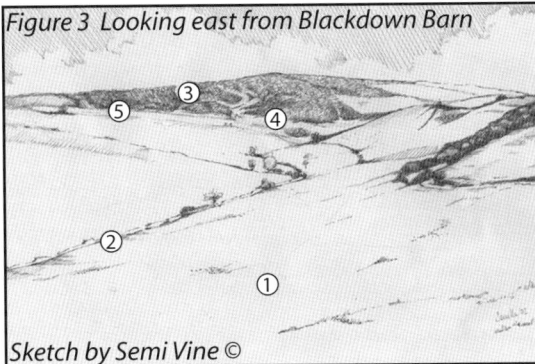

Figure 3 Looking east from Blackdown Barn

Sketch by Semi Vine ©

1. Rolling Chalk downland, typically used for sheep pasture or for cereals
2. Dry valley, with dry stone wall of Purbeck or Portland limestone
3. Heathland developed on Tertiary sand and gravel
4. Dry valley leading from Hell Bottom up to the Hardy Monument
5. Approximate edge of sand and gravel deposits

where heathland gives way to pasture, a natural progression linked to soil fertility.

Follow the footpath south towards Portesham Farm *(SY 611861)*. As the track drops slightly towards the farm you cross the Abbotsbury/Ridgeway Fault at SY 611864 *(Figure 4)*. This is a major fracture along which significant vertical movement of the rocks has taken place. The movement was probably, at least in part, linked to earth movements which occurred during the Alpine **Orogeny** which occurred between 45 and 25**Ma**. The Upper Chalk is on the north side of the fault with the Lower Purbeck Beds to the south. Much of the Cretaceous sequence, which is largely restricted to the Upper Cretaceous in this area, has been faulted out possibly by as much as 200m of rock *(Figure 4)*.

Location 4 *(SY 610859)* Rocket Quarry

Follow the farm road downhill to Rocket Quarry where Portland and Purbeck Limestone have been extracted over many years and which supplied Portesham with much of its building stone. The remains of the tracks leading from the quarry to Portesham can be seen in the dry valley to the north of the village. The bedded nature of the rocks can be seen, identifying them as being sedimentary. They dip gently into the quarry face at 10 - 15° to the north. The massive beds of Portland Limestone were largely formed in shallow tropical seas during long periods of continuous sedimentation. The more thinly-bedded Purbeck rocks at the top of the quarry were formed during intermittent and variable sedimentation at the end of the Jurassic and the beginning of the Cretaceous.

Figure 4 Sketch section to show rocks associated with the Abbotsbury Fault, from the Hardy Monument to the Upwey-Abbotsbury Valley

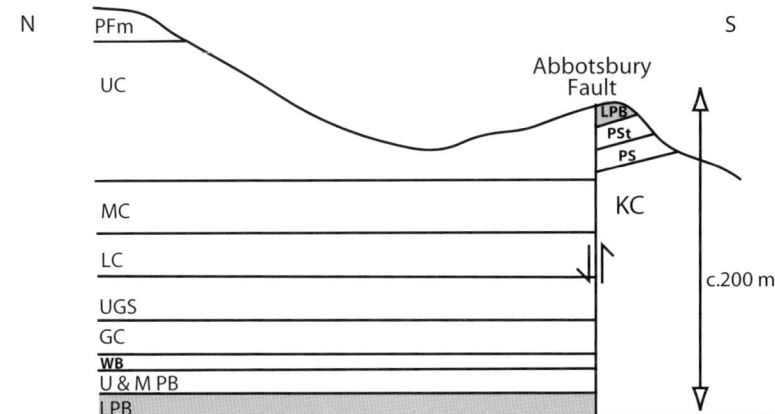

PFm	= Poole Formation	(9m)	Tertiary
UC	= Upper Chalk	(137m)	
MC	= Middle Chalk	(30m)	
LC	= Lower Chalk	(50m)	
UGS	= Upper Greensand	(50m)	Cretaceous
GC	= Gault Clay	(12m)	
WB	= Wealden Beds	(2m?)	
U & MPB	= Upper and Middle Purbeck Beds	(16m)	
LPB	= Lower Purbeck Beds	(35m)	
PSt	= Portland Stone	(18m)	
PS	= Portland Sand	(30m)	Jurassic
KC	= Kimmeridge Clay	(350m)	
		base not seen	

To the south of the quarry there are outstanding views across the Weymouth Anticline *(Figure 5).* Further information on the anticline and Rocket Quarry can be obtained from the information boards put on site by DIGS.

Figure 5 Aerial photograph by kind permission of Mrs Francesca Radcliffe©

The broad valley immediately in front of you is developed on the Kimmeridge Clay. Within the Kimmeridge Clay is a shale layer *(thinly bedded clay)*, rich in organic material, which was utilised in the late 19th and early 20th centuries. It was processed for the extraction of oil and used for lubricants and paraffin. The Kimmeridge Clay, in the northern North Sea, is one of the main source rocks for UK petroleum reserves. The organic-rich nature is from deposition of the sediment in deep oxygen-deficient waters. With no significant break down of organic material kerogen was formed, from which the oil and gas were derived.

Walk back up the hill to the footpath, go through the gate on the right and follow the ridge east for about 1km. The steep face below the path exposes Portland Limestone in several places and the contrast between the thin grassland of the ridge and the fertile Kimmeridge Clay vale is obvious.

©Mrs Francesca Radcliffe

Corton

Figure 6

Figure 6 shows the importance of the underlying rock formations to the shape of the landscape. The hard bands of Portland Sand and Stone form the prominent ridge while the softer rocks have weathered into the low-lying vales on either side. To the south *(right)* is Kimmeridge Clay, north *(left)* is the thinly-bedded Purbeck Limestone, also much more easily eroded.

The escarpment continues as the Corton and Friar Waddon Hills beyond the small gorge occupied by the road. Follow the not-obvious steep path off the ridge down to the road taking care as the stile is directly on to the road. Go left to the Coryates lane and over the stile on to Corton Hill.

Location 5 *(SY 630855)* There is a good view from the permissive path on the shoulder of the hill *(at the top of the Kimmeridge Clay)* and exposures of Portland Sand on the steep south-west facing slope. The sand is weakly cemented and crumbles away in the hand. Portland Sand is above the Kimmeridge Clay and below Portland Limestone in the succession. The Portland Sand formed in shallow tropical seas with a good supply of land-derived sediment whereas the Kimmeridge Clay formed in deeper water and lower energy conditions. The Portland Limestone was formed in shallow seas, with little sediment input from the land. Now dominantly calcite, it was made mainly by organisms secreting calcium carbonate in the sea.

Location 6 *(SY 636855)* Corton Farm and Chapel

Follow the path round Corton Hill until you reach Corton Farm and

Corton Chapel *(Figure 7)*. The path comes out just by the chapel, which is delightful.

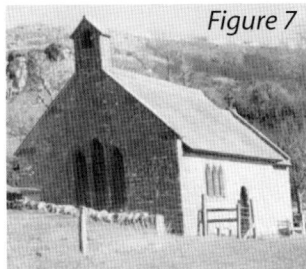

Figure 7

The farm road takes you on to the lane running north through the Corton cutting. Note the exposures of Portland Sand, much better cemented here than those seen earlier. Follow the road west nearly back to the Coryates lane and take the track to the right *(northward)*. 50m up the track turn west. After a further 50m go through the gate on the left, turn right and keep the wall on your right.

Location 7 *(SAY 630857)* Hell Bottom

This dry valley in the Chalk leads you back to the Hardy Monument, which can be seen on the skyline. One explanation for the formation of the dry valley is that during the Pleistocene much of Britain was periodically covered by glacier ice. The rest, including Dorset, was experiencing permafrost conditions similar to the present day Arctic tundra. Permafrost is impermeable so large volumes of melt water, from thawing snow in the late spring and summer, flowed over the landscape and eroded out the valleys. Nowadays the ground is permeable, the water table is lower and the valleys are presently dry.

Location 8 *(SAY 616877)* As you reach the road at the end of Hell Bottom there is a pit to the west *(left)* which, at the time of writing, is partly filled with rubbish. This pit exposes the Chalk and must be very close to the boundary with the Tertiary sands and gravels. This is indicated by the change of vegetation and land use from productive pasture to heathland and conifer trees. Walking up the road to the Hardy Monument you will see deep pits that resemble bomb craters. The pits are dolines and entirely natural. Dolines are solution hollows formed by the percolation of acid rainwater through the sands and gravels. The sands and gravels are also acidic, helped by the acidity of the humus formed from decay of vegetation. The acid waters, passing down through the rock, reach the alkaline Chalk which is then dissolved. The Chalk surface underneath the gravels is irregular so that the rainwater collects in some places more than in others and preferentially dissolves the Chalk at those points. The overlying sands and gravels collapse into the spaces and the dolines are formed. Culpepper's Dish *(SY 814925)* near Briantspuddle, is probably the best developed of such features in Dorset.

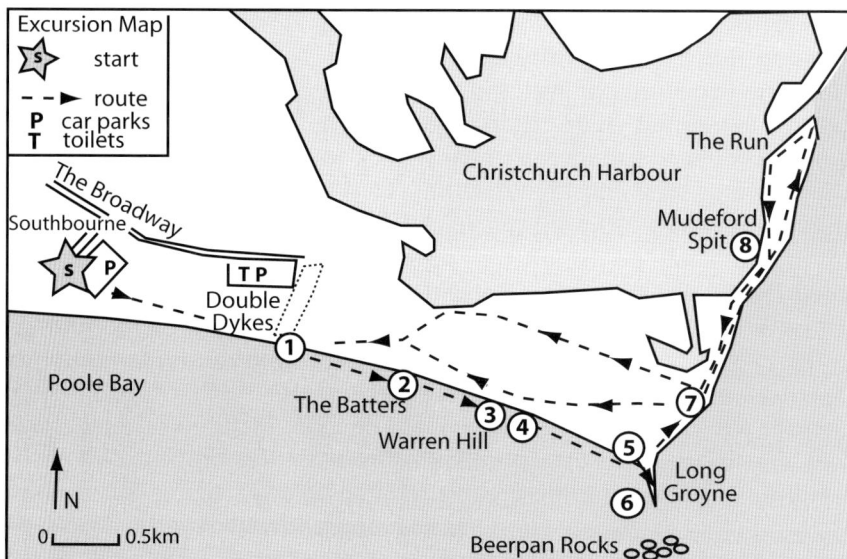

PURPOSE: To examine the Eocene succession on the coast at Hengistbury Head: to study aspects of marine erosion and deposition on the coast between Double Dykes and the distal end of Mudeford Sandspit and to study the nature and effectiveness of coastal management on this coast.

PRACTICAL DETAILS: The walk from the car park at SZ 158912 to The Run at Mudeford Sandspit should take about three hours, including stops. The return walk, which may be taken over the top of Hengistbury Head via Warren Hill need only take one hour. All of the cliff sections are accessible at most states of the tide, unless there are exceptionally stormy conditions. Parking is only available at the two car parks on the map. Toilets and refreshments are available at the Hengistbury Head Information Centre and café *(café open only at weekends in the winter)*. Toilets are also available along Mudeford Sandspit *(some may be closed in the winter)*. The Hut on Mudeford Sandspit serves refreshments during the summer.

GEOLOGICAL SETTING: The rocks exposed in the Hengistbury Head sequence belong to the Tertiary strata of the western part of the Hampshire Basin. The Basin structure here is an elongated asymmetrical downwarp, with steep to near-vertical dips on the southern limb and gentle southerly dips on the northern limb. With the exception of a small exposure of the Branksome Sand at the base of the cliffs near Double Dykes, the rocks exposed in the cliffs of Hengistbury Head belong to the Eocene Barton Group. The Branksome Sand probably represents estuarine channel deposits but the Barton Group, including the Boscombe Sands and the overlying Barton Clay, was deposited during a series of **marine transgressions**. The Solent River and its tributaries deposited the overlying Pleistocene gravels.

Hengistbury Head lies at the eastern end of Poole Bay and forms a promontory that separates it from Christchurch Bay to the east. To the north lies Christchurch Harbour into which the Rivers Stour and Avon flow. They make their exit from Christchurch Harbour through The Run into Christchurch Bay. Several miles to the south the Needles, off the Isle of Wight, and the Old Harry cliffs in Purbeck form the two ends of the now lost Chalk ridge between them. The precise time of the breaching of the Chalk ridge between them is still uncertain. Recent workers have suggested that the breaches could have occurred in either Devensian or Flandrian times *(a wide time span from 100,000 years BP to 7500 BP)*. To the north, the Solent River was a well-established arterial river in mid Pleistocene times. It drained an area between the Wiltshire and North Dorset Downs to the north and the Purbeck Hills-Isle of Wight Chalk ridge to the south. During the post-glacial rise in sea level the lower parts of its catchment were drowned. Poole and Christchurch Bays appear to have developed during the Flandrian transgression with recent work concluding that Poole Bay was the first to be submerged and that Christchurch Bay was probably formed between 7500-7000 BP.

EXCURSION DETAILS

Location 1 *(SZ 164908)* Double Dykes

The low cliffs to either side of Double Dykes are composed of river gravels, probably deposited by the Solent River or one of its tributaries, and capped with wind blown sand. The narrow isthmus inland from the cliff edge, separating Hengistbury Head from the Bournemouth gravel plateaux to the west, is now thought to be the former course of the River Bourne, which at present enters Poole Bay near Bournemouth Pier. Its former course, now lost to marine erosion, followed the present coast from Bournemouth to Double Dykes, where it turned north to enter the Stour in the present position of Christchurch Harbour.

This section of coast is particularly vulnerable to marine erosion since it is exposed to waves that have a long **fetch** up the English Channel. Current rates of erosion are estimated to be in excess of one metre a year. An additional concern is that during a storm surge, waves might overtop the low cliffs and break through to Christchurch Harbour, effectively isolating Hengistbury Head *(as almost happened in 1976)*. Coastal defence measures are therefore of crucial importance on this section of the coast. The seaward end of Double Dykes is protected by gabion cages emplaced in 1976 and replaced in 1984. These have proved successful to date as the cliff line has retreated several metres on either side since their construction. Three rubble groynes were built along this section in 1987, an extension of the system that extends along the whole frontage of Poole Bay from Sandbanks to Solent Road, to the west of Double Dykes. It is unlikely that a further set of groynes, planned for the stretch of coastline as far as Warren Hill, will now be built. Beach nourishment has also been carried out along this section of the coast.

Location 2 *(SZ 167907)* The Batters

This location is approximately 200m to the east of Double Dykes. The cliff section *(Figure 1)* displays the Boscombe Sand overlain by Barton Clay. At the top of the cliff section quarry spoil is exposed above the

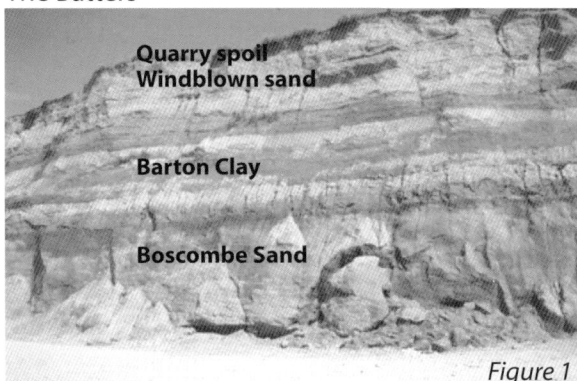

Figure 1

original line of wind blown sand which is marked by a greyish horizon. The Boscombe Sand is generally buff, brown, or greyish brown fine to medium-grained sand. Two clear bands of flint cobbles occur at the top of the Boscombe Sand. The sands were probably deposited in a tidal estuary but the cobble layers are likely to represent shoreline conditions with the flint pebbles being derived from storm beaches. At the eastern end of The Batters dark brown to black bituminous sand is found near the base of the cliff.

Above the Boscombe Sand the Barton Clay is exposed in the upper part of the cliff below the quarry spoil. It is greenish-grey clay, often glauconitic, with a varying content of fine-grained sand. The glauconite *(a potassium iron alumino-silicate)* indicates that the Barton Clay was deposited in open marine conditions, possibly sub-tropical. The lower part of these cliffs is much gullied and "splash-back" action within the lower part of the gullies is responsible for their widening and deepening and for eventual cliff collapse.

Location 3 *(SZ 175905)* Warren Hill

This cliff section *(Figure 2)* affords the most complete vertical section of the rocks exposed at Hengistbury Head. The Boscombe Sand is exposed at the base and is succeeded in the middle part of the cliff by the Barton Clay. The main sequence is again composed of glauconitic sandy clay. The foraminifer *Nummulites prestwichianus* has been found some 4.5m above the base of the Barton Clay, but specimens are now

Figure 2

Pleistocene Gravels

Warren Hill Sands

Ironstone nodules

Barton Clay

Boscombe Sand

difficult to locate. A dominant feature of the Barton Clay is the presence of a number of sideritic ironstone nodule layers (*'doggers'*). These nodules were quarried on the inland side of the Head and also collected from the base of Warren Hill between 1847 and 1865. The removal of the ironstone boulders from the base of the cliff led to much increased erosion. It is estimated that nearly half of Hengistbury Head was lost to the sea between 1852 and 1932 as a result of losing the protective apron of ironstone boulders. Overlying the glauconitic clays there are 10 metres of yellowish fine-grained sands, originally known as the Highcliffe Sands, now renamed as The Warren Hill Sands. The highest part of the sequence on Warren Hill consists of gravel deposits of the "proto Solent" now described as the Tenth River Terrace deposits.

Location 4 *(SZ 176905)* The Barton Beds are cut here by a remarkable gully, the largest seen anywhere on the face of Hengistbury Head. Close examination will reveal that there is seepage at the base of the Pleistocene gravels and the steady dripping of water from this source has been responsible for "splash-back" erosion in the Barton Clay below. This erosion has had the effect of undermining the layers of doggers and several boulders now clog the lower part of the gully, forcing the little stream to erode sideways. This seepage is permanent, and there has been a trickle of water even during the driest periods of recent summers.

To the east of the gully the lower part of the Barton Clay has been protected by an old storm ridge for most of the 1990s, but nearly all of this shingle has now been eroded away. Two small earthflows occurred in this section of the cliffs during the 2000-2001 winter, because of heavy rains, which indicates a measure of cliff-face instability that has not been apparent for over a decade.

Location 5 *(SZ 177904)* The accumulation of the sand dunes at the base of the cliff here is a consequence of the arresting of the drift of beach material eastwards after the building of the Long Groyne in 1938-1939. The construction of the Groyne has led to the build-up of a wide beach to the west and sand has been blown towards the base of the cliffs. These dunes first began to appear in the early 1950s and have grown at a steady rate ever since. They have now been fenced off, which has aided the growth of a dune ecosystem (*psammosere*) with the usual plant association. The cliff has become more stable as a result of the protection from marine erosion afforded by the dunes. It has become increasingly vegetated with invasion by heathland species from the open area of Hengistbury Head above.

Location 6 *(SZ 178903)* The Long Groyne

The effect of the Long Groyne in arresting the eastward drift of beach material has been noted above. Another less welcome effect of its construction has been the starving of the beaches to the east of material. This has inevitably meant that the cliffs beyond the Long Groyne have had no protection from wave attack and have suffered considerable erosion. Similarly, beach material has failed to reach Mudeford Sandspit which has also become vulnerable to wave attack. New groynes were built to the east of the Long Groyne in 1987 and they have helped in the accumulation of a new beach in this section of the Head.

Location 7 *(SZ 179904)* This section of the coast displays the eastern-most exposure of the Barton Clay. The western end of this section has become obscured as the result of defence works carried out in the early 1990s. At one time there was a large gully in the cliffs just to the east of the sand dunes. In the 1980s attempts were made to halt erosion within the gully by the emplacement of a series of gabion boxes but this was not really successful in stopping the enlargement of the gully.

In the early 1990s a new Purbeck Stone cascade was installed. Drains laid beneath the ground immediately inland from the cliff brought water to the cascade where it was discharged through pipes. Regrading of the cliff was completed on either side of the gully, together with some re-facing of the upper cliff with geotextile material and some planting of marram grass. Ten years later the cascade has become clogged by sand and the lower parts of the regraded cliff have become gullied again.

Location 8 *(SZ 182910)* Mudeford Sandspit

The Sandspit *(Figure 3)* is best viewed from the Grid Reference indicated above. This depositional feature was formed by frontal building by waves from the east-south-east of beach material carried around the end of Hengistbury Head by longshore drift.

Figure 3

The spit has had an unstable past and, during some phases, it has grown as far northeast as Highcliffe Castle *(in the 1880s and again in the early 1900s)*. The spit has been breached near its roots on several occasions *(in 1883, 1911, 1924 and 1935)*. After the last of these breachings the distal end became detached and drifted onshore at Friars Cliff enclosing a lagoon *(late 1930s)*. As a result of the building of the Long Groyne, the spit became unstable again and, during the second half of the twentieth century, numerous attempts have been made to restore its stability. Small seawalls were built in the most vulnerable sections and, more recently, a series of rubble groynes have been emplaced to encourage a wide beach to develop. With the building of a series of beach chalets along the spit in the twentieth century, the need for stability has become an even more vital part of coastal protection policy.

From the viewpoint on Hengistbury Head the spit may be visited by walking along the seaward side to The Run and returning along the landward side. The return walk can either be taken across the top of Hengistbury Head, where a different view of shoreline development may be obtained or, alternatively, the route taken by the land train, along the northern side of Hengistbury Head, may be followed.

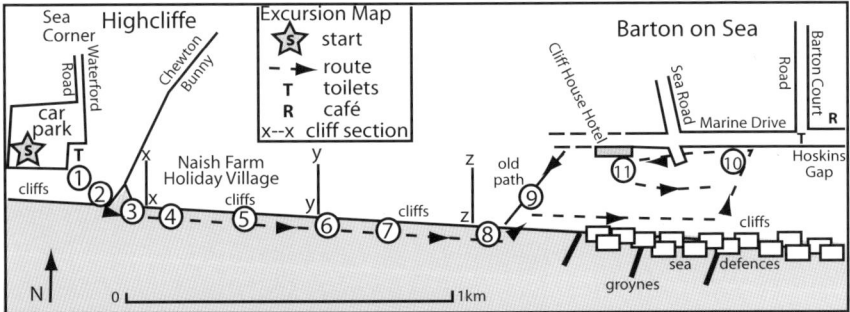

PURPOSE: To examine the Eocene succession along the coast between Chewton Bunny *(Highcliffe)* and Barton on Sea: to study the landslips, slumping and varying lithology of the clays and to find some of the many marine fossils along the way.

PRACTICAL DETAILS: The walk from the car park at SZ 217932 to Barton on Sea is 2km and should take about 2 hours allowing for stops or longer if any serious fossil hunting is undertaken. The return walk, if along the beach, can be done in an hour with no stops.

Safety: This walk should be undertaken on a falling tide, check with tide tables or a local authority. In the winter, and at spring tides, the approach to the beach and other areas can be cut off at high tides and, if the clays are liquid, it is not possible to go overland. It is inadvisable to explore the upper levels, certainly not alone, as the clays are treacherous when wet. There may be adders on the upper vegetated levels. Some of the cliffs are unstable and liable to fall.

Fossil collecting can be carried out with a small trowel and a suitable container. Shark teeth, for instance, can be found in the shingle at the water's edge at low tide. Parking is available at the above car park, free in winter. Refreshments are available in Highcliffe village. Toilets and refreshments are available at Barton on Sea in the summer. The cliffs are a Site of Special Scientific Interest (SSSI). Useful maps: British Geological Survey 329 and 330, Ordnance Survey Landranger 195

GEOLOGICAL SETTING: The clays and sands of the Barton Beds are Eocene, deposited between *c.* 42 and 37**Ma**. At that time Britain was some 10° latitude further south than today and the climate was generally warmer. Conditions were similar to those in the Bahamas today. The marine sands and clays were deposited, over an area of coastal swamps and lagoons, in a series of marine incursions from the east. The geology covered in this walk is fully marine but further to the east, at Hordle, it becomes lagoonal and **fluvial**. The beds can be traced along the Avon Valley in the west, to Bransgore and Crow in the east, northwards to near Bramshaw in the New Forest and, running south easterly, towards Southampton. There are fourteen beds identified in the Barton Beds *(Burton) Figure 1*, J, K and L are not seen on this trip. The first two A1 & A2 were exposed to the west of Chewton Bunny but are now covered by sea defences. A3 to I may be seen in this excursion progressively from Chewton Bunny to Hoskins Gap at Barton on Sea. The whole sequence is capped by Plateau Gravels deposited by braided rivers in Pleistocene post glacial conditions, or possibly during a pulsed high-stand sea level period. The gravels are interspersed in some areas with **brickearth**. The beds have an apparent dip to the east of c. $1°$

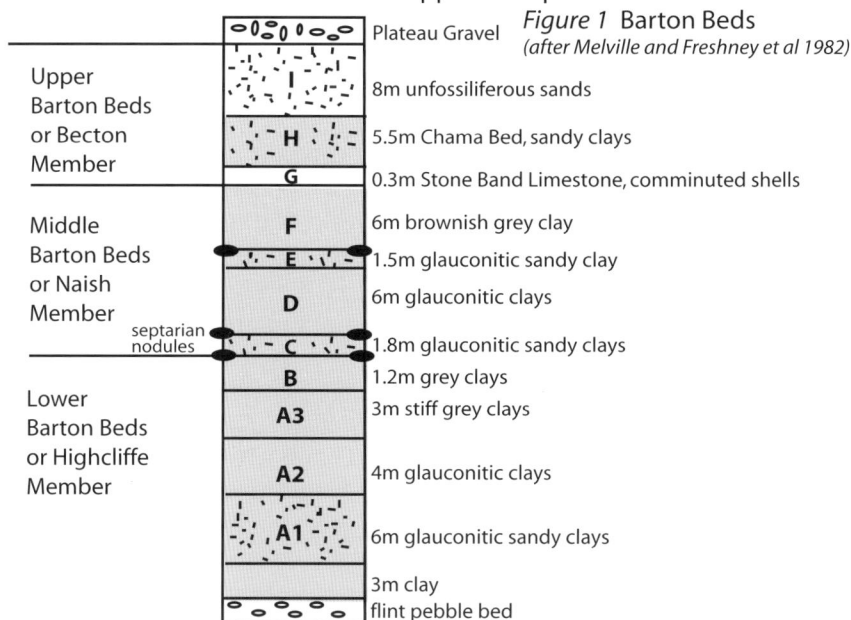

Figure 1 Barton Beds
(after Melville and Freshney et al 1982)

	Plateau Gravel	
Upper Barton Beds or Becton Member	I	8m unfossiliferous sands
	H	5.5m Chama Bed, sandy clays
	G	0.3m Stone Band Limestone, comminuted shells
Middle Barton Beds or Naish Member	F	6m brownish grey clay
	E	1.5m glauconitic sandy clay
	D	6m glauconitic clays
septarian nodules	C	1.8m glauconitic sandy clays
	B	1.2m grey clays
Lower Barton Beds or Highcliffe Member	A3	3m stiff grey clays
	A2	4m glauconitic clays
	A1	6m glauconitic sandy clays
		3m clay
		flint pebble bed

The majority of the beds are highly fossiliferous *(Figure 4, page 91 & Figure 5 pages 93/94)* with shells similar to subtropical shells today. The original aragonite remains although the colouration has been lost. Gastropods and bivalves predominate. Shark teeth are common with both shark and **teleost** vertebrae frequent. Turtle remains and ray spines and dentition can be found. Collecting has been taking place here for over two hundred years. The first major collection recognised was by Gustavus Brander who presented the collection to the British Museum in 1776. Erosion of the beds is significant with rates of up to one metre a year. The beds are shown in *Figure 3* on page 89.

EXCURSION DETAILS

Location 1 *(SZ 217932)* Shelter on seaward side of car park

From here, to the west, Hengistbury Head can be seen and beyond it, on a clear day, the Purbeck hills. The Boscombe Sands of Friars Cliff are to the east of Hengistbury. The cliffs between there and Chewton Bunny are graded and few exposures can be seen now. To the south east is the Isle of Wight. Turn to the east and walk down the gravel path to the information board *(no longer legible)* above the beach .

Location 2 *(Figure 2)* The beds can be seen, stretching from Chewton Bunny to Barton on Sea, from near the information board. There are at least three different levels of slipped and slumped clay with the Plateau Gravel capping at the top. The shearing and slumping occur at different levels in the strata. One is in the upper part of Bed F with gravel and brickearth **colluvium** falling onto the shear near the base of Bed

Figure 2

D and mixing with clay from Beds E & F. The final level is a shear at the base of Bed A3 which collects colluvium from all of the upper beds. This level extends to the beach level and is partly covered by beach sand and shingle. A3 is currently covered by this deposit and by beach sand and shingle with Bed A2 below it. Go down the path to groyne H12.

Location 3 At the west end of the cliffs, where they slide into the valley and just below the plateau gravel, there are **septarian nodules** which mark the top of Bed E *(Figure 3 Section X-X)*. Some 200m to the east, Bed G, the Stone Band, can be seen as a thin red band with some nodules 6m above Bed E. The main identifying feature is Bed C which has septarian nodules at its base and top with a thin grey sandy layer in between them. The septaria at the base are frequently covered by slipped clays from above. Walk past groyne H12 and some 50m along the beach.

Location 4 From here the slipped levels can be seen more clearly and it is possible to note the variation in the lithology of the sediments. They vary from grey clays interspersed with grey sands of A3, glauconitic sandy clay of Bed B and glauconitic clay of Bed C weathering to a rusty colour. This may be better seen some 100m to the east. Fossils can be found in all of these beds although those in C are frequently crushed, particularly the gastropod *Clavilithes longaevus*. 200m to the east, Location 5, there is a slumped gully with material from the middle beds running onto the lower beds. It is said that vertebrae of the archaeocete whale *Basilosaurus* were collected from here. Moving east Beds B and C are *in situ* in the cliff with Bed D, a dark clay, slipping over them.

Location 6 *(Figure 3)* Section Y-Y
100m past the fallen pill box *(now almost covered by sand)* the Plateau Gravel has reached the lower cliff level having slumped from above Bed H.

Location 7 100m to the east the waterfall flows all year and was recently considerably larger. Further east Bed C reaches beach level with D slumping above it with many fallen septaria on the beach. The higher beds are now further inland with vegetation, pools, mudflows and rotational slumping forming an undercliff. Further along the cliff Bed E, a glauconitic sandy clay with selenite crystals, reaches to beach level.

Location 8 *(Figure 3)* Section Z-Z
The sea defences, with Portland Stone groynes and large blocks, are beyond this section and the path. Climb up from the beach and turn east along the path.

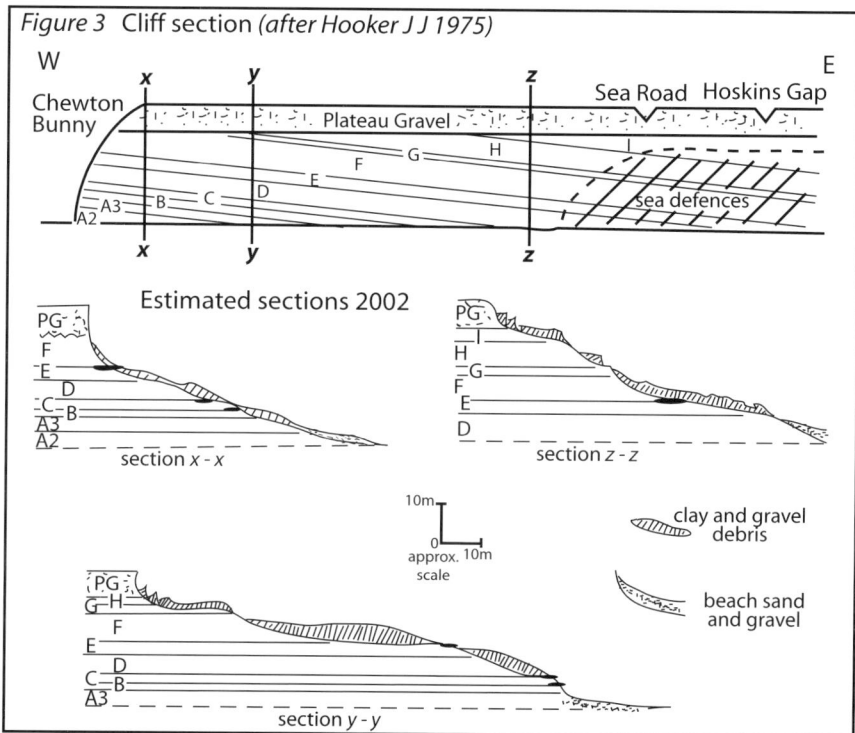

Figure 3 Cliff section *(after Hooker J J 1975)*

Location 9 A brief detour up the old path to the north east gives a view of the recently slumped Beds H & I. The path finally collapsed after the rains of 2000. The sheet steel piling has been rotated by the force of the slipping sediments. Return to the lower path and continue toward

Barton on Sea. Beds F & G can be seen to the left. F is a brown clay with thin shell drifts in it. G is a comminuted shell bed, forming a red limestone and marking the start of the Upper Barton Beds or Becton Member. The sea defences consist in part of Portland Stone with several blocks of the 'Roach' and also Carboniferous Limestone from the Mendips. The Carboniferous Limestone is fossiliferous and looking for the corals and molluscs in the blocks brightens up this somewhat drab stretch *(it is reported that a trilobite has been spotted but I am unable to confirm this)*. Further on, to the left, the beds have been regraded after the slippages. Bed H, the Chama Bed, can be seen in various places with patches of Bed I, a light coloured sand. Take the path sharp left up the slope and follow it right until you can see the path going up the cliff.

Location 10 *(SZ 238928)*   Bed I can be more closely seen on each side of the path but is a bright yellow micaceous sand at this level. Above Bed I the Plateau Gravels, which consist of flint pebbles with interspersed sand, can be examined. Bedding structures can be seen and, in places, **cryoturbation** structures. Water runs through the gravels and the lower sands contributing to the slipping and rotational slumping of the beds. Further views of these structures can be seen to the east of Hoskins Gap. Climb the steps up Hoskins Gap and follow the path to the road, turn east to the village where refreshments and toilets are available. Suitably refreshed it is worth walking 500m to the west to the Cliff House Hotel *(SZ 236929)*.

Location 11 Looking over the cliff, with care as the Plateau Gravels can be undercut, the engineering works to stabilise the cliffs can be observed. You can also see the rotational slumps with Bed I capped by the gravels and overlain by brickearth and grass. Looking west the whole of the Barton Beds that you have traversed are visible. There are two options for the return journey *(unfortunately the cliff path passes through the Naish Farm Holiday Village and the notice on the gate restricts entrance to occupants)*. Bus No 123 runs approximately every hour *(two hours on Sundays)*, from the café at Barton *(SZ 239928)* to Sea Corner at the top of Waterford Road in Highcliffe *(SZ 215936)*. Alternatively, descend the path by the Hotel near Sea Road then head east until you reach the path that you climbed to reach Barton on Sea. Retrace your steps along the sea defences. When you reach the groynes by the old steps you can descend to the beach and retrace your steps to Highcliffe. **Don't forget to watch the tide.**

My thanks to Paul Clasby for reading and checking this excursion

Figure 4 Bed	A3	B	C	D	E	F	G	H	I
Foraminifera									
Nummulites elegans (J de C Sowerby)	c	nc	r						
Nummulites prestwichianus (Jones)	c								
Anthozoa									
Turbinolia sp.	c				f	c	c	vc	
Bivalvia									
Cardiocardita sulcata (Solander)	c	f	c	vc	vc	c		f	
Chama squamosa (Solander)								vc	
Corbula ficus (Solander)					c	c			
Corbula pisum (J Sowerby)	vc	c	c	vc	vc	vc			
Crassatella sulcata (Solander)	c	c	c	f	vc	f			
Cubitostrea plicata (Solander)	c	c	c	f	vc	f	c	f	
Glycymerita deleta (Solander)	f							vc	
Nemocardium turgidum (Solander)			c	f	f				
Pectuculina scalaris (J de C Sowerby)					c	c		f	
Potamomya plana (J Sowerby)		f	f	c	c	f			
Gastropoda									
Ampullonatica ambulacrum (J Sowerby)	nc	nc			nc			vc	
Athleta athleta (Solander)	f	c	nc			nc			
Athleta luctator (Solander)		f	vc	f	vc	f		nc	
Bathytoma turbida (Solander)	c	f	c	c	vc	nc		f	
Bonellitia evulsa (Solander)		f	c	f	c	f	f	f	
Clavilithes longaevus (Solander)		nc	c	vr					
Clavilithes macrospira (Cossman)		nc		c	c			f	
Euthriofusus regularis (J Sowerby)	f	nc	nc		vc				
Fusinus porrectus (Solander)	nc				c	f		nc	
Globularia grossa (Deshayes)	nc				c				
Globularia patula (Lamarck)			f		f	nc			
Pterynotus tricarinatus (Lamarck)	c	nc	f	r	c	r			
Rimella rimosa (Solander)	c	f	f		vc	f		c	
Sycostoma pyrus (Solander)	c	f	vc	c	vc	c	f	f	
Turricula rostrata (Solander)		nc			c	nc			
Turritella edita (Solander)								vc	
Turritella imbricataria (Lamarck)	c	c	c	f	vc	f		c	
Volutocorbis ambigua (Solander)	vc	f	f	vc				nc	
Annelida									
Protula extensa (Solander)	nc	f	c	f	c	f		nc	
Scaphopoda									
Dentalium bartonense (Palmer)	f	f	f	nc	c	c		nc	
Pisces									
Jaekelotodus trigonalis (Jaekel)	f				f				
Striatolamia macrota (Agassiz)	f		f	f	f	f	f	nc	
Odontaspis winkleri (Leriche)	c		f	nc	c	nc			
Vertebrae	c	c	c	f	c				
Turtle shell and bone		f	f	r	c				

vc - very common, c - common, f - frequent, nc - not common, r - rare   after E St J Burton

Figure 5 Fossils from Barton *(scale100%)*

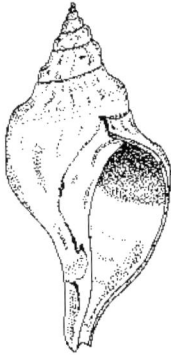

Syscostoma pyrus

Sassia arguta

Cryptoconus priscus

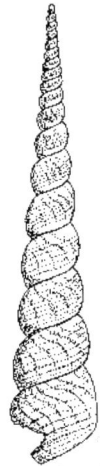

Turritella edita

Pterynotus tricarinatus

Rimella rimosa

Odontaspis winkleri

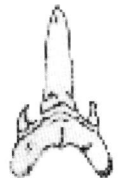

Daphnobela juncea

Crassatella sulcata

Cubitostrea plicata

©RJC

Athleta scalaris

Fusinus porrectus

Olivelli branderi

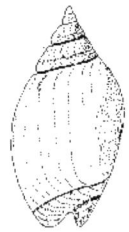

Figure 5 cont. Fossils from Barton *(scale 50%)*

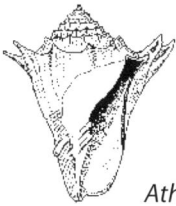

Athleta athleta

Cornulina minux

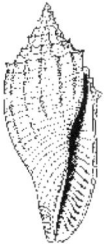

*Volutocorbis ambigua
var. compressa*

Volutocorbis ambigua

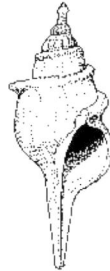

Clavilithes scalaris

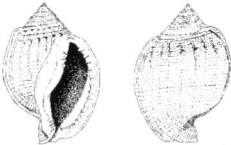

Sconsia ambigua

Globularia grossa

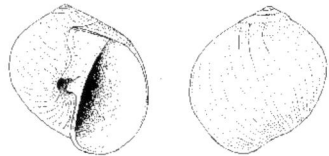

Sigatica hantoniensis

Globularia patula

Ampullonatica ambulacrum

Globularia sigaretina

©RJC

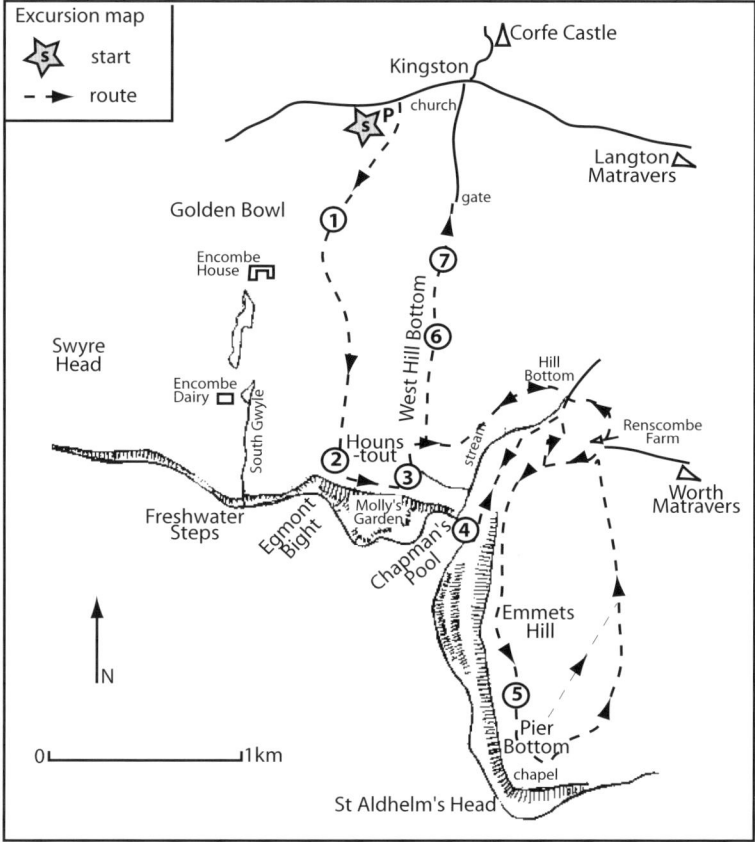

PURPOSE : To study the evolution of coastal scenery along the south
Purbeck coast between Houns-tout and St. Aldhelm's Head.

PRACTICAL DETAILS : The walk from the car park at Kingston *(SY 954795)*
to St. Aldhelm's Head, via Chapman's Pool, and return to Kingston via West
Hill Bottom is approximately 13 kilometres, and should take about six
hours, including stops. Considerable stretches of the walk are along
exposed cliff-tops and paths leading into Chapman's Pool are often
muddy and slippery. Great care should be taken at all times. When visiting
Chapman's Pool it must be remembered that the cliffs of Kimmeridge Clay
are extremely unstable and cliff falls are common at all seasons: the foot of
the cliffs should be avoided. There are some steep climbs on this walk,
notably the ascent of St. Aldhelm's Head from Pier Bottom - there is an
alternative; using the footpath that ascends Pier Bottom to the track that

leads from the coast *(SY 959759)* to the track from St Aldhelm's Head to Renscombe Farm. Refreshments are available in both Kingston *(The Scott Arms)* and Worth Matravers *(The Square and Compass and the Craft Centre)*. Toilets are available in Worth Matravers. There is a very infrequent bus service from Worth Matravers to Kingston. Useful maps are the Ordnance Survey 1:25,000 Explorer Purbeck and South Dorset, and the 1:50,000 BGS Sheet Swanage 342(East) and 343.

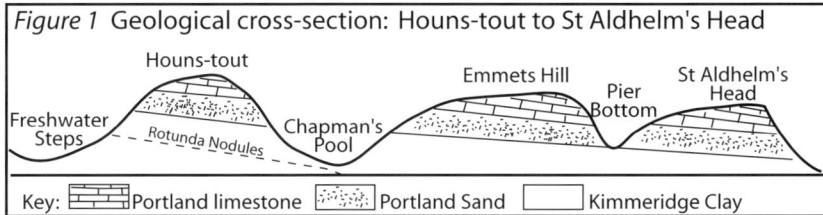

Figure 1 Geological cross-section: Houns-tout to St Aldhelm's Head

Key: Portland limestone | Portland Sand | Kimmeridge Clay

GEOLOGICAL SETTING: the rocks exposed in this coastal section are Upper Jurassic in age *(Figure 1)*: the Upper Kimmeridge Clay is exposed in the lower part of the cliffs but is almost completely obscured by landslide debris on the lower slopes of Houns-tout, Emmetts Hill and St Aldhelm's Head. The Kimmeridge Clay is overlain by the Portland Sand which forms much of the very steep face of Houns-tout. Portland Sand is also prominent in the middle section of the cliffs of Emmetts Hill and St. Aldhelm's Head. All three of these major cliffs carry a capping of Portland Limestone: on Houns-tout the lower Cherty member crowns the highest part of the cliff, on Emmetts Hill the Cherty member forms the free face of the cliffs. The axis of an anticline runs out to sea west-south-west from the eastern side of Chapman's Pool but as **dips** on either side of this structure are minimal, for most purposes the rocks may be regarded as almost horizontal. The slight dip, however, brings increasingly higher horizons of the Portland Limestone into the upper levels of the cliff as St. Aldhelm's Head is approached. Poorly stratified Pleistocene **solifluction** debris mantles the lower sides of the main valleys of the area.

EXCURSION DETAILS: Cars may be parked in the small unsurfaced area at SY 954795 and the signposted route to Houns-tout should be followed to the first viewing point at

Location 1 *(SY 949787)* From this vantage point there is an excellent view of the whole area known as the Golden Bowl, with Encombe House occupying a central position. An escarpment formed of the Portland Sand and capped by Portland Limestone surrounds the Golden Bowl which is floored with Kimmeridge Clay. The Kimmeridge Clay is obscured almost everywhere by landslide remnants or periglacial debris. The hummocky area at the base of Swyre Head is the result of past landslides, caused by the sliding of Portland Sand and Limestone over the underlying unstable Kimmeridge Clay. Small hollows in the escarpment, particularly seen below Polar Wood, are likely to have developed as **nivation hollows** during periglacial times.

Location 2 *(SY 950773)* Houns-tout Cliff

Portland Limestone here forms a capping to the cliff and has been weathered into a series of castellated forms, many of which are likely to collapse due to the underlying instability of Kimmeridge Clay which forms the lower part of the cliff. Most of the base of the cliff is a tumbled mass of former landslide debris, known locally as Molly's Garden.

The view to the west *(Figure 2)* embraces the seaward end of The Golden Bowl, through which threads the wooded incised valley of South Gwyle. 'Gwyle' is an old Purbeck word meaning deep wooded valley. Its stream reaches the sea at Freshwater Steps where it plunges

Figure 2

some ten metres to the Kimmeridge shale ledges on the foreshore. The formation of these gwyles will be discussed later. Beyond are the cliffs of Kimmeridge Clay, particularly prominent at Rope Lake Head and continuing westwards to Kimmeridge Bay

Location 3 *(SY 953773)* Eastern end of Houns-tout Cliff

Figure 3

The view from this cliff top takes in almost all of the stretch of coast visited on this excursion. Immediately below is Chapman's Pool *(Figure 3)* carved in the less resistant upper Kimmeridge Clay. Inland are the deep valleys of Hill Bottom and West Hill Bottom and, stretching seawards, the great cliffs of

Emmets Hill and St Aldhelm's Head. The view gives a most instructive view of the main physical processes at work on this coast.

Landslides are prominent along the face of both the eastern edge of Houns-tout below and along the whole of the face of Emmetts Hill. Water percolates down through the Portland Limestone and the underlying Portland Sand until it reaches the impermeable Kimmeridge Clay, causing the latter to become unstable. This results in a series of rotational slides, which bring large slices of the upper cliff of Portland Sand and Limestone downwards into the undercliff. Boulder arcs indicate the former position of these slides, now partly eroded away by the sea.

Erosion in Chapman's Pool has forced the small stream draining Hill Bottom, and its tributary from West Hill Bottom, to incise their valleys rapidly. Both gwyles display the **valley-in-valley** form resulting from such incision remarkably well. Continued downcutting means that the valley sides are very unstable and the site of much slumping. At one stage the stream immediately upstream from its exit into Chapman's Pool was blocked by a rotational slide from the western end of Emmetts Hill and a temporary lake was formed. It soon silted up and the stream re-established its former course.

From Location 3 the eastern side of Houns-tout may be descended by the steps, and at the bottom the stile can be crossed and the ill- defined path northwards can be followed to the small embankment that carries the path across the West Hill Bottom stream. The main track descending West Hill Bottom can then be joined and followed round to Hill Bottom itself. Beyond the hamlet of Hill Bottom the signposted track to the right over the bridge can be followed to Chapman's Pool.

Location 4 *(SY 956770)* Chapman's Pool

This small semi-circular inlet is fringed at its outer limits by boulder arcs from past landslides. Most of the cliffs in Chapman's Pool are cut in the *Pavlovia rotunda* zone of the Kimmeridge Clay and it is possible to collect specimens of *Pavlovia* from recent debris on the beach *(please do not hammer the cliffs!)*. From the eastern side of Chapman's Pool *(Figure 4)* there are are excellent views of the face of Houns-tout, particularly of the Portland Sand in the middle zone of the cliff. Recent prominent mudslides in the north-west corner of the beach mean that the area should be avoided since the whole cliff is unstable and therefore, is liable to fall again.

Figure 4

The track can be followed back towards Hill Bottom, but just before the bridge the Coast Path forks off to the right and this should be ascended. Eventually *(300 metres)* the Path emerges on to the western end of Emmetts Hill, giving superb views over Chapman's Pool and Houns-tout. The Path can be followed southwards, past the Royal Marines monument to Pier Bottom, where steps descend to this dry valley and then ascend steeply to St Aldhelm's Head. Only the very fit should attempt this ascent without a break!

Location 5 *(SY 958757)* St Aldhelm's Head

The viewpoint *(Figure 5)* gives a different perspective on the whole coast from west of Houns-tout to the immediate foreground of Pier Bottom. Portland Sand is exposed in the lowest parts of Pier Bottom, which has a mantle of periglacial debris, with a hint of solifluction

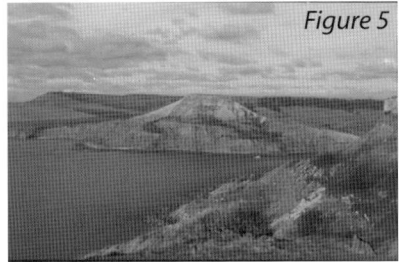

Figure 5

lobes extending into the valley in places. It is interesting that, whilst the stream at Chapman's Pool has cut down to sea level, Pier Bottom hangs some 40 metres above sea level. It probably became dry in post -glacial times before it could keep pace with marine erosion.

From Location 5 there are different options for the return to Kingston. The Coast Path is best followed to the Coastguard Cottages on St Aldhelm's Head. From the cottages the track back to Renscombe Farm can be followed, and then the tarmac road to the hamlet of Hill Bottom *(SY 962777)* can be taken. Alternatively the field can be crossed from the car park and the Coast Path regained at SY 959773 and followed to Hill Bottom. From Hill Bottom the track to Kingston is reached through the gate and stile. The track follows round the prominent feature separating Hill Bottom and West Hill Bottom.

Location 6 *(SY 955778)* Disused quarry

This old quarry reveals that there is a thick mantle of periglacial **head** draped over the sides of West Hill Bottom. The limited exposures within the quarry show very angular limestone debris *(mostly Portland limestone)* set within a matrix of much finer material. In places there is a hint of **cryoturbation** activity within the head. Looking south-westwards towards Houns-tout a small rotational slide may be seen on the valley side at approximately SY 954775 with a crescent-shaped toe and a well-developed backscar.

Location 7 *(SY 955784)* At this point in the course of West Hill Bottom there is a small steep tributary valley, which joins it from the west. At the point where this valley debouches onto the main valley there appears to be a small alluvial fan, now completely grassed over. This could possibly be a periglacial feature where a summer meltwater stream brought considerable amounts of debris into the main valley, depositing it rapidly as its energy was reduced.

Follow the track northwards to Kingston Church and the car park is about 150 metres to the left *(west)*.

Dorset hillforts and their geology
(measurements are approximate)

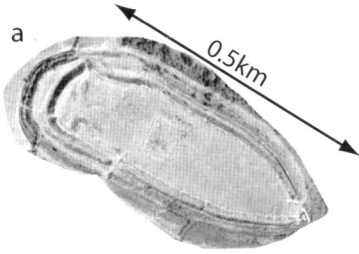

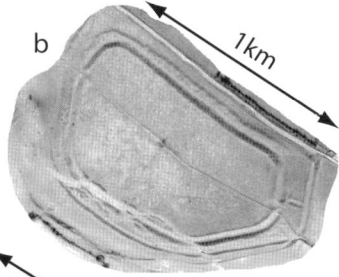

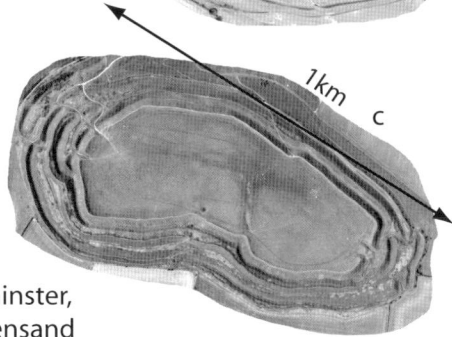

a

0.5km

b

1km

c

1km

The familiar outlines of the many
hill forts across Dorset are worth
looking at geologically as well as
historically. From their lofty
viewpoints the geology of much
of the County is also very visible.

a. **Pilsdon Pen** ST 413013 nr Beaminster,
(8km from Chapter 17) Upper Greensand
b. **Eggardon** SY 542946 nr Powerstock
(RIGS see www.dorsetrigs.com) Upper Chalk
c. **Maiden Castle** SY 667885 nr Dorchester,
Upper Chalk *(worth a visit with Chapter 8)*
d. **Rawlesbury** ST 767058 nr Bulbarrow
Upper Chalk *(and superb views across the
Kimmeridge Clay of the Blackmoor Vale)*
e. **Hambledon Hill** ST 845124 nr Child Oakford,
Upper Chalk *(near Hod Hill ST 855108 location 2, Chapter 15)*
f. **Hengistbury Head** SZ 175907 Eocene *(and guarding Christchurch
Harbour, Chapter 11)*

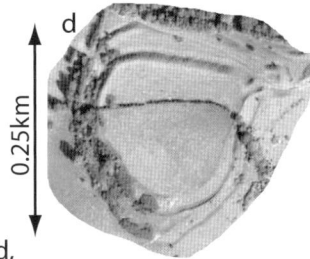

d

0.25km

The photographs are from
Dorset. A Photographic Atlas
© Dorset County Council 2000

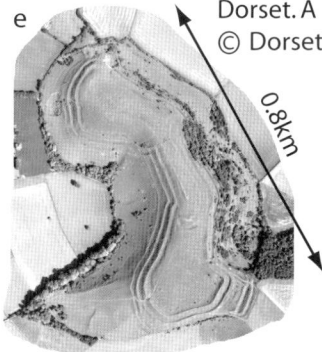

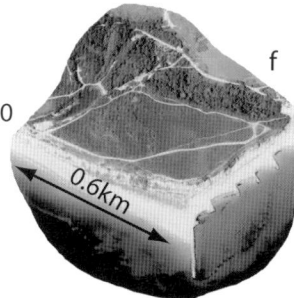

e

0.8km

f

0.6km

Information on all these sites is available from
The Prehistoric Age by Bill Putnam
(see bibliography)

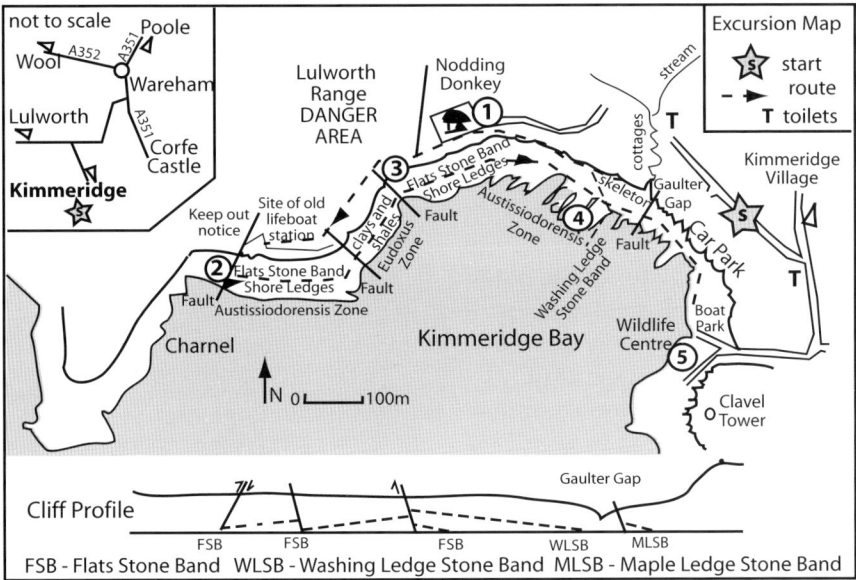

Excursion Map

not to scale — Poole
Wool
Wareham
Lulworth
Corfe Castle
Kimmeridge

Lulworth Range DANGER AREA

Nodding Donkey

stream

start
route
T toilets

Kimmeridge Village

Kimmeridge Bay

Charnel

Cliff Profile

FSB   FSB   FSB   WLSB   MLSB
FSB - Flats Stone Band WLSB - Washing Ledge Stone Band MLSB - Maple Ledge Stone Band

PURPOSE: To examine the upper two zones of the Lower Kimmeridge Clay at Kimmeridge Bay *(Figure 1)*.

PRACTICAL DETAILS: The walk can only be undertaken when the army ranges are open which is most weekends and school holidays. To check times, telephone 01929 404819 *(recorded message)*. The walk is about 2km and takes about 11/2 hours; the first half over the cliff top is level walking but the return along the beach *(tide dependent)* involves rock-hopping, sometimes over very slippery rocks. Hard hats and tough walking boots are recommended. The nearest café is in Kimmeridge Village where drinks, snacks and full meals can be enjoyed. Access to the beach is via a toll road with a fee per car. There are narrow country roads to Kimmeridge from Wareham, Corfe Castle and Lulworth.

Figure 1
Kimmeridge Bay

The bay is best viewed at low water when the shale ledges are exposed

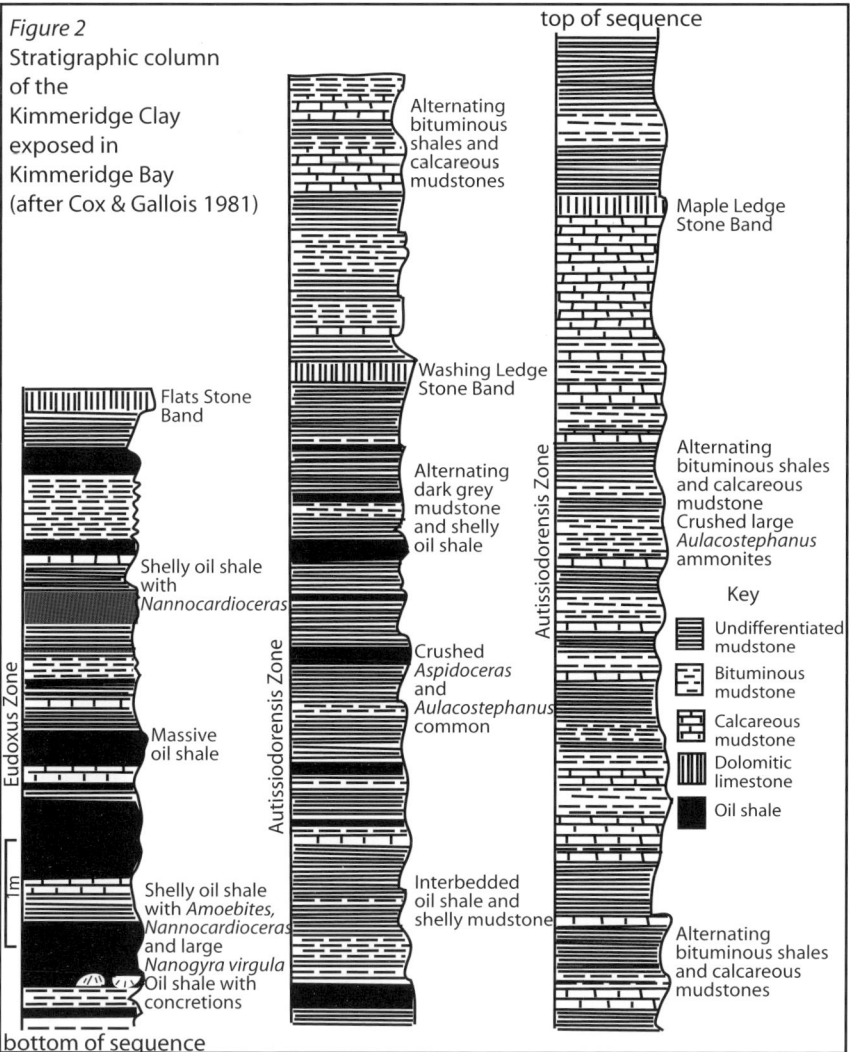

Figure 2
Stratigraphic column of the Kimmeridge Clay exposed in Kimmeridge Bay (after Cox & Gallois 1981)

top of sequence

Alternating bituminous shales and calcareous mudstones

Maple Ledge Stone Band

Flats Stone Band

Washing Ledge Stone Band

Alternating dark grey mudstone and shelly oil shale

Alternating bituminous shales and calcareous mudstone
Crushed large *Aulacostephanus* ammonites

Shelly oil shale with *Nannocardioceras*

Crushed *Aspidoceras* and *Aulacostephanus* common

Key

Undifferentiated mudstone
Bituminous mudstone
Calcareous mudstone
Dolomitic limestone
Oil shale

Massive oil shale

Eudoxus Zone

Autissiodorensis Zone

Shelly oil shale with *Amoebites*, *Nannocardioceras* and large *Nanogyra virgula*
Oil shale with concretions

Interbedded oil shale and shelly mudstone

Alternating bituminous shales and calcareous mudstones

bottom of sequence

1m

GEOLOGICAL SETTING: The Kimmeridge Clay was laid down in anoxic conditions in a subsiding marine basin 150 million years ago in the late Jurassic. It is composed of some 500m of clays, oil shales, bituminous shales, coccolith limestones and dolomites, the latter known locally as stone bands *(Figure 2)*. The sequence is divided into the Upper and Lower Kimmeridge Clay and into 13 ammonite zones, five in the Lower and eight in the Upper. The rocks exposed at Kimmeridge Bay are the top of the Eudoxus Zone and the entire Autissiodorensis Zone, the two uppermost ammonite zones of the Lower Kimmeridge Clay.

EXCURSION DETAILS

From the car park *(SY 778791)* take the track towards the beach at Gaulter Gap but, instead of turning left towards the beach after the wooden bridge, fork right, climb to the top of the cliff and join the road behind the row of fishermen's cottages.

Location 1 *(SY 904792)* Nodding Donkey

This is a service road for the Nodding Donkey oil well. Due to cliff erosion, the original road became unsafe and had to be moved back from the cliff edge. Before construction of the new road, an archaeological dig was carried out and several archaeological artefacts were unearthed dating from the late Iron Age and from the time of the Roman occupation. The artefacts included flint lathe tools, "coal money" (the discarded centres of lathe-turned shale bracelets and rings), several antler tools highly polished with sharpened tips for engraving, pottery shards and animal bones. Most of the artefacts are now in the Dorset Natural History and Archaeological Society Museum in Dorchester.

The Nodding Donkey is atop an oil reservoir which BP have been tapping for the last 45 years. The well was initially predicted to dry up after 20 years but has confounded all the experts and still produces 4.6 million gallons per year. This is somewhat of an enigma as several other bore-holes have been sunk in the vicinity, all of which have proved to be dry. It is proposed to install a gas turbine to utilise the natural gas *(at the present time it is wasted)* and generate electricity to drive the donkey and other equipment on the site; any surplus electricity will be fed into the National Grid.

Continue westwards along the cliff-top path until the security fence surrounding Lulworth Army Ranges is reached. To venture further the Range walks must be open and the gate unlocked. Continue along the cliff path, cross a cattle grid and walk on for approximately 100m, then turn left. Pass through a gate and down the steps to the site of the old lifeboat station; there is very little left, just a flat area with a retaining wall. Descend the footpath, which gives access to the beach, to the east of the Army "Danger Keep Out" notice.

Location 2 *(SY 901790)* At the bottom of the cliff pause a moment to look across the Bay to Clavel Tower on Hen Cliff, the high point of the cliff to the east. This folly was built in the 1800s by Mansell-Pleydell, the landowner, well away from the cliff edge but the cliff has receded and the tower is now very near the edge. It has fallen into disrepair and has been fenced off for safety reasons. There is a proposal to move it to a safer site inland but it will be very expensive to move and some local opinion wishes it to remain where it is for as long as it lasts.

While looking eastwards the gentle **dip** of the eastern arm of an **anticline** can be observed in the cliffs. The crest of the anticline is westwards, out of bounds in Hobarrow Bay, but the dip can be clearly seen in the exposed cliffs of Kimmeridge Bay.

To the right of where we are standing there is a **fault** which brings the Flats Stone Band to outcrop as the ledge at the base of the cliff and which can be seen, running out to sea, at low tide. The Flats Stone Band is one of the **dolomitic** beds. The surface is rumpled with adjacent slabs of the bed thrusting over each other. Moulds of ammonites can be seen which are often distorted due to deformation of the rocks. There is a theory that the bed was laid down and **dolomitised** relatively early which caused shrinkage. It later **dedolomitised** and expanded but, due to the pressure of the overlying beds, the expansion was confined to the bed itself causing lateral rumpling rather than upwards expansion.

In the past the Kimmeridge Clay has yielded several superb specimens of fossilised marine reptiles which are now in the Natural History Museum in London and the Dorset Natural History and Archaeological Museum in Dorchester. Fossils can be found all round the bay but there are notices prohibiting fossil collecting and the use of hammers. There is a warden who patrols the beach, ensuring that the rules are adhered to, so it is wise to confine your search amongst the boulders and shingle on the beach.

Aspidoceras ammonites *(Figure 3a)* are distinctive in appearance as they are fat and have two rows of protruding spines. They are often be found in the Eudoxus Zone and are also in the Autissiodorensis Zone above the Flats Stone Band. Aptychi *(Figure 3b)*, thought to be the mouthparts of ammonites, can be found either singly or in pairs; occasionally they are found inside the body chambers of *Aspidoceras*. They are often mistaken for bivalves but are flatter and do not have the paired hinges of bivalves. Other ammonites to be seen include *Aulacostephanus*. These fossils are thought to display dimorphism *(differences between the sexes)*. The microconch, smaller and thought

1cm   *Figure 3a*
       Aspidoceras

©SE

Figure 3b
Aptychi

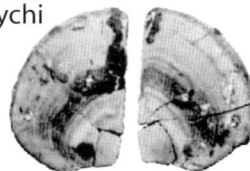

1cm

possibly to be male *(Figure 3c)*, is coarse ribbed and has a smooth venter. The macroconch, possibly female *(Figure 3d)*, is very much larger and more coarsely ribbed. Bivalves and oysters are common throughout the sequence.

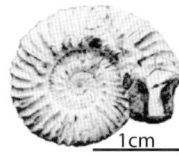

Figure 3c
Aulacostephanus
(microconch)

©SE

Keeping a lookout for fossils, start to make your way eastward back into the bay across the boulders which are strewn over the beach. Care is needed as some of these boulders are not stable and are often covered in green algae, which makes them very slippery.

Figure 3d
Aulacostephanus
(macroconch)

The Flats Stone Band is the uppermost bed in the Eudoxus Zone and is rising up into the cliff as you round the corner into Kimmeridge Bay. On the corner there is a small fault which hardly disturbs the beds. The beach is littered with boulders which obscure the underlying shales and must be traversed with care. The shales are softer than the Stone Band and wear away faster so the beach is narrower at this point. Another fault brings the Flats Stone Band down to beach level again. Rounding the corner you are walking on the Flats Stone Band which then dips below the overlying shales forming the exposed shore ledges.

Location 3 *(SY 904792)*

The Washing Ledge Stone Band now appears in the cliff top. The cliff profile is worth studying as the stone bands and shales weather differentially. The Washing Ledge Stone Band descends gently towards the beach, arriving at shore level just about under the fishermen's cottages. At low water this band forms the ledge which stretches furthest into the bay. As the Washing Stone Band dips beneath the overlying shales, the beach is again narrower due to their faster erosion.

Location 4 *(SY 907791)*

If you glance up to the cliff top above your head there is a horizontal gap just below the earth and grass top. This was the site of the discovery of a human female skeleton in the spring of 2000. Apparently a small cliff fall had dislodged the stones from around her grave and the skull and limb bones were visible from the shore. As is always the case with human remains, the police removed the skeleton and sent it for forensic examination. Eventually it was established that it was a Bronze Age burial of a twenty-five year old pregnant female. Originally the shallow grave would have been some way back from the clifftop. Over the four thousand years since her death the cliff has gradually receded and eventually revealed her remains.

Passing Gaulter Gap most of the ledges are usually covered by seaweed but occasionally a storm clears the beach and ammonites are exposed. Sometimes *Trigonia* bivalves are also seen. Occasionally the large ammonite *Gravesia (Figure 4),* which has prominent coarse ribs, is uncovered. Exposed ammonites on the ledges do not last long as they are worn by the incoming tide. Small pebbles and sand are carried across the fragile fossils by the water. After scouring by a couple of tides, the ammonites have lost a great deal of their surface definition.

©SE

1cm

Figure 4

A fault to the east of Gaulter Gap brings the Maple Ledge Stone Band up into the cliff. It runs below the car park, dipping gently, until it is covered by the overlying shale. It forms the ledge that runs across the eastern corner of the bay and then dips beneath the slipway. This band marks the top limit of the range of *Aspidoceras* ammonites; other ammonites, *Aulacostephanus* and *Propectinitites*, are common but no *Aspidoceras* have been found higher in the sequence.

Location 5 *(SY 909787)* Wildlife Centre

At the eastern side of the bay there are a few small boat sheds and a landing stage. Alongside these buildings is a splendid new Wildlife Centre which houses displays of the rocks, fossils, butterflies, plants and animals to be found in the area. There are also three saltwater tanks full of marine fauna and a video link to an underwater camera, out in the bay, which is fully operational during the summer months.

To the north of the Wildlife Centre is the site of a 17th century glass works which used the oil shale as fuel for the kilns. Slag glass and red coloured burnt oil shale can still be seen in the low banks that front the fishermen's huts in the lower car park. Prior to the glassworks alum was produced on the site but no indication of this enterprise remains.

In the 19th century oil shale was mined from the cliffs to the east. It was transported overland, via tramways, to the harbour where it was loaded onto barges. The remains of a stone pier, constructed for this enterprise, can still be seen at the end of the lower car park.

Thanks are due to Jane Clarke for assistance in compiling this chapter

Chapter 15 John Chaffey

LANDFORMS of NORTH -EAST DORSET
Geology and Scenery

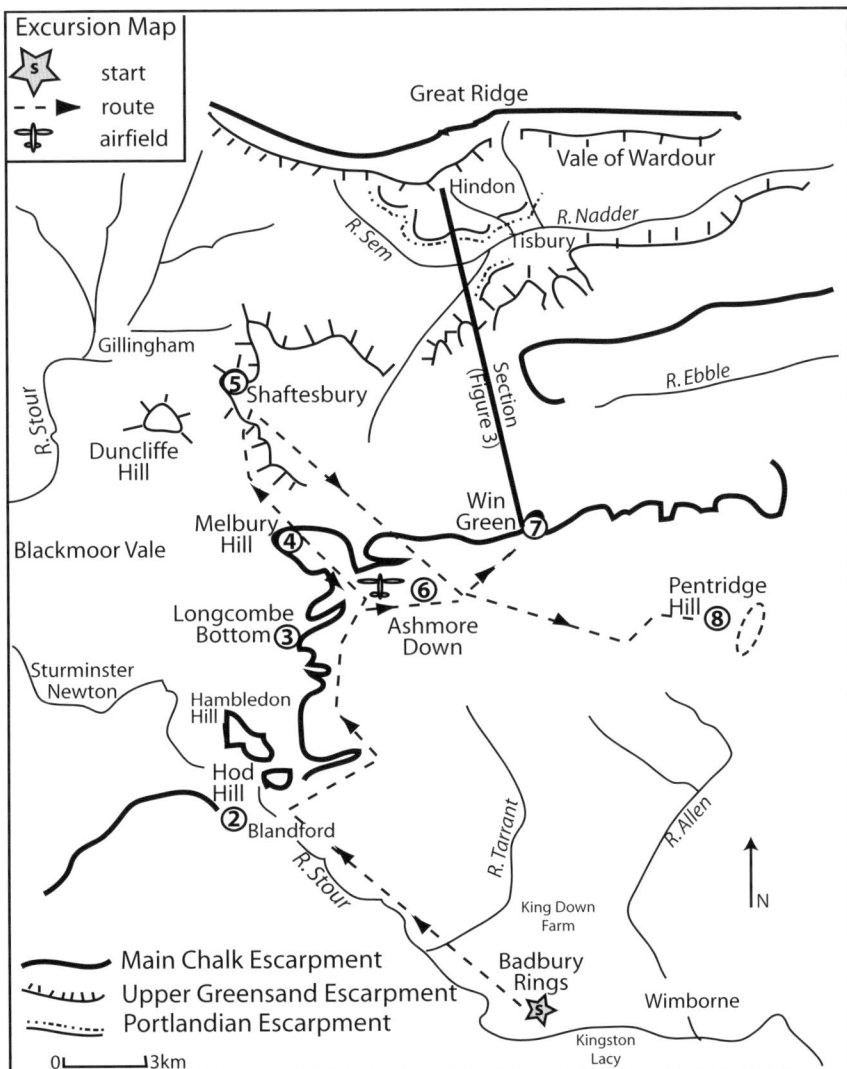

Excursion Map

⬟ s start
- - ▶ route
⬥ airfield

Great Ridge

Vale of Wardour

Hindon

R. Sem

R. Nadder

Tisbury

R. Ebble

Gillingham

⑤ Shaftesbury

R. Stour

Duncliffe
Hill

Section (Figure 3)

Win
Green ⑦

Melbury
Hill ④

Blackmoor Vale

Pentridge
Hill ⑧

⑥

Longcombe
Bottom ③

Ashmore
Down

Sturminster
Newton

Hambledon
Hill

Hod
Hill

② Blandford

R. Stour

R. Tarant

R. Allen

↑ N

King Down
Farm

Badbury
Rings

Wimborne

⬟ s

Kingston
Lacy

━━━ Main Chalk Escarpment
⊥⊥⊥⊥ Upper Greensand Escarpment
········· Portlandian Escarpment

0 �·⌐3km

PURPOSE: To examine the relationship between geology and scenery in
north-east Dorset and to examine some aspects of the erosional history
of the area

PRACTICAL DETAILS: This is a car excursion, which takes in eight
different sites in north-east Dorset, with an overall distance of about
64km between the first site to be visited and the last. The whole

excursion will take up to five hours depending on the length of time spent at each stop. All of the sites are accessible by rights of way, and paths are clearly signposted at each location. Refreshments and toilets are available at Compton Abbas airfield restaurant *(ST 890185)* which is on the route between sites, and in Shaftesbury. At the second location *(Hod Hill)* there is a steep climb from the car park up to the viewpoint: at Melbury Hill there is a climb from the car park to the summit of the hill but it is relatively easily graded. The most suitable topographical map is the Ordnance Survey 1: 25,000 Explorer, Sheet 118 Shaftesbury and Cranborne Chase: all of the localities are on this sheet. The relevant British Geological Survey maps are Sheet 313 Shaftesbury, Sheet 314 Ringwood and Sheet 329 Bournemouth.

GEOLOGICAL SETTING: The rocks exposed in this itinerary are mainly of Cretaceous age, with **outliers** of Tertiary material, and Quaternary superficial deposits. The main formation exposed in north-east Dorset is the Upper Cretaceous Chalk. This is bounded in the west by the Lower Cretaceous and Jurassic rocks of Blackmoor Vale, in the north by the Lower Cretaceous and Jurassic rocks exposed by the unroofing of the Vale of Wardour Anticline and in the south-east, by the Tertiary deposits of the Hampshire Basin. Over most of its outcrop the Chalk is dipping very gently towards the south-east. Topographically the area studied on this excursion is bounded on the west by the north-south escarpment formed by the Upper and Middle Chalk, on the north by the Chalk escarpments overlooking the Vale of Wardour and on the south-east, by the lower-lying country developed on the Tertiary Beds.

EXCURSION DETAILS

Location 1 *(ST 965030)* Badbury Rings

Badbury Rings is owned by the National Trust, and cars may be parked at the National Trust car park which is reached by the gravel track from the B3082 road from Wimborne to Blandford. Badbury Rings, capped by an Iron Age hill fort, is a locality of considerable geological interest. It is an erosion remnant on the dip-slope of the Chalk of north-east Dorset. It stands out as a prominent feature above the surrounding Upper Chalk downland, because of the slightly harder, more resistant Belemnite Chalk, part of the Upper Chalk, of which it is composed. Capping the summit of the Rings are rocks of an entirely different nature. On the footpaths leading through the ramparts there are many small, rounded flint pebbles present which belong to beds that are younger than the Chalk, the so-called West Park Farm Member *(Reading Beds)*. The flints were eroded from the Chalk and redeposited by a new sea flooding into the area in earliest Tertiary times *(marine transgression)*. It is possible that these pebble beds originally covered a much wider area, but they only remain as outliers at Badbury Rings, nearby at King Down Farm and Kingston Lacy. The pebble beds have been eroded away from the surrounding area to reveal the original Chalk surface on which they were deposited, known as the sub-Eocene surface. Follow the B3082 and the A350 to Hod Hill.

Location 2 *(ST 854108)* Hod Hill

Hod Hill is an isolated feature, with the River Stour flowing along its western slopes and the Iwerne Brook flowing in the valley to the east. It is built of Middle Chalk, with a capping of Upper Chalk. On its summit there are both Iron Age and Roman fortifications, the latter occupying a site in the north-west corner of the larger Iron Age structure. Cars may be parked in the small car park *(ST 853112)* at the roadside where the minor road passes between Hod Hill and the larger Hambledon Hill to the north-west. A steep path leads upwards to the north-west corner of the Iron Age fort and the ramparts here may be used as a vantage point to study the relationship between the geology and the scenery. The River Stour immediately below Hod Hill has cut a deep valley leading into the Chalk from the Kimmeridge Clay outcrop of Blackmoor Vale. On the other side of the Stour valley the prominent Chalk escarpment formed of the Middle and Upper Chalk may be seen extending away westwards towards Bulbarrow Hill. The long dip slope of the Upper Chalk *(Blandford Chalk)* slopes down to the south-east with its thick cover of Clay-with-Flints supporting dense woodland. Continue on the A350 to either Sutton Waldron or Fontmell Magna and turn east. Both roads climb steeply. At the top of either hill turn north again toward Shaftesbury.

Location 3 *(ST 886180)* Longcombe Bottom

Approximately 2km along the hill top road, turn east on to the lane signposted Compton Abbas airfield *(ST 890185 refreshments available to the public- open until sunset every day)* then turn left *(north)* and park on the side of the road. Cross the A350 to the stile with care and follow the footpath to the viewpoint.

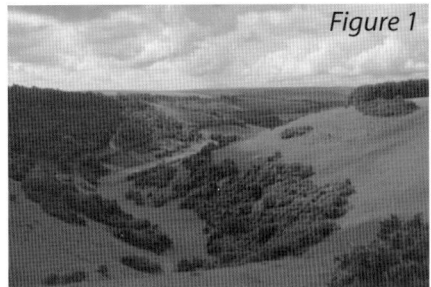

Figure 1

Longcombe Bottom *(Figure 1)* is an escarpment dry valley cut down into the West Melbury Chalk *(Lower Chalk)* by the small stream that now rises lower down the valley about a kilometre to the east of Fontmell Magna. The valley exhibits a sharp bend about 300m from its head. It is likely that the spring at the head of the valley may have eroded headwards along a well-marked joint, and then, at the bend in the valley, it may have selected another major joint to erode along - in a different direction. Meltwater from the crest of the escarpment may have coursed down this valley in Pleistocene times, causing it to be much deepened. Drying out of the valley would have occurred later, with a falling water table, resulting partly from scarp retreat, and the lowering of the height of the spring at the head of the valley.

Location 4 *(ST 873197)* Melbury Hill

Continue toward Shaftesbury to where there is a convenient car park on Clubman's Down *(ST 887187)* though space is limited. From the car park a path may be taken to the summit of Melbury Hill via Compton Down *(ST 883194)*. Melbury Hill *(263m)* is one of the highest points on the Chalk escarpment. It rises above the surrounding chalklands which here display the planed-off features of a **peneplain**. It is possible that this peneplain surface was cut in Mid-Tertiary times *(Mio-Pliocene)* by sub-aerial erosion. The near level surface is plainly evident over much of the surrounding area. (*Compton Abbas Airfield operates its aircraft from a grass landing strip which displays the peneplain perfectly. From the restaurant at the airfield the view of Melbury Hill clearly indicates how it rises above the peneplain as a residual eminence or* **monadnock**). From the summit of Melbury Hill there are magnificent views in all directions. To the north, the Shaftesbury Plateau is clearly visible, developed on the Shaftesbury Sandstone with its capping of resistant Chert Beds. The Chert Beds are found throughout south-west England but are locally described as the Boyne Hollow Chert. To the west the Upper Greensand outlier of Duncliffe Hill is seen surrounded by its apron of landslipped surfaces. It has been suggested that the summit of Duncliffe Hill may also carry a remnant of the Mio-Pliocene peneplain.

Location 5 *(ST 862230)* The Shaftesbury Plateau

The town of Shaftesbury occupies one of the most dominant positions in Dorset. It is built on the Shaftesbury Plateau which overlooks the Vale of Blackmoor to the west. In Shaftesbury two main viewpoints are worth visiting. Park Walk *(ST 862228)* affords stunning views to the south with Melbury Hill in the middle distance and the Mio-Pliocene peneplain to the east. Immediately below Park Walk is the steep escarpment formed by the Shaftesbury Sandstone and this is fringed by the so-called Shaftesbury Platform developed on the Cann Sand. Beyond is the Undercliff, a much-slipped area, with many shallow **rotational slips** developed on the underlying Gault Clay. To see the Undercliff a suitable viewpoint is Breach Common *(ST 853227)* which can easily be reached by car from Shaftesbury. The other main viewpoint is at Castle Hill *(ST 858229)* on the north of the Shaftesbury Plateau. From here there is an excellent view of Duncliffe Hill to the west and the continuation of the Greensand escarpment to the north, with the western extension of the Wiltshire Chalk beyond, which also carries remnants of the high level peneplain.

Location 6 *(ST 914194)* Ashmore Down

Either retrace your steps and go to the north east end of the Compton Abbas airfield lane, or follow the B3081 up ZigZag Hill *(892208),* turning right at the airfield sign. There are a number of laybys where a car may be parked along this road but those nearest the above Grid Reference will afford the best view westwards over Melbury Bottom and to Melbury Hill beyond *(Figure 2).* Melbury Bottom is one of a series of deep, dry valleys that dissect the high Chalk plateau in this area. Melbury Bottom displays an exceptionally fine series of **interlocking spurs**, the result of the original stream meandering in the valley bottom. All of these dry valley systems in the western part of Cranborne Chase were cut during the Pleistocene period, when the Chalk

Figure 2

would have been rendered impermeable by permafrost. During the brief tundra summers of that time meltwater would have poured down these valleys which would have been rapidly deepened. Beyond Melbury Bottom the peneplain at Compton Abbas airfield is again well displayed and Melbury Hill, the monadnock, rises clearly above the planed off surface in the distance.

Location 7 *(ST 926206)* Win Green

Win Green is 300m on the right back across the B3081. This fine viewpoint lies just inside Wiltshire and gives magnificent views over the Shaftesbury Plateau to the west, the Vale of Wardour to the north, and the dip slope of Cranborne Chase to the south-east. It is the view northwards over the western end of the Vale of Wardour that offers the most instructive insight into the relationship of geology and scenery in southern Wiltshire. The Vale of Wardour has been excavated by erosion along the axis of the Wardour Anticline. Today it displays the classic features of **inverted relief**, where the Chalk roof of the anticline has been stripped away by erosion to reveal the older Lower Cretaceous and Jurassic rocks beneath.

Figure 3   Section across the Vale of Wardour - Hindon to Win Green

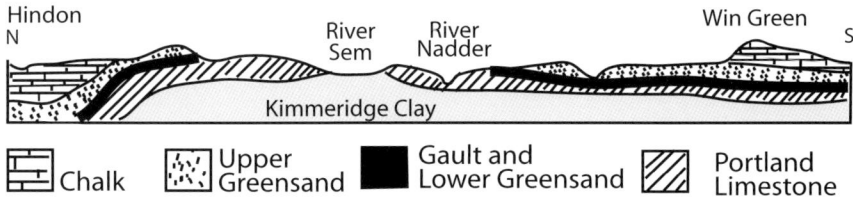

When rocks are uplifted in an anticline, structural weaknesses in the upfold are exploited by erosion, which cuts down into the core of the anticline. The relief is therefore lowered so that the zone along the axis, formerly occupied by the highest ground, now forms the most low-lying terrain. The headwaters of the River Nadder have cut down deeply through the Cretaceous rocks to reveal the underlying Jurassic rocks as far down as the Kimmeridge Clay. The Vale of Wardour now displays a series of inward facing escarpments *(Figure 3)*, revealed by the unroofing of the anticline, which are the result of the varying resistance of the rocks to erosion.

Win Green is the northwards facing Chalk escarpment and this is succeeded to the north by the Upper Greensand *(Shaftesbury Sandstone)* bench and escarpment. Beyond these Wardour Castle occupies a site on the Portland Limestone escarpment. The south-facing escarpments on the northern side of the Vale of Wardour are less prominent because of the steeper **dips** though usually the steeper the dip the more prominent the scarp as with the Purbeck ridge *(chapter 20)*.

Location 8 *(SU 039171)* Pentridge Hill

This locality is reached from Win Green by following the B3081 to the A354 Blandford-Salisbury road, turning north and then driving to the village of Pentridge, east of the road at SU 033178. A footpath leads from the centre of the village to the summit of Penbury Knoll *(0.5km)*. Pentridge Hill is a remnant of the secondary escarpment formed by the resistant Belemnite Chalk and it forms a north-eastern continuation of the much broken escarpment farther to the south-west as at Badbury Rings. Other remnants of the escarpment, such as Windmill Hill *(SU 082191)*, occur to the north-east. On the summit of Penbury Knoll there is an outlier of Tertiary beds similar to that found on Badbury Rings. Rounded flint pebbles can be found in the fields surrounding Penbury Knoll and in places amongst the pine trees on the summit, indicating again the presence of the basal beds of the West Park Farm Member *(Reading Beds)*.

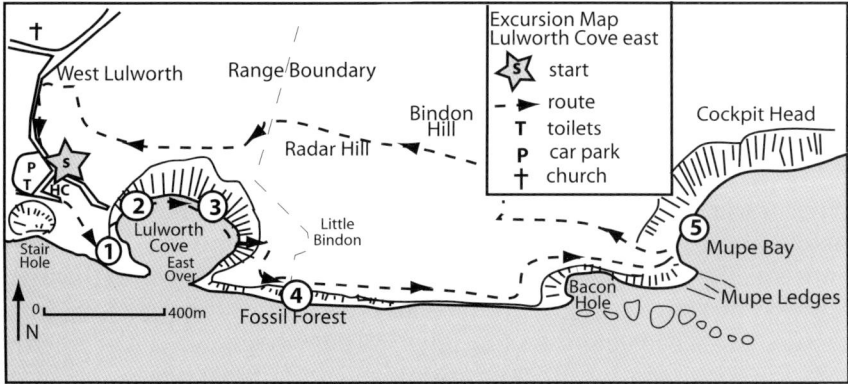

PURPOSE: To examine the sequence of Jurassic and Cretaceous rocks between Lulworth Cove and Mupe Bay to the east and Lulworth Cove and Durdle Cove to the west. To examine the variety of structures affecting the Jurassic and Cretaceous rocks along the Lulworth Coast and to study the geomorphology of the coastal features between Mupe Bay and Bat's Head to the west *(see map page117)*

PRACTICAL DETAILS: The visit to the Lulworth Coast needs to be undertaken as two separate excursions. It would be difficult to explore thoroughly the coast eastwards from Lulworth Cove as far as Mupe Bay and the coast westwards as far as Bat's Head, during the course of one day. It is, however, possible to reduce the amount of time spent at various locations and thus complete both excursions in a day.

The walk from Lulworth Cove car park *(SY 822802)* to Mupe Bay, along the coast and returning via Radar Hill, takes about four hours including stops. It can only be undertaken at weekends, Easter, Christmas and during the schools' summer holidays as most of the excursion is within the Lulworth Firing Range. Details of when the Ranges are open can be obtained from 01929 404819 *(recorded message)*. The walk westwards to Durdle Cove takes about three hours including stops.

Note: Man o' War Head cannot be negotiated at high tide.

The Heritage Centre in West Lulworth is well worth a visit as it has a particularly interesting display on coastal geology and scenery. Park at the Heritage Centre car park *(parking meters)* although there is some road parking near the church. Refreshments and toilets are available in the Heritage Centre and at the Cove. Useful maps are OS Landranger 194 and, if available, BGS 342 (East) and 343 Swanage.

GEOLOGICAL SETTING: The rocks exposed along the Lulworth Coast are of Jurassic and Cretaceous age with Tertiary material and Quaternary superficial deposits on top *(Figure 1)*. The oldest rock exposed is the Portland Limestone which outcrops along the coast from Mupe Bay in the east to Dungy Head in the west. It reappears further west in the Durdle Promontory where it forms Durdle Door. It also forms *(together with basal Purbeck material)* the isolated stumps to the west of Durdle Door, Man o' War Rocks to the east and Mupe Rocks to the south of Mupe Bay. On the landward side of the Portland Limestone, rocks of the Jurassic and Cretaceous outcrop in a series of east-west bands which tend to widen, to the east, as the strata thicken. Going north, the Purbeck Beds are the first encountered and are followed by the Wealden Beds, the Lower Greensand *(very thin or absent)*, Gault, Upper Greensand and the Chalk.

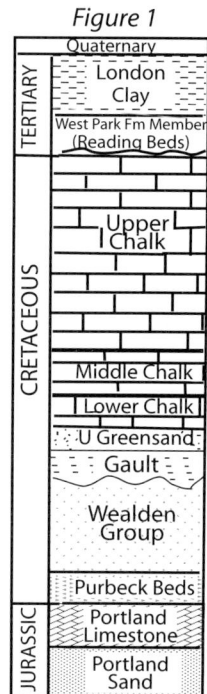

Figure 1

The rocks of the Lulworth coast form the northern limb of the asymmetrical Lulworth Banks **Anticline**. There are moderate to steep **dips** to the north throughout the sequence where the Upper Chalk is vertical or even overturned. The gentle east-plunging axis of the anticline is offshore at the Lulworth Banks. The east-west Purbeck Fault cuts the strata along the northern limb of the Lulworth Banks Anticline and small scale folds, such as the Lulworth Crumple, occur adjacent to this fault.

The geomorphological evolution of this coast has long been of interest. It is a classic example of a **concordant coastline** under attack by marine processes. Between Durdle Door and Worbarrow Bay *(east of Mupe Bay)* there are a series of coves which may represent different stages in the same process of coastal development. The simplest interpretation of coastal development suggests that Stair Hole may represent the earliest stage with the Portland barrier breached and the sea now scouring out the Purbeck and Wealden Beds to the north. Lulworth Cove is at an intermediate stage of development with a near perfect bay eroded out principally in the Wealden Beds. Durdle Cove, Man o' War Cove, Mupe Bay and Worbarrow Bay suggest a further stage of development where erosion has removed much of the controlling geology. This basic model is now regarded as oversimplified and in need of considerable refinement. Details of factors that need to be considered will be discussed later in this excursion.

EXCURSION DETAILS Lulworth Cove to Mupe Bay
Location 1 *(SY 824798)* Overview of Lulworth Cove
The main physical features of the Cove can be seen from the grassy
slopes rising seawards above the Heritage Centre *(Figure 2)*.

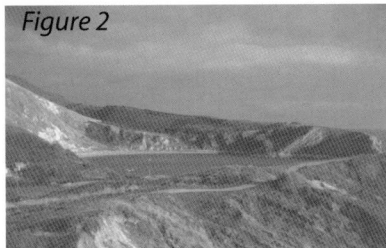

Figure 2

The two enclosing arms of the Cove
are cut in Portland limestone and the
Purbeck Beds. Marine erosion has
opened up the Cove in the softer and
less resistant Wealden Beds behind.
The steeply inclined and sheared
Chalk is much more difficult to erode
and has proved to be another
barrier at the back of the Cove. It is likely that the small stream that
drains into the Cove has played some part in its development. In the
past it must have cut through the Portland Limestone barrier on its
course southwards to the sea. Rising sea levels in post-glacial times
would have broken through this gap to begin eroding away the softer
Wealden Beds beyond, a process which would have been aided by
mass-movement on the latter rocks.

Location 2 *(SY 825799-828799)* Inner cliffs of Lulworth Cove
The Upper Greensand *(dipping steeply northwards)* is soon encountered
after leaving the café and traversing the northern side of the Cove. The
lower part of the Upper Greensand is a clayey sand with obvious
greenish-black grains of glauconite which indicate its marine origin. The
bivalve *Exogyra* may be found here. The upper part of the Upper
Greensand contains much chert, with a bed of glauconitic sandstone
boulders rounded by marine action, completing the sequence.
The Chalk now forms the cliffs to the east, in the middle of Lulworth
Cove. The cyclical beds of flintless Lower Chalk *(pure chalk alternating
with more **argillaceous** material)* are the first encountered. The Plenus
Marl *(another clearly argillaceous horizon)* separates the Lower Chalk
from the Middle Chalk which is nodular and also lacking in flints. Dips
to the north, in the Lower and Middle Chalk, are steep. The overturned
Upper Chalk, with its bands of flints, is only seen in the upper parts of
the cliff, north of a fault. At beach level, in the middle of the Cove,
freshwater springs may be seen emerging from the Chalk at low tide.
As progress is made around the Cove the same beds will be
encountered, in reverse order, until the soft grey Gault Clay with its
landslides, is reached.
Location 3 *(SY 828798)* Outcrop of the Wealden Beds
The Wealden Beds, on the eastern side of Lulworth Cove, dip steeply

- they are almost vertical in places. They consist of variegated marls and sands, bands of soft ironstone and some quartz grit horizons. The marls were formerly worked for bricks and remains of the old kilns can be seen near the mouth of the small stream that drains into Lulworth Cove. The deposits are fluvial, laid down by a large river that drained into the area from the west. The marls were deposited as floodplain sediments by the river. The sandstones may represent deposits which resulted from the river breaking out of its channel and laying down sands on the floodplain. The quartz grit layers are channel deposits with lignite *(fossil wood)* indicating that logs, and other plant debris, were originally washed into the channel. Most of the small pebbles in the grit are vein quartz: black fragments are **tourmalinised** quartzite which can be dated isotopically as Precambrian *(570Ma+)* so may have come from Britanny or Galicia in Spain, where there are rocks of that age.

It is worthwhile continuing the traverse around the beach to the section where the Purbeck Beds are encountered after a small **fault**. After crossing a boulder strewn stretch of beach, the small promontory of East Over is reached and, immediately beyond it, a small **syncline** and anticline are exposed at beach level at low tide. The structures are best traced using the bluish grey Cinder Bed, full of oyster shells, as a marker horizon. This is a continuation of the 'Lulworth Crumple' best exposed in Stair Hole. The 'Crumple' is more fully described and explained at location 2a in the second part of this excursion which is westward from Lulworth Cove. There are good exposures of the underlying Purbeck Beds to the south but it is not advisable to examine them there as the cliffs are unsafe and rockfalls are frequent.

Location 4 *(832796)* The Fossil Forest *(Figure 3)*

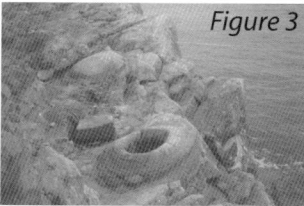

Figure 3

This famous locality is reached from Lulworth Cove by ascending the steps at the old brick kilns in the Cove. Follow the path east towards Little Bindon and then fork off to the south to reach the Fossil Forest gate which gives access to the Ranges. After descending the steps, the Ledges, along which the Fossil Forest is exposed, are all accessible. The Portland Beds form the cliffs to seaward of the Ledges and are overlain by the Purbeck Beds. The lowest of the Purbeck Beds is the Hard Cap, made up of laminated limestones and **oolitic** limestones. These limestones are overlain by the fossil soil of the Great Dirt Bed which can be easily traced along the Ledges. The ancient coniferous trees of the Fossil Forest were rooted in this soil which contains organic matter and limestone fragments. The 'trees' are in fact moulds which are surrounded by the Soft Cap composed of **stromatolitic limestone**. The space within the mould was originally occupied by the trunk of the tree, silicified in some cases, but they have mostly been removed by collectors. The trees appear to have been killed by a flood of very saline water, then 'pickled' and later coated with the algal limestone. **Please do not hammer or collect from these ledges**. Above the trees are the Broken Beds which are well exposed at the landward side of the Ledges. These very distinctive beds owe their broken nature to the dissolving out of evaporite horizons within the sequence and their subsequent collapse. Further fragmenting of the limestone could have been caused by later earth movements.

Location 5 *(SY 844797)* Mupe Bay
To reach Mupe Bay *(Figure 4)* ascend the steps from the Fossil Forest Ledges and then follow the coastal footpath eastwards past Bacon Hole. From Bacon Hole there is a fine view of the Purbeck Beds exposed in the

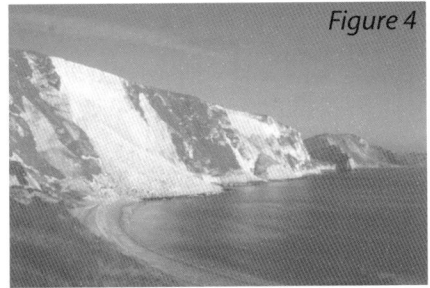

Figure 4

cliffs of Bacon Hole. Eastwards the series of stacks known as Mupe Rocks, composed of Portland Limestone and the basal Purbeck Beds, can be seen. The path descends to the grassy slopes above Mupe Bay and from there a series of steps lead down to the Bay itself.

Mupe Bay is cut in the Wealden Beds with the Purbeck Beds exposed at the southern end of the Bay and the Chalk at the northern end. All of the strata dips steeply to the north. The Wealden Beds are composed of mottled red, purple and yellow coloured sands and clays. As at Lulworth Cove these deposits are fluvial, laid down by a river flowing into the area from the west. Coarse sandstones and grits occur and, in some places, form prominent buttresses in the cliffs which are unstable elsewhere as a result of landslides in the clays.

Probably the most interesting of the Wealden strata is a conglomeratic oil sand which can be examined just to the north of the point where the steps lead on to the beach. It is thought to be an example of 'palaeo-pollution' *i.e.* a Cretaceous stream was polluted by oil seeping up along a fault plane which extended downwards into Liassic shales. The oil would have migrated upwards and seeped into Wealden Sands. The Wealden river subsequently eroded the oil-saturated sand and then deposited the intraformational oil sand conglomerate on its bed. A very large rockfall occurred at the northern end of Mupe Bay in the spring of 2001. This has profoundly altered the shape of the bay with a quarter of the length of the beach being buried by the rockfall. A large number of chalk boulders are now resting on the beach. The northern end of the bay is highly dangerous, being vulnerable to further falls, and should not be visited by groups or individuals.

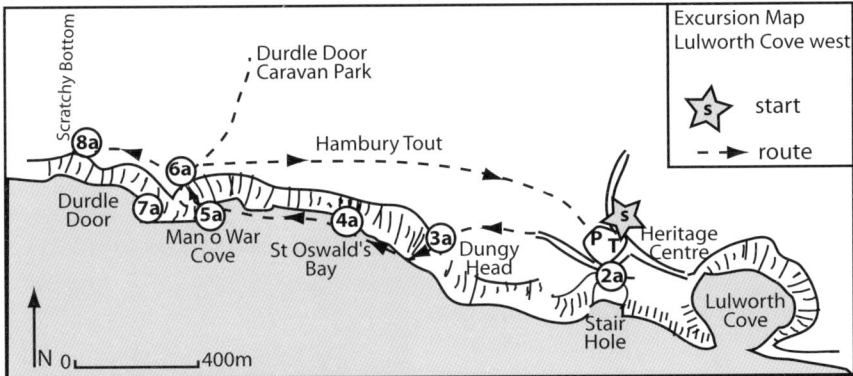

Lulworth Cove to Scratchy Bottom

This excursion begins at the same **Location 1** *(SY 824798)* as the excursion from Lulworth Cove to Mupe Bay. It is important to check tide times before setting out since the base of Man o' War Head cannot be negotiated at high tide.

Location 2a *(SY 823798)* Stair Hole

Stair Hole represents an early stage in the breakdown of the Portland Limestone barrier by marine erosion. The sea has broken through the northward dipping limestone at several locations on the seaward side of Stair Hole producing a number of caves, two small arches and a complete breach at its western end. Thus the sea has access to the Purbeck and the Wealden Beds on the northern side of the limestone rampart and it is in these formations that Stair Hole is being excavated by the sea. The Wealden Beds on the landward side of Stair Hole are much affected by landslides and mudflows. These movements deliver the sands and clays to the foot of the cliff in Stair Hole from whence they are eroded by the sea. It is unlikely that Stair Hole represents an early stage of the development of Lulworth Cove simply because no stream flows into Stair Hole so it is probably a unique feature on this coastline. At either end of Stair Hole, the famous 'Lulworth Crumple' is seen in the Middle and Upper Purbeck Beds.

The Crumple is an asymmetrical minor fold within the main northern limb of the anticline. The origin of the 'Crumple' is still imperfectly understood. The beds have been deformed by the reactivation of an earlier **Hercynian/Variscan** fault. The pre-Hercynian basement *(>285Mya)* was affected by folding and faulting. The rocks were then uplifted and eroded and later the Mesozoic sediments were deposited on top. With the **Alpine Orogeny** *(25Mya),* movement on the earlier fault caused the overlying sediments to be deformed *(Figure 5).*

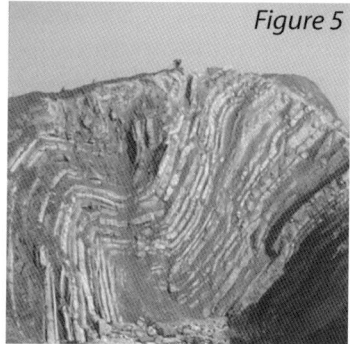

Figure 5

Location 3a *(SY 816801)* Western side of Dungy Head, St. Oswald's Bay

This location provides one of the best views of the whole of the coast westwards from Dungy Head, looking towards Bat's Head and White Nothe *(Figure 6).* It is reached by following the road up from the cottages at Lulworth Cove and then taking the path which descends to St. Oswald's Bay. A brief diversion southwards, from the path towards Dungy Head, leads to the viewpoint. The Bay, with its cliffs of much faulted,

Figure 6

overturned Upper Chalk, forms the foreground. It may have developed as a cove similar to Lulworth Cove with the Portland Stone barrier only remaining as offshore rocks. St. Oswald's Bay is separated from Man o' War Cove beyond by Man o' War Head which is made of much sheared vertical Middle Chalk. Man O' War Cove may also have originated like Lulworth Cove although the role of a stream, both here and in St. Oswald's Bay, is difficult to demonstrate. Man o' War Rocks represent the remnants of the Portland Limestone barrier. Beyond Man o' War Cove is the Durdle peninsula where the Durdle promontory is linked to the main coast by cliffs formed mainly of the Wealden Beds.

Location 4a *(SY 814800 - 809803)* Traverse of St. Oswald's Bay

From the last locality, the footpath leading to St. Oswald's Bay may be regained and then followed down to beach level. The Wealden Beds are first encountered at the base of the steps leading to the beach. To the west the Gault is encountered although it is much obscured by slipped material. The Upper Greensand is next encountered with chert abundant in the bouldery beds exposed at beach level. From here westwards the Chalk is best examined in relation to the **shear planes** and faults that cut it at different angles.

> Group 1: Shear planes dipping 60-70° south, which coincide
>   with overturned bedding
> Group 2: Shear planes dipping 50-70° north, created by tension
> Group 3: Shear planes dipping 25-40° south but becoming true
>   thrust planes, in places dipping 0-20° south
> Group 4: Steep **reverse faults** with dips 70-40° south - often
>   displaying thick **crush breccias**
> Group 5: Reverse faults with dips 35-55° north
> Group 6: Reverse faults dipping 35° north

In the cliffs of St. Oswald's Bay, below Hambury Tout, overturned Upper Chalk with flint layers is cut into well-recognised blocks by Group 1 and 2 shears. The planes are well characterised by slickensides, a series of grooves caused by one block of rock *(in this case Chalk)* moving over another, under pressure. At the base of the cliffs a well-marked notch has been cut by marine erosion. About half way along St. Oswald's Bay there is a solution pipe *(see page 164)* which reaches down to about four metres above beach level. This is one of several prominent examples in the cliffs of St. Oswald's Bay. They are filled with rust coloured sands, probably of Eocene age and some ground up flints.

At Man o' War Head, at the western end of St. Oswald's Bay, a Group 4 fault running through a well-marked crush breccia, brings vertical Middle Chalk against the overturned Upper Chalk. The Middle Chalk is cut by a prominent series of Group 3 shears which tend to cut the rock up into rhomb-shaped blocks. At the base of Man o' War Head a series of ribs of Lower Chalk are exposed. The Chalk here is cyclical with bands of marly chalk alternating with bands of purer, more resistant chalk and the former being eroded away by the sea.

Location 5a *(SY 807803)* Man o' War Bay

As in St. Oswald's Bay, the main northern cliffs in Man o' War Bay are formed of overturned Upper Chalk, cut by Group 1 and 2 shears, giving the typical blocky appearance to the cliff. The remainder of the cliffs in Man o' War Bay *(traversing to the west and south-west)* reveal sections from the Gault *(much slipped and rarely yielding a good section)* down to the Lower Purbeck Beds. The Lower Wealden Beds and the Upper Purbeck Beds are cut out by a **strike fault**. In the south-west corner of Man o' War Cove the Purbeck Beds, from the Cinder Bed down to the Broken Beds, can be examined. They are almost vertical and affected by the 'Lulworth Crumple'. Excellent examples of **ripple marks** can be observed in the cliff face of the Durdle Promontory just to the east.

Location 6a *(SY 806803)* The Durdle Peninsula and views westward
The steps leading upwards from Man o' War Bay may be ascended to gain access to the Durdle Peninsula. From the top of the steps there is a magnificent view westwards to Bat's Head *(Figure 7)*. Durdle Cove is in the foreground with Durdle Door on the seaward side and cliffs cut in

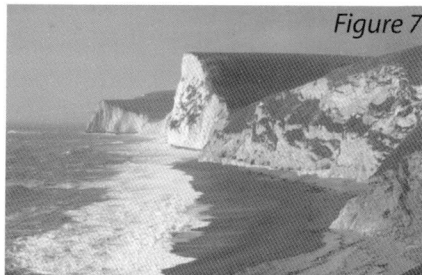

Figure 7

Upper Greensand and Lower Chalk on the western side. Most of the cliffs to the west of Durdle Cove are of vertical Upper Chalk with flint bands. The prominent set of caves just to the west of Durdle Cove have been excavated, by the sea, along a low thrust fault dipping south at various angles from 0 - 20°. Beyond the dry valley of Scratchy Bottom, Swyre Head is composed of much sheared vertical Upper Chalk. At the end of the beach running from Durdle Cove to Bat's Head, there is a chalk stack called Butter Rock, which is gradually being eroded away. Bat's Head is eroded in vertical Upper Chalk cut by a series of Group 3 shears. The streams originally draining the two dry valleys, Scratchy Bottom and the unnamed feature between Swyre Head and Bat's Head, may have aided the development of what were originally two coves, now coalesced to form the Durdle Cove-Bat's Head beach.

Location 7a *(SY 805803)* Durdle Cove
Durdle Cove may be reached by descending the steps from the Durdle Peninsula. Durdle Door, a much photographed natural arch, has been eroded by the sea through the Portland Stone and the Purbeck Hard Cap *(which are seen in the view from Durdle Cove)*. The actual shape of the opening of the arch is controlled by two oblique sets of joints. There is evidence, best seen with binoculars, of the sites of former trees in the Purbeck Caps, seen now as holes in the stromatolitic limestone. Further remnants of the Portland Limestone barrier occur as stumps to the west, from The Bull to The Calf. It is possible that a former natural arch connected Bat's Head to the stump of The Cow offshore.
In the south-east corner of Durdle Cove the Lower Purbeck Beds are again seen as in Man o' War Bay. They are almost vertical and are affected by the 'Lulworth Crumple'. Traversing north along the Cove, the Wealden Beds are encountered, here much thinned and containing lignite *(fossil wood)*. The outcrop of the Gault, much affected by landslides as usual, is seen beyond the Wealden Beds. If exposure conditions are right, the basal pebble bed of the Gault, resting on the

Wealden, can be examined. The Upper Greensand is the next formation to the north including the prominent Exogyra Bed. Chert beds, similar to those at the western end of Lulworth Cove and the eastern end of St. Oswald's Bay, can also be seen. The Basement Bed of the Lower Chalk, which is glauconitic with phosphatic nodules, is the next outcrop to the north.

Location 8a *(SY 803803)* Scratchy Bottom

Scratchy Bottom is a remarkable truncated dry valley that 'hangs' some 10 metres above the beach in the small cove to the east of Swyre Head. If traced inland, for about 500 metres, it turns through a right angle before heading steeply some 500 metres further east, near Newlands Farm. Surface weathered Chalk debris can be seen in the cliff section on the eastern side of Swyre Head just to the west of the small cove. This material was moved down the valley slopes by **solifluction** during the Pleistocene. Similar debris can be observed in the cliffs at the seaward end of Swyre Bottom to the west. Higher up the valley there is some evidence of solifluction lobes extending out into the valley from the sides.

In common with the dry valleys to the west at Swyre Bottom and Middle Bottom, Scratchy Bottom is truncated by the sea. The valley would appear to have been cut, during the Pleistocene, when the Chalk was impermeable as a result of permafrost sealing. Frost shattering, under very cold conditions, would have broken up the Chalk in the valley bottom making it easy to transport when meltwater coursed through the valley in the brief Pleistocene summer. The right angle bend could be explained if we regard the original spring as cutting back northwards along a joint. It then changed direction along another joint at right angles eventually cutting the steep valley head, at Newlands Farm, by spring-head sapping. The truncation of the valley may be due to two factors: the stream perhaps was unable to keep pace with marine erosion and was left hanging or the valley may have dried out before the stream had time to adjust to marine erosion.

This excursion can make the return journey to Lulworth Cove by going back to the Durdle peninsula, over Hambury Tout and down the new footpath to the Cove car park. Alternatively, transport could be arranged to meet the party at Durdle Door Caravan Park.

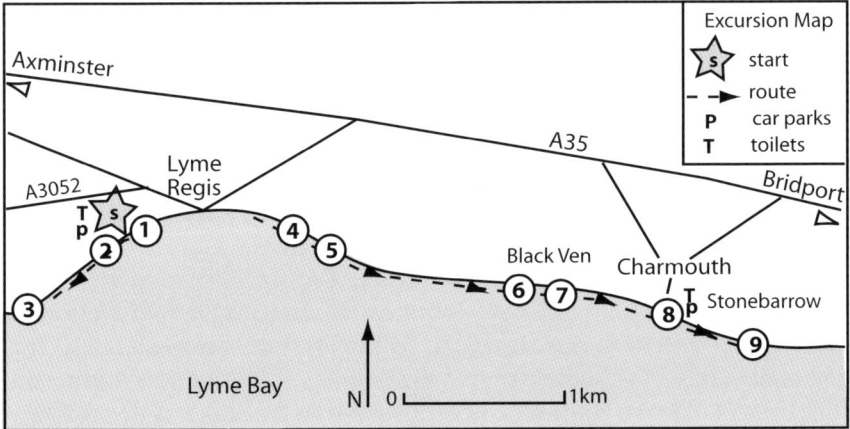

PURPOSE: To explore the Lower Jurassic rocks, fossils and landslides of the coast at Lyme Regis and Charmouth.

PRACTICAL DETAILS: Three excursions are covered here with some options for circular walks. All should be undertaken on low tides. Monmouth Beach at Lyme Regis is best accessed from the car parks west of the Cobb (the harbour) and lies within the Axmouth to Lyme Regis National Nature Reserve. The Lyme Regis Philpot Museum and Dinosaurland both contain displays about the geology and fossils of the area.

Charmouth Beach is best reached from the beach car park. The Charmouth Heritage Coast Centre is located above the Beach Café and offers excellent displays about the rocks and fossils. At the time of writing the Coast Path between Charmouth and Lyme Regis was closed due to cliff retreat. A inland diversion is in place. A bus service runs between Charmouth and Lyme. All grid references are on the OS Landranger sheet 193 'Taunton and Lyme Regis'. Monmouth Beach to Pinhay Bay is 1km, Church Cliffs to Charmouth is 2km, Charmouth to Stonebarrow is 0.5km

Due to the high erosion rates, the value of some specimens, both scientific and commercial, and the important role that collectors play in their recovery, a fossil collecting code of conduct is in operation along the West Dorset coast. Details are available from the Earth Science Manager for the World Heritage Team, Tel 01305 224477 or from the Charmouth Heritage Coast Centre web site at www.charmouth.org.

Safety: As with any beach and cliff it is important to stay well clear of the cliffs at all times. Within this area mudflows are a further hazard and it is advisable to stay on the beaches and not to venture into the landslides. Beware of mudflows that may extend across the beaches. Always check the tides and aim to be out on the beach at low tide. The beach just east of Lyme Regis is cut shortly after low tide. Always aim to pass this point around low water and beware especially during rough weather. If you want to find fossils then rough, winter weather is the best time but all of these hazards are greater so take care! Monmouth Beach and part of the beach below Black Ven are formed from large boulders which can make walking difficult.

GEOLOGICAL SETTING: The cliffs *(Figure 1)* and foreshore display magnificent sections through the Lower Jurassic, Lower Lias and represent a **marine transgression** that flooded the Triassic desert between about 200 and 185**Ma**. At this point along the coast all of the Middle and Upper Jurassic rocks, together with much of the Lower Cretaceous, have been eroded away and the Upper Greensand lies **unconformably** on the Lower Lias *(Figure 2)*.

Figure 1 The cliffs are dominated by dark Lower Jurassic clays capped by striking Lower Cretaceous sandstones

Figure 2 The stratigraphic column:

Upper Greensand		Lower Cretaceous
		Unconformity
Green Ammonite Beds	Charmouth Mudstone	Lower Jurassic, Lias Group
Belemnite Marls		
Black Ven Marls		
Shales with Beef		
Blue Lias		
Blue Lias (lowest beds)	Blue Lias Group	Triassic
Penarth Group		

Palaeontology: The Lower Jurassic rocks contain the most diverse fauna of marine reptiles, fish and insects of this age known in the world and, despite over 200 years of collecting, species new to science continue to be found each year. Some specimens are important for exceptional soft part preservation such as stomach contents and skin. Exceptional preservation is due to the environment in which the rocks formed. At times the sea floor became stagnant and unfavourable to life while deposition rates were rapid. Animals such as ichthyosaurs, living in the open water, died and sank to the sea floor where there were no scavenging animals to eat and break up the body before they were buried. As a result many skeletons are well articulated and, at times, the environment was so unfavourable to life that even the process of decay was slowed long enough for the soft parts to be preserved.

Geomorphology: The cliffs are dominated by landslides that occur because permeable sandstone overlie impermeable clay. Rainwater can percolate through the sandstone but not the clay. After periods of prolonged wet weather the cliff top becomes saturated with water and the clay surface is lubricated, allowing huge sections of cliff top to break away. The blocks tend to rotate back towards the cliff but the seaward side also breaks up into dangerous sand and mudslides that fall into the undercliff.

The relationship between the geology, landslides and late glacial history, particularly sea level change, has been the subject of considerable research that has led to new thinking on the formation of Chesil Beach and the management of coast defences at Lyme Regis and West Bay.

The raised beach on the western side of Portland Bill indicates that 125,000 years ago sea levels were several metres higher than they are today. At that time the cliffs would have looked much the same, if a little further out to sea. Then, with the onset of the last glacial episode, sea levels dropped by over 100 metres, leaving the coastline exposed to 100,000 years of weathering, degrading the cliffs into huge **debris fans**. Later, only about 20,000 years ago, the ice sheets began to melt and sea levels rose until, probably only about 10,000 years ago, they encountered the degraded cliffs releasing vast volumes of chert and flint. Longshore drift then transported the pebbles to the east essentially forming the bulk of Chesil Beach. With continuing sea level rise, the beaches have been driven onshore to the point where headlands, such as Golden Cap, have emerged trapping pocket beaches such as at Seatown.

Such a scenario has profound implications on management of this coast. The bulk of Chesil Beach may be very young indeed, while the supply of shingle that formed it has essentially stopped. Furthermore the cliffs we see today were active more than 125,000 years ago and ancient landslides lie dormant within towns such as Lyme Regis just waiting to be 'unzipped' by renewed erosion. This is of major concern and is being addressed by West Dorset District Council Engineers' Department.

Excursion 1 Lyme Regis and Pinhay Bay

Location 1 Monmouth Beach *(SY 332913)*

The Blue Lias consists of a striking sequence of hard limestones and softer clays that form vertical cliffs and extensive rocky ledges. Fossils are common, particularly large specimens of the ammonite *Arietites* and nautiloids.

Location 2 The Ammonite Graveyard *(SY 329910)*

One limestone surface is packed with ammonites. Did some catastrophe overtake a shoal of these creatures or is there another explanation? Please do not attempt to extract the ammonites here or in the large boulders *(Figure 3)*; attempts to do so only lead to damage and deprive other people of the opportunity to enjoy them.

Figure 3 Large ammonites can be found on the beach but please leave them for others to enjoy.

A closer examination of the rock sequence poses more questions. The rocks display a striking cyclic repetition of the layers. A typical cycle starts with black, laminated shale passing into grey marls and then harder limestone that often reverts to pale marl. The black shale is virtually devoid of fossils though these are the beds in which superbly preserved fish and ichthyosaurs can be found. They formed on a stagnant and anoxic sea floor. The upper two units are quite the opposite and contain abundant burrows *(Thalassinoides* and *Chondrites)* and a **benthic** fauna of bivalves and brachiopods. The top surfaces of the limestones may be smooth or highly irregular while some are nodular. The cyclicity has attracted considerable debate but it is generally accepted that these cycles relate to periodicity in the earth's orbit around the sun, the famous 'Milankovitch Cycles' that affect the climate and therefore the sediment supply.

Location 3 Pinhay Bay *(SY 318908)*

The oldest rocks, the Penarth Group, rise through the foreshore and lower cliffs of Pinhay Bay before being faulted down at this locality. Only the top of the Group, the White Lias, is clearly seen and consist of creamy micritic limestone with algal structures, conglomerates and desiccation cracks. The interpretation is of a shallow marine lagoonal environment that became exposed to weathering for a brief period of time. The original Triassic/Jurassic boundary was placed at the top of the White Lias but this has now been revised upwards by several metres into the Blue Lias based on the appearance of *Psiloceras planorbis* which defines the first ammonite zone in the Jurassic.

There is no formal access off the beach within the National Nature Reserve and although it is possible to walk further around Pinhay Bay, it is advisable to return to Lyme Regis along the beach.

Excursion 2 Church Cliffs and Black Ven

Location 4 Long Entry *(SY 344922)*

This location is approached from the new sea walls at the lower end of Lyme Regis. The Blue Lias forms Church Cliffs but the continued easterly dip has the effect of bringing the Shales-with-Beef, Black Ven Marls and Belemnite Marls into the cliffs between Lyme Regis, Charmouth and Stonebarrow.

Location 5 Church Cliffs *(SY 346926)*

The effect of erosion can be seen at the end of the sea wall that was constructed in the early 1950's. Since then the cliffs have retreated by over 20m and rock armour has been placed as a temporary measure to protect the end of the sea wall.

Location 6 The Black Ven Landslide *(SY 355929)*

Black Ven is the site of the largest coastal mudflow in Europe which took place in the winter of 1958/9. The extensive landslipped area is composed from a series of stepped terraces created by hard bands of limestone within the shale, rising to the sandstone cliff top. During the winter of 2000/01, a large section of cliff top on the western side of Black Ven fell away and cracks extended into the wooded Spittles, just east of Lyme Regis. The beach below Black Ven is an excellent place to look for fossils on the beach; ammonites, belemnites, tube worms and even reptile bones can be found here.

Location 7 Black Ven *(SY 356930)*

The Shales-with-Beef form the lower cliffs from here to Charmouth and consist of finely laminated clays with numerous layers of fibrous 'beef' calcite crystals. The formation of beef has been associated with the presence of high organic matter and the Lower Lias which includes the Shales-with-Beef are the source rock for the Wytch Farm Oil Field below Poole Harbour. The overlying Black Ven Marls begin above the striking Birchi Bed, a layer of large limestone nodules that forms the top of the first cliff terrace. The Black Ven Marls contain a number of nodular horizons some of which yield superbly preserved fossils, particularly the ammonite *Asteroceras*. These nodules can be found on the beach but are difficult to identify without practice.

Location 8 Charmouth *(SY 364930 Figures 4 and 5)*
Just west of the sea front the Shales-with-Beef are well exposed and the beef layers can clearly be seen. The bedding is contorted here, the result of **valley bulge**, deep-seated periglacial weathering which is of interest when regarding the stability of inland slopes. On the foreshore, and within the river, a late glacial fossil forest is occasionally exposed and this has yielded mammal remains such as deer antlers and bones.

Figure 4 (photo: Doreen Smith)
Charmouth, looking
west to Black Ven and Lyme Regis

Figure 5 (photo: Doreen Smith)
Charmouth, looking east
to Stonebarrow and Golden Cap

Excursion 3 Stonebarrow
Location 9 Stonebarrow *(SY 375927)*
To the east of Charmouth the Black Ven Marls dip below the sea and the Belemnite Marls form towering cliffs that are occasionally prone to spectacular cliff falls.....stay well clear! If conditions are right masses of dark metallic lumps of pyrites can be found on the beach and ammonites, preserved in the pyrite, can be collected.
It is possible to walk to St Gabriel's Mouth and return via the Coast Path to Charmouth. Low water is essential and it is important to stay well away from the high Belemnite Marl cliffs. The path up from the beach can be difficult particularly in the winter months.

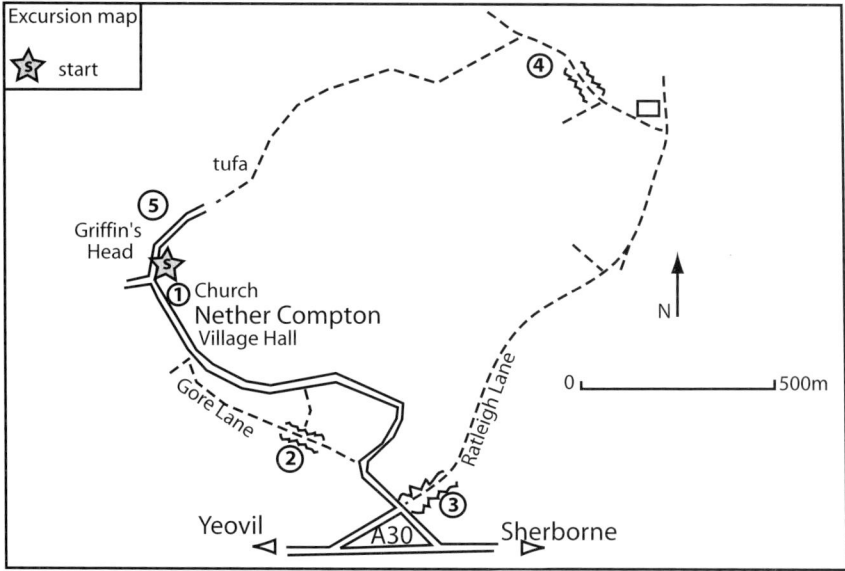

PURPOSE: An introduction to the Yeovil Sands of the Lower Jurassic and associated landforms in northwest Dorset.

PRACTICAL DETAILS: The following maps will enhance the visit: OS Explorer series 1:25,000 Yeovil and Sherborne (129); OS Landranger series 1:50,000 Yeovil and Frome (183); BGS 1:50,000 Yeovil (312). Boots recommended. Distance 5.5km. Allow 2-3 hours. There is a Pub in Nether Compton. Access to Nether Compton is easiest off the A30 near Halfway House at ST 604163 and there is street parking near the parish church. Combine with a visit to the Butterfly Farm at Over Compton *(ST 595168)* and/or the deep Babylon Hill Holloway *(ST 578155)* cut in the Yeovil Sands. Access to the latter is by a footpath leading up the escarpment from near the Matalan store.

GEOLOGICAL SETTING: The escarpment and **dip** slope of the Yeovil Sands is a dominant landform feature on the south and east side of Yeovil. There are exposures in the many holloways. Nether Compton is an attractive village situated where the regional line of **strike** turns from E-W to NE-SW and then N-S. The strata are disturbed by a large number of variable, small mainly north-south **faults** that are thought to be the result of wrenching during the Tertiary Era. The British Geological Survey has now abandoned the term 'Yeovil Sands' in favour of 'Bridport Sands'.

Location 1 *(ST 598173)* St Nicholas
The church of St Nicholas shows yellow-brown, sandy **ferruginous** limestones *(the local Inferior Oolite)* and dressings of golden, **bioclastic** limestone *(Ham Hill Stone)*. The nave, chancel and entrance porch date from the 13th century. Note the attractive 15th century Ham Hill Stone screen.

Location 2 *(ST 601169)* Turn left out of the churchyard and then right, opposite the Memorial Hall, to Gore Lane and bear to the left up the picturesque holloway. Note the fine grain-size of the sands that are generally poorly cemented. Wear and tear plus heavy rainstorms have washed away the floor of the holloway yet, paradoxically, the walls are able to maintain steep sides partly owing to their dryness, weak cement and the interlocking of the sand grains. An intermittent stream continues to slowly deepen the holloway. There appears to be the remains of a lime kiln, and possibly an ice house, on the north side.

The cutting in the Yeovil Sands widens out towards the top and is worth a close inspection. Try to make out the features shown in *Figure 1* below and see if you agree with the interpretation. Three distinctive faces are shown and labelled. They appear to be separated by steeply dipping faults. The right hand side of the middle section appears to be highly disturbed. The Yeovil geological map shows a fault *(downthrow to the west)* on the same line extending to the A30 where, previously, large tilted blocks of Inferior Oolite were seen to be dragged down against the Yeovil Sands on the downthrow side. The faults appear to trend N-S/NNW-SSE. The orientation, wedging and disturbed zone all point to lateral, as well as a vertical, component of movement.

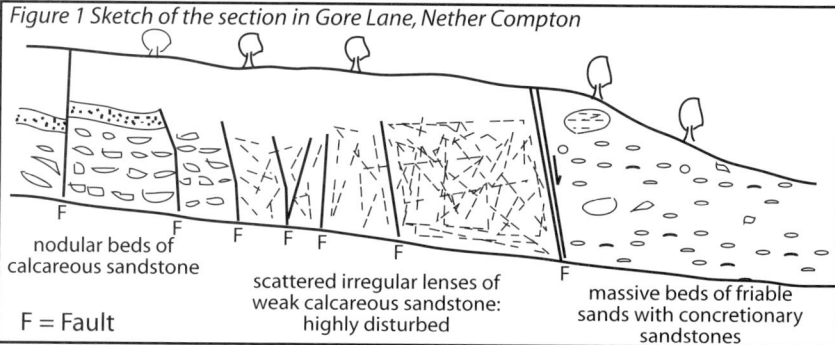

Figure 1 Sketch of the section in Gore Lane, Nether Compton

nodular beds of calcareous sandstone

scattered irregular lenses of weak calcareous sandstone: highly disturbed

massive beds of friable sands with concretionary sandstones

F = Fault

If the Yeovil geological map is to hand, note the complex pattern of small faults to the north and south of Nether Compton. Many of these are approximately N-S and orientated in narrow elongate zones; mini **horsts** and **graben**. Some 6km to the east is the NNW-SSE Poyntington

Fault - a **wrench fault** with some 2km of **dextral displacement**. This evidence for north-south compressive tectonics and wrenching *(with associated joint patterns)* is widespread in Somerset and north Dorset. These displacements may well be the result of the reactivation of **Hercynian/Variscan** wrench faults in the basement rocks. These faults can be related to the **Alpine Orogeny** as they cut rocks as young as the Upper Chalk. *(See the BGS Shaftesbury Memoir for details).*

Location 3 *(ST 168608)* Continue along Gore Lane to the metalled road, turn right for 200m, left at Court Ash Cottage and ascend Ratleigh Lane where one can pass up through some 30m of Yeovil Sands. Note the variations in the shapes of the concretionary 'doggers' plus the occurrence of more regular beds. The sandstones have over 50% $CaCO_3$ compared with 5% in the friable sands. NNE-SSW joints may indicate the incipient development of **gulls** parallel to the adjacent hillside.

Location 4 *(ST 611185)* Continue along the track and then turn west to pass the group of isolated buildings. Descend the short, steep-sided valley where the track is being actively eroded during storms. There appears to be a fan-shaped depositional feature at the exit to the holloway. Where has all the material eroded from the holloways gone? Brown, structureless sandy **colluvium** near the hydraulic ram suggests soil wash at a time when the field may have been cultivated.

Examine the exposure of Yeovil Sands to the east of the path *(ST 611185)*. The reason for the exposure is not clear but it may be an old marl pit. Compare the friable sands with the calcareous sandstones. Weathering of the latter has picked out sedimentary structures and a variety of **trace fossils**. The Yeovil Sands are massively **bioturbated**. The dip of the beds can be assessed as can the direction and amount of movement *(throw)* on the low angle fault. The fault may be associated with E-W extensional faulting.

Take the track to the left for Nether Compton. The track skirts the foot of the winding escarpment and passes a number of springs where ground water is thrown out by impermeable beds in the Yeovil Sands. The Yeovil sheet shows a deposit of **tufa** at ST 600775. Please keep to the track.

Location 5 The Griffin's Head
The grey rough-textured building stone in the walls of the Griffin's Head is interesting. Note the ammonites at various angles, orange-brown algal concretions with concentric rings and conglomeratic material. These stones are from the local Upper Lias Junction Bed; a thin condensed deposit associated with the 'Yeovil High', an example of local shallowing of the Jurassic seas. The Inferior Oolite shows similar thinning in the Yeovil area, presumably due to **tectonic** factors.

If you have enjoyed this walk I recommend Chapter 3 'Upper Lias mostly Yeovil Sands' to be found in the Reverend J. Fowler's 'Sherborne behind the Seen' (*sic*) (Fowler, 1936) *(see bibliography)*. The book is a lovingly-written appreciation of the rocks and scenery around Sherborne. The interpretation of the geomorphology may be dated but Fowler's sensitive account is something to relish.

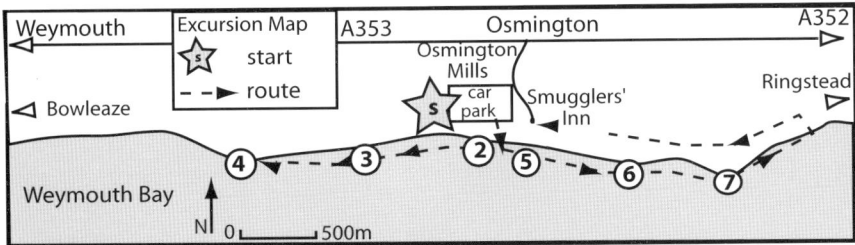

PURPOSE: To examine the geological structure of the Corallian rocks outcropping in the bays east and west of Osmington Mills, near Weymouth. To also examine the fossils and bed forms that give clues to their environment during deposition and the relationships with younger and older rocks.

PRACTICAL DETAILS: This locality is best viewed in two parts, the first walking westwards along the beach from Osmington Mills *(SY 735816)* as far as a point just west of Black Head and then back again - about 3.5km taking 3 hours. The second is again from Osmington Mills but trekking eastwards along the beach to Bran Point at the western end of Ringstead Bay, returning via the cliff top path - about 3km, 2.5 hours. The tides are only a problem at Location 2 where a scramble over the vegetated part of any new landslips may be required at high tide.

There is parking for individual cars in the Smugglers Inn car park if you use the facilities in the pub during your visit, otherwise in the road leading down to it. There are additional public toilets and a tearoom which is open in the summer season.

Walking on the beach involves some rock hopping and shingle crunching so strong walking boots are recommended, as is a hard hat, for both sections of the walk. Invaluable aids are a hand lens for examining rock and fossil specimens, plastic bags for packing and labelling *(location and date essential minimum)* and a table knife or small trowel. A geological hammer would be useful for reducing the size of rock specimens, most of which can easily be collected from the recent falls on the beach, but wear eye shields when hammering.

GEOLOGICAL SETTING: The generalised stratigraphic column and cross-sections *(Figures 1 and 6)* show the whole sequence of rocks exposed in this area. The oldest is Oxford Clay to the west and the youngest Lower Chalk, brought down to beach level by slumping and erosion at various points. In between there is the whole sequence of the sedimentary Corallian rocks, deposited in various marine environments in the late

Figure 1 Sequence of rocks seen at Osmington Mills

		Division	Description	Environment
Cretaceous		Lower Chalk	pure coccolith limestone	deep sea
		Upper Greensand	grey green sandstones	open marine
		Gault	concretions	off shore shelf
Jurassic		Unconformity		
		Kimmeridge Clay	dark clays and concretions	deep off shore shelf
	CORALLIAN	Sandsfoot Grit	red sands and clays	sub tidal
		Trigonia clavellata	shelly sands, limestones and clays	sub tidal
		Osmington Oolite	oolitic & shelly limestones with clay bands	lagoonal and near shore bar
		Bencliff Grit	cross-bedded sands with doggers and oil seeps	intertidal
		Nothe Clay	grey clay	offshore shelf
		Preston Grit	shelly sandstone	near shore sub tidal
		Nothe Grit	grey sandstones, bioturbated	near shore sub tidal
		Oxford Clay	dark grey clay	offshore shelf

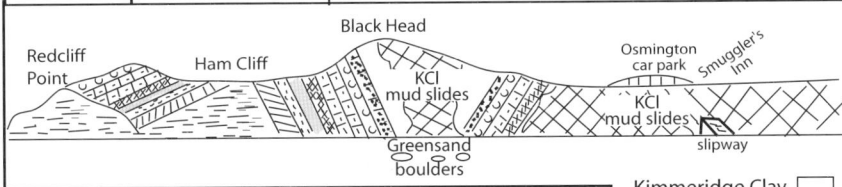

Jurassic, some 150**Ma** when the locality would have been much nearer to the Equator. The area formed the southern margin of the Hampshire Basin, affected by **eustatic** worldwide changes in sea level as well as more localised **tectonics**. These events gave rise to folds and **fault** structures which partly determined the rates and types of depositional environments.

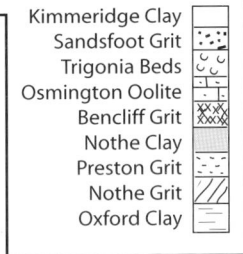

The end result was a sequence of repeating rhythms of clays, limestone and sands as water depth varied from deeper, offshore low energy environments and passed through shallowing upwards periods when limestone and near shore carbonate sands could accumulate.

These environments supported a diverse marine fauna and there are abundant fossils throughout the sequence. After **lithification** of these sedimentary sequences, folding and faulting, followed by millions of years of erosion, have produced the landscape and complicated rock exposures we see today.

EXCURSION DETAILS
Location 1 *(SY 735816)* The Smugglers Inn car park *(Figures 2 and 2a)*

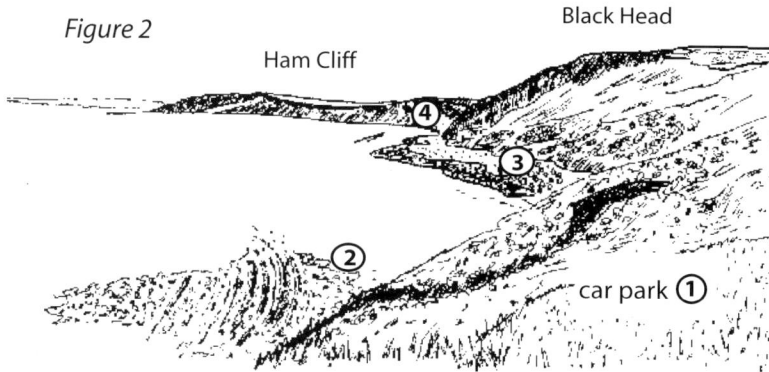

Figure 2

Black Head

Ham Cliff

car park ①

Figure 2a

This is a wonderful vantage point for an overview of the area.   Looking south-west there is the Isle of Portland, capped by Portland Limestone with a gentle southerly dip, then the lowland area surrounding Weymouth Bay. At the far end of Osmington Bay is Redcliff Point and Ham Cliff. On most days you should be able to see paler coloured bands of rock, dipping in opposite directions, either side of the concave shape of the cliff line. This is the Ham Cliff Anticline. The darker rock, making up the core, is the softer Oxford Clay which is more susceptible to erosion. The paler bands are the limbs of an upward arching fold structure, with the apex eroded away, which would previously have continued across the bay towards you. At low tide the remnants of the structure can be seen curving out to sea, just off-shore below you.

In the middle distance the highest cliff is Black Head, formed in Kimmeridge Clay, with evidence of recent mudslides on the steep slopes. In the lower cliffs, just to the east, are older landslips that have since stabilised as evidenced by the extensive vegetation. These slips have brought down much younger, down faulted Chalk and Upper Greensand rocks, originating inland but cascading through gaps and gullies in the Kimmeridge Clay cliffs. At low tide, you can see that the beach in front of these cliffs is strewn with large round boulders in an arc, delineating the toe of the earlier land slips. The roundness of the boulders is testimony to the many years that they have been exposed to the sea and wave action. Towards you, to the east of the boulders, there are further big slips in the Kimmeridge Clay which have occurred since 1999. Immediately adjacent to the car park there is a big scar in the cliffs exposing the cream/yellow coloured rocks of the Osmington Oolite. Take the opportunity to examine these pale coloured rocks that outcrop at the back of the car park. With a hand lens you can easily see that these limestones are made up of individual spherical grains, or ooliths, resembling fish roe. They are formed by calcium carbonate precipitating around a nucleus of sand or shell debris in an off shore shoal environment similar to that of today in the Bahamas. Worm burrows *(Skolithos)* are also apparent.

Although quite weathered you can determine that these rocks dip roughly north-eastwards. In the sea cliffs, to the east of the car park, you can see the damage to the coast path and slipway caused by landslips in 2001. From here you can descend carefully to the beach following recently trodden paths or take the path behind the pub, then turn immediately right to the beach and work your way round to the foot of crumbly, dark Kimmeridge Clay immediately west of the slipway.

Location 2 *(SY 735817)* West of the Slipway - Kimmeridge Clay

On the beach look out for larger, hand sized lumps of soft dark clay and use a knife, trowel or bare fingers to prise them apart. From what seems to be unfossiliferous material, you can find a large variety of **phosphatised** shells and ammonites, preserving some good detail although always crushed. The clay formed in quite deep water that must have teemed with life despite there being little oxygen at the bottom. Larger "D" shaped shells of the oyster *Deltoideum delta* can sometimes be found amongst the cobbles on the beach.

Moving westwards to the next slip, examine the large fallen blocks of oolite with some wonderful trace fossils of worm burrows going right through and, in places, ripple marks preserved on the surfaces *(Figure 3)*. Most of these seem to be symmetrical which is indicative of wave formed ripples where the bottom water oscillates forward and back as the wave passes. On some surfaces you can find small oyster shells, *Nanogyra* and *Pecten* shells and, infrequently, the irregular echinoid *Nucleolites* which can be recovered

Figure 3

with careful hammering. Continue another 100m to the next slip in the Kimmeridge Clay. It has larger blocks of clay in front of it which can be split with a hammer to reveal more bivalve shells and crushed ammonites. There are large septarian nodules which have cracked open since their formation and the spaces have then filled with calcite. Other, more homogeneous nodules sometimes preserve larger, uncrushed ammonites. Look out for smooth, grey brick-sized nodules with tiny white ammonites in cross section on the surface, often in thin lines. Careful hammering of these can reveal channel wash deposits of a mass of juvenile ammonites. Just above you in the cliffs, the prominent bands of Corallian rocks are picked out. This is the reappearance of the eastern limb of the Ham Cliff anticline but now as the western limb of a syncline.

Location 3 *(SY 730818)*   Upper Greensand boulder field

A hundred metres further west, the beach is strewn with large, rounded grey/green boulders. The texture is not as smooth as the nodules seen in the Kimmeridge Clay. These are water worn blocks of Upper Greensand, very well cemented and thus hard to hammer. At the foot of the low cliffs there is some softer, eroded sandy material with a characteristic green colouring from the weathering of the mineral glauconite. In the wet sandy ooze you can often find the brown, phosphatised internal moulds of bivalves and gastropods. There are also weathered exposures of Lower Chalk with, occasionally,   small ammonites lying on the surface of the scree.

The main interest here though is with the Upper Greensand boulders which have some lovely examples of large bivalve shells and the irregular sea urchin *Cardiaster lattisimus* *(Figure 4)*.

The thin pink/cream coloured shell and tests are visible in cross-section at various angles and the diverse results can be as informative as a whole specimen. There are a few specimens of echinoids preserved whole in the blocks but they are quite difficult to collect due to the hardness of the boulders. It is better

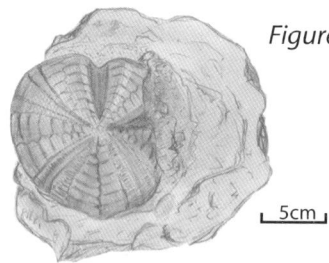

Figure 4

5cm

to leave them for others to see rather than damage them by unsuccessful hammering. Often visible in these rocks, particularly when they are wet, are masses of small, coiled worm tubes called *Rotularia*, other serpulids and moulds of large ammonites.

Location 4 *(SY 728818)* Black Head

At the base of the cliff on the east side of the head is the first outcrop of the red/grey coloured *Trigonia clavellata* Beds. These are packed with shells of *Myophorella clavellata* *(Figure 5a)*, a large ribbed and tuberculate bivalve with modern equivalents that use their strong muscular foot to "jump" over the substrate. Look out for patches of

©RJC

Figure 5a
Myophorella clavellata x 0.25%

dried out, light grey mud layers, on the lower slopes of the Head, which often contain fragments of large, club like echinoid spines from *Plegiocidaris florigemma* together with large, twisted serpulid worm tubes. To the west of the Head the rocks clearly dip to the northeast so that successively older beds are seen as you work westwards.

On the beach there are fallen blocks of dark red Sandsfoot Grit, speckled with large white and grey ooliths, which contain collectable specimens of *Myophorella* and many other types of marine shells. They include *Pinna* and the strongly ribbed oysters *Lopha gregarea*. More rarely regular echinoids, belemnites, the gastropod *Bathrotomaria* and lobster *Glyphea* can be found and collected. There are often large Y-shaped burrows of the **trace fossil** *Thalassinoides,* probably formed by a crustacean, on the surfaces. See also the 2.5m thick, grey, nodular sandy limestone section of the cliff in which **bioturbation** has destroyed all lamination. Moulds of the large burrowing bivalve *Pholadomya (Figure 5b)* smaller *Pleuromya*, elongate gastropod *Pseudomelania* and more rounded *Natica* can be seen, preserved in life position. Fairly large Perisphinctid ammonites are also found in the red blocks on the beach, the coloration arising from the iron-bearing mineral ankerite.

©RJC

Figure 5b Pholadomya x 0.25%

At low tide the Osmington Oolite is clearly visible. The beds **dip** steeply north-east, **strike** parallel to the beach and run on into the eastern limb of the Ham Cliff anticline. Here the Middle White Oolites have some well preserved current **cross-bedding** picked out by iron staining and variations in grain size. These beds have yielded fossilised fir cones, indicative of land not far away when they were formed. Note also that the thicker beds are separated by thinner bands of clay, evidence of quite rapid changes in conditions of deposition.

Return to Osmington. Note the distinct change in the dip angle of the Corallian beds in the cliffs beyond the slipway in the distance. This is partly related to a large fault which runs obliquely through the beach and cliff, passes behind the pub and continues parallel to the coast.

Location 5 *(SY 737817)* East of slipway *(Figures 6 and 6a)*

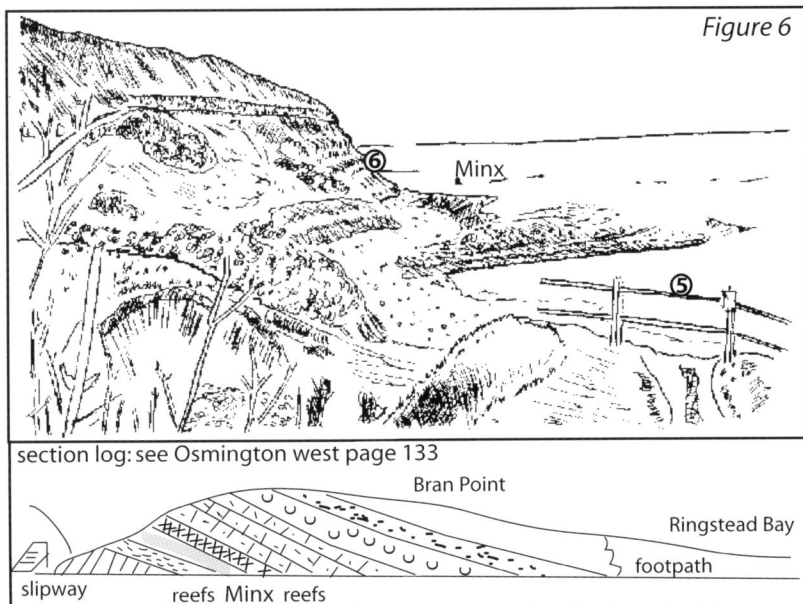
Figure 6

section log: see Osmington west page 133

Bran Point

Ringstead Bay

footpath

slipway   reefs Minx reefs

Figure 6a

The change, to hard ledges in grey, bioturbated well cemented Nothe Grit, is obvious here. There are abundant large oysters and loose very large, elliptical shaped **doggers**, the fresher ones having good examples of quite large scale cross-bedding. Also note the smaller 'cannon ball' concretions that are *in situ* in the ledge. The low cliffs include fine grained, poorly cemented yellow/brown sands containing examples of the oyster *Gryphea dilatata* in some horizons and harder, well cemented shelly sandstones. A little further on a stream cascades over a waterfall in a more resistant band of the Preston Grit where a small fault displacement can be seen. Walking 20m east the beach is strewn with blocks of pure white oolite, some with calcite veins cutting the bedding and a few small oysters and occasional *Nucleolites* on the surface. On some exposed bedding planes there are squashed 25mm sized mud pellets probably ripped up and redeposited during a local storm event. A little further on are the low cliffs of slumped, grey Nothe Clay which has brought down the material on the beach from higher in the cliffs. Here and there are small blocks of a gravelly, grey/brown limestone called a pisolite and made up of pea sized grains. The individual grains *(pisoliths)* look similar to ooliths *(see page 135)* but are larger and not quite so well rounded. Their formation is due to algae depositing calcium carbonate. Look out for slabs of rock with good examples of ripple marks as you continue around this embayment until the cliff profile appears, showing a series of stepped terraces where harder bands of limestone and sandstone stand proud.

Location 6 *(SY 739813)* Bencliff Grit and oil seeps.

As you round this headland, opposite the wreck of the Minx *(a 20th century coal barge)*, you can see the origin of the large doggers seen earlier. However here, *in situ* in the steep cliffs of Bencliff Grit, it is mainly a loosely cemented sandstone. There are some good sections showing medium scale **cross-bedding** *(swaley, hummocky cross-bedding)* which is also preserved in the much harder doggers. Thin clay bands interrupt the deposition of these sands in places. On particularly warm, still days there is a strong smell of bitumen and you can easily locate the source as a dark band of sand containing an oil seep, mostly dry now but with a greasy feel. Beware of loose blocks from above the first hard limestone ledge when examining the cliff face close up and note the erosion surface between the top of the sands and this ledge. Some of the thin slabs of grey sandy beds on the beach have small particles of black lignite *(fossil wood)* and plant material again showing that vegetation was not far away at the time of deposition.

Location 7 *(SY 742813)* Bran Point

The beds in the cliff section here dip to the east so that successively younger beds are seen as you approach the headland at Bran Point. Midway between the Point and the Minx the pisolite bed outcrops on the beach but better examples are found in fallen blocks on the dry ledges. On other fresher surfaces, and in fallen blocks, you can identify the grey Qualicosta Bed full of *Nanogyra* with good examples of *Chlamys qualicosta.* The ledge, at chest height from the beach as you round the Point, has some clear examples of the U shaped burrows of the trace fossil *Arenicolites.* To the east of the Point you should recognise the Trigonia Beds and the red Sandsfoot Grits and Clay, seen in the first part of the walk. The water worn, grey oolites on the beach are shot through with calcite veining and a hand lens reveals the concentric growth layering of the grains seen in cross section.

Continue 300m east, towards Ringstead and White Nothe in the distance, before turning left at the boathouse *(SY 744813)* to follow the stream up to the coast path that will take you back to Osmington Mills.

Chapter 20 Mike Cosgrove and John Chaffey   **PURBECK CHALK RIDGE**

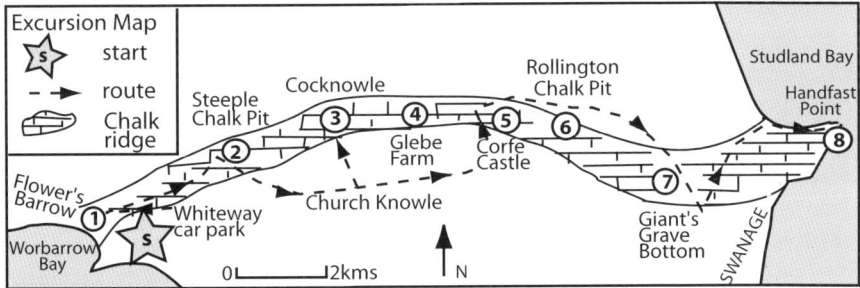

PURPOSE: To study the geomorphology of the Purbeck Chalk Ridge from Flower's Barrow to Handfast Point: to examine aspects of the structural geology of the Chalk at various locations on the Chalk Ridge: to establish any relationships between the structural geology and the geomorphology of the ridge.

PRACTICAL DETAILS: This excursion is best done with a car although there is some walking involved. The most westerly location *(Flower's Barrow)* is half an hour's walk from the car park at Whiteway in the Lulworth Ranges and can only be visited during some weekends or in the main holiday periods *(for times when the Ranges are open telephone 01929 404819).* The most easterly location *(Handfast Point and Old Harry Rocks)* can be reached from either the National Trust Car park at Studland *(SZ 037825)* or the layby on the road from Studland to Swanage at Ulwell *(SZ 022809)* - the latter requires a steep climb up the steps to the summit of Ballard Down. Refreshments and toilets are available in Corfe Castle village and at the Bankes Arms, Studland *(toilets at the bottom of the hill to the south of the Bankes Arms).*

GEOLOGICAL SETTING: The Purbeck Chalk Ridge runs from Arish Mell in the west to Handfast Point in the east. The Chalk, together with all of the other rocks in the area, has been affected by folding that produced the Purbeck monocline. Throughout its length the Chalk is steeply dipping 70-90° north and is cut by a number of faults. The high dips in the Chalk are responsible for the narrow outcrop, resulting in the hog-back nature of the ridge. The dips are steepest in the central part of the ridge where it bulges northwards. This is also the section where the Chalk outcrop is at its narrowest. It reaches a height of 198m at Grange Arch in the west and 199m at Godlingston Hill in the east. The continuity of the ridge is broken by three high level cols, or wind gaps, in the west at Tyneham, Lutton and Cocknowle. Further gaps are cut by three flowing streams at

Arish Mell at the western end, at the double water gap at Corfe Castle in the centre and at Ulwell in the east where the stream rises just to the south-east of the gap. All of these features cut across the structural grain of the ridge. It is thought that they may have originated on an uplifted Pliocene sea floor and have been **superimposed** on the east-west trend of the ridge.

However, it is quite possible that the water gaps and other dry valleys owe their orientations to **fault** structures in the Chalk. *Figure 1* shows the Chalk outcrop and the alignment of these features across or within the ridge. Allowing for the arc-shape outcrop of the ridge *(it is not strictly*

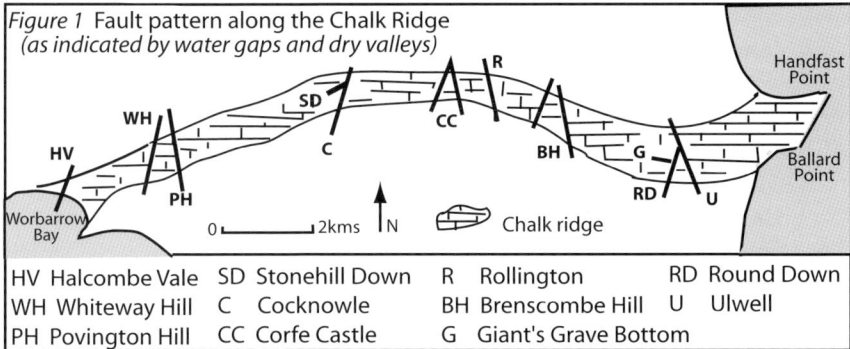

Figure 1 Fault pattern along the Chalk Ridge (as indicated by water gaps and dry valleys)

HV Halcombe Vale	SD Stonehill Down	R Rollington	RD Round Down
WH Whiteway Hill	C Cocknowle	BH Brenscombe Hill	U Ulwell
PH Povington Hill	CC Corfe Castle	G Giant's Grave Bottom	

east-west) the valleys or gaps are approximately orientated either north-west to south-east or north-east to south-west. This suggests a classic fault pattern, produced by the deformation of the strata during the **Alpine Orogeny.** After folding *(plastic deformation)* the hardened Chalk could fault *(brittle deformation)* in response to a maintained pressure from the south, with relief of the strain thus produced in the rock being horizontal *(east-west)*, high-angle **transverse faults** would result *(Figure 2)*. Should the greater relief of strain be vertical *(a factor probably controlled by the amount of overburden - the overlying Tertiary strata)* then low-angle fractures could occur striking parallel to the Chalk **(thrust faults, *Figure 3*)**. These

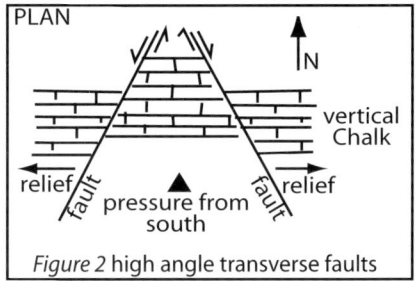

Figure 2 high angle transverse faults

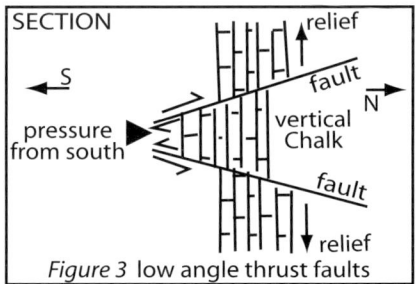

Figure 3 low angle thrust faults

latter structures may well play a part in the formation of the unusual "parallel to ridge" valleys at Stonehill Down and Giant's Grave Bottom *(see geomorphological details in later location descriptions).*

EXCURSION DETAILS

Location 1 *(SY 865805)* Flower's Barrow

Cars are best parked at Whiteway Car Park *(SY 888812)*. The walk to Flower's Barrow affords extensive views over the western part of the Purbeck Vale to the south and the heathlands to the north. After descending from the car park the most westerly of the high level cols is encountered before the walk rises to Whiteway Hill. Flower's Barrow is an exceptionally fine viewpoint with Worbarrow Bay immediately to the south and with Arish Mell and Mupe Bay just visible to the west.

Worbarrow Bay and Mupe Bay are both eroded in the Wealden Beds and Worbarrow Tout, beyond Worbarrow Bay, displays a magnificent section of the Purbeck Beds. On the seaward side of Flower's Barrow there is much landsliding as a result of water saturated Chalk and Upper Greensand sliding over the impermeable Gault.

Location 2 *(SY 904816)* Steeple Chalk Pit

There is a large public car park and picnic site on the top of the ridge at SY 905817. Access to this site is via the bridleway to the east of the car park, down the hill to the road and then a short walk up the road to the north-west. This small outcrop of grey Lower and Middle Chalk was probably worked for lime. The Chalk is thin-bedded and somewhat nodular, dipping into the hillside at about 55°. There is very little flint and fossils are rare. Three shear planes *(south-dipping thrust faults)* can be discerned by their marly-white appearance in the grey Chalk. Movement along these shears has crushed the rock to produce shaly, clay-like bands running parallel to the bedding. These are the low-angle fractures referred to in the Geological Setting section and *Figure 3.*

Location 3 *(SY 928822)* The Cocknowle Gap

Cars may be parked at the entrance to the Nature Reserve *(SY 930821)*. This location marks the lowest point of the high level col at Cocknowle. This col marks the former south-north course of a stream that was initiated on an uplifted Pliocene sea floor, tilted to the north. The course of this stream may have become disrupted as drainage developed in the less resistant Wealden Beds to the south, leaving the col at a height of approximately 100m as the only evidence of its high-level course. To the north of the col there is a remarkable dry valley that can be reached by following the path along the former tramway, originally used for transporting marl dug from pits near the high level col *(SY 932822)*. The dry valley heads, at a height of nearly 170m, to the west of the high level col and then descends, steeply parallel to the ridge, south of Stonehill Down. After the hairpin bend in the road, the gradient of the valley eases and after a hundred metres the valley makes a clear change in direction to the north-east and exits through the ridge in an almost gorge-like feature. Although the valley is now dry it is clearly a stream-cut feature; it may have developed in pre-glacial times through a spring cutting back along structural lines of weakness *(the faults referred to in the Geological Settings section, with a low-angle strike fault intersecting a north-east to south-west fracture)* and then, at a later stage, it was deepened by periglacial meltwater. The still active quarry on the north side of the valley is in hard sheared Upper Chalk with many **slickensided** surfaces evident in the constantly changing exposure.

Location 4 *(SZ 950822)* Glebe Farm Chalk pit

This may be reached by parking at Castle View Car Park, Corfe Castle *(SZ 959825)*. Cross the main road and follow the path to the bridge over the Corfe River and take the track that leaves the road at SZ 957822. To the right of the path two small hollows may be noticed in the flank of the Chalk ridge: these are nivation hollows caused by the accumulation of snow during periglacial times and subsequent freeze-thaw action enlarging the hollow. After 600 metres a small quarry exposes a section in the Lower Chalk, characteristically grey and with shaly partings, dipping 45-50° north. The southern end of the outcrop shows thin-bedded nodular Chalk but this passes upwards into more massive beds, 300-400mm thick. These show a well-developed fracture cleavage cutting across the beds dipping south at 50-60°. A low-angle, northward dipping shear occurs high in the face at the northern end of the exposure. There is a well-developed weathering profile, with the north-dipping beds curving over towards the horizontal *(sometimes referred to as terminal curvature)*, as a result of weathering and soil creep.

Location 5 (*SZ 959824*) Corfe Castle

Figure 4

Corfe Castle *(Figure 4)* stands on the hillock isolated by the two valleys, cut through the Chalk ridge by the Corfe River and the Byle Brook. Double water-gaps such as this one are not common and it is often cited as further evidence of the superimposition of Purbeck's drainage system from an uplifted Pliocene sea floor. The steep slopes that terminate the ridge to the west of Corfe Castle are probably a meander scar, cut when the Corfe River was flowing farther to the north-west.

Location 6 *(SZ 970824)* Rollington Farm Chalk Quarry

The quarry may be reached via the B3351 road from Corfe Castle to Studland. Take the turning south at SZ 968828 to Rollington Farm where there is parking for a few cars in the yard area. The quarry is then a short walk up a well-defined north-west to south-east trending valley cutting into the ridge. The quarry is still occasionally worked so the exposures change but it is sometimes possible to make out the essentially vertical dip of the beds. The Chalk is very hard and much shattered by faulting. There are numerous slickensided surfaces, large pipes of Tertiary material and some well-developed fault breccias of Chalk and flint. It is highly probable that the shattered nature of the Chalk reflects its close proximity to a north-west to south-east fault zone, now the site of the prominent valley.

Location 7 *(SZ 015810)* Giant's Grave Bottom

Cars may be parked in the Ulwell Gap in the layby *(SZ 022809)*. Giant's Grave Bottom is another unusual dry valley *(Figure 5)* and is a tributary of the main valley that forms the Ulwell Gap. It heads steeply under

Figure 5

Godlingston Hill and then trends east-south-east before turning through a right angle and continuing north-east to join the main Ulwell valley. Although there is a gap between Round Down and Godlingston Hill it seems unlikely that the stream that cut the upper stretch of Giant's Grave Bottom, ever flowed through it. If it did follow this course, then the only explanation of the present course of Giant's Grave Bottom would be to invoke river capture by a small stream cutting back from the Ulwell Gap, in which case there should be a steepening of the long profile of Giant's Grave Bottom at or near the right angle bend. Such a break does not exist. It therefore seems that the stream cut back from the Ulwell gap along one line of weakness and then encountered another, which was responsible for the change in direction. It seems that such a steep-sided valley was probably cut during periglacial times when the Chalk was sealed by permafrost. It is possible that these complex features owe their origin to the interplay of north-west to south-east *(Ulwell)*, north-east to south-west *(Round Down-Godlingston*

Hill gap) and strike thrust fault fractures *(Giant's Grave Bottom)*.

Location 8 *(SZ 054824)* Handfast Point and Old Harry Rocks

This is best approached from the National Trust car park at the Bankes Arms and is approximately half an hour's walk. Along the walk there are splendid views to the north over Studland Bay, and the distant cliffs of Poole Bay, with Hengistbury Head beyond. At Handfast Point the upper Chalk has a recorded dip of 8° north-west. Marine erosion has carved the whole of this headland into a complex of caves, stacks and arches along the lines of weakness afforded by joints and bedding planes. Just to the west of Handfast Point there is a series of well-marked buttresses that protrude northwards, more possible evidence of differential marine erosion. It is worth noting that the cliff-line between Handfast Point and Ballard Point has a north-east to south-west alignment suggesting perhaps that it is fault-controlled.

The outcrops at Steeple, Glebe Farm and Rollington Farm together with the geomorphological features at Cocknowle (Stonehill Down), Corfe Castle and Giant's Grave Bottom are all Regionally Important Geological/Geomorphological Sites (RIGS) designated by the Dorset Important Geological Sites (DIGS) group.

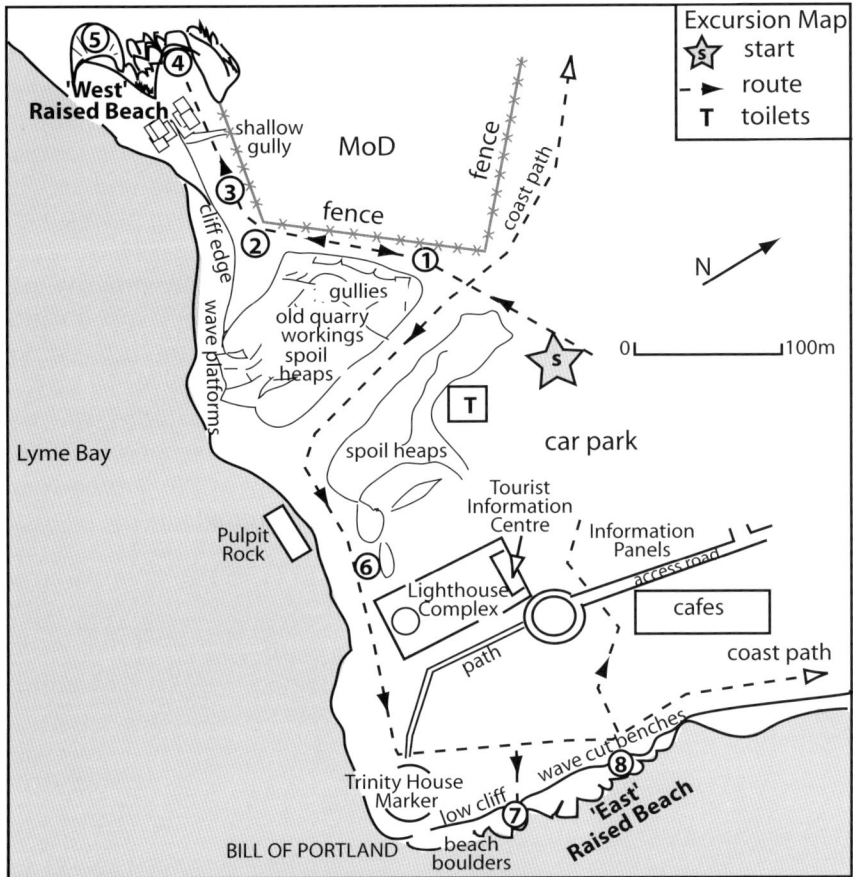

PURPOSE: To see and explore some of Portland's more recent geology, two raised beaches of differing ages and character. Both beaches are of national and international importance and are classed as Sites of Special Scientific Interest (SSSI). **Note:** Digging into the structures of the beaches is not permitted.

PRACTICAL DETAILS: Portland Bill *(SY 677681)* is accessible by car, bus and foot *(coast path)*. Ample parking is available *(but very busy in summer)*. Cafes, toilets and local information are close to hand. Please remember cliff edges, spoil heaps and gullies can be dangerous so take care. Portland Bill has very thin soils and a fragile ecosystem, easily damaged. Please avoid trampling and disturbing the very vulnerable flora. With stops and exploration the walk should take about 1¼ hours.

GEOLOGICAL SETTING: Both raised beaches are of Late Pleistocene age, the west beach being deposited approximately 210,000 years ago and the east beach about 125,000 years ago. The west beach correlates in age to the raised beach at Hope's Nose, Torquay and the east beach with deposits in Jersey. Sea levels would probably have been higher than at present and the land mass lower. Some authors talk about sea temperatures probably 3°C lower than at the present time. During glacial episodes in the Devensian *(Pleistocene)* this area was very wet and covered with ponds and marshy places *(evidence from overlying silty **head** and loams i.e. fossil soils. This aspect is not fully dealt with in this excursion).*

EXCURSION DETAILS West Raised Beach

Location 1 *(SY 678688)* Most people walking around the Bill would not give this section a second glance as it looks like a purpose laid gravel path. In fact it is residual material from the west beach, left from erosion and man's influence in the area.

Location 2 One of the better spots to explore residual material from the west beach with water worn clasts of Purbeck, Portland limestone and chert. A few exotic clasts and fragments dot the area; occasional quartzites, quartz and Devonian limestone but Chalk flints and Greensand chert are common. The exotics were previously deposited on a low lying area by river systems before being redeposited and incorporated into the raised beach when sea levels rose in interglacial periods.

Location 3 *(SY 677690)* A good spot to see the head and loam deposits plus the raised beach. The deposits are not directly accessible but can be viewed through the fence. A simple explanatory notice is viewable just inside the fence. Use *Figure 1* to work out the types of deposits.

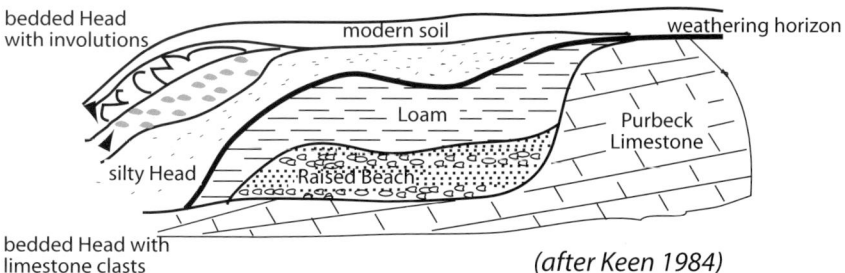

(after Keen 1984)

Figure 1 West Raised Beach, Head and Loam

Location 4 An accessible area of the raised beach *(Figure 2)* with well cemented pebbles, grit and some carbonate rich areas with locally sourced clasts. Note the angular polished grit, the well-rounded pebbles and the rounded, washed nature of the local material all indicating deposition in a high energy

Figure 2 West Raised Beach

environment *(substantial wave action)*. All the material is well-cemented with calcium carbonate derived from the local limestone, almost like a pudding stone. The locally sourced limestone material is often pierced by the borings of marine sponges, evidence of previously being on a shoreline. Shell material is not obvious as it would have been smashed during deposition in this high energy environment. The carbonate cement originates from percolating waters dissolving the calcium carbonate content of the limestone and re-depositing it. The water would have originated from the ponds, marshy areas, possibly rain water and, no doubt, spray and water from wave action possibly during the Ipswichian interglacial and through the Devensian glacial periods. Look for pebbles of a more exotic nature as at location 2.

Location 5 This area cannot be accessed and it would be foolhardy to try. It can only be viewed from location 4. Note the often jumbled nature of Purbeck Limestone Slatt *(thinly laminated, used as tiles or 'slates')* mixed with large pieces of limestone. Sands and grits are also evident where they have been pounded into cavities between the stones and then cemented by percolating ground waters, again evidence of a high energy environment.

Location 6 *(SY 676684)* You will need to retrace your steps part of the way to reach this location. The low banks and surrounding area show evidence of being affected by previous sea levels, wave action and water. The limestone is often rounded, water worn and also encrusted and cemented by calcium carbonate deposits. Some limestones have been bored by marine sponges. The area is strewn with harder chert and flint pebbles as at location 2.

Location 7 *(SY 678682)* East Raised Beach

It is possible here, with care, to gain access to the modern boulder beach. Use the beach's wave cut benches to traverse along the low cliff section. Note the sandy deposits with clasts of local limestone above the limestone bedrock. Also observe the large numbers of marine shells, mostly intact periwinkles and limpets, evidence of a lower energy environment than at the west beach and indicating a low lying beach similar to a strand area.

Location 8 *(Figure 3)* This is probably the best locality to explore and examine the east raised beach as the deposits are accessible from the wave cut benches, with care. The deposits contain local Slatt and boulders, showing evidence of water wear if not all rounded. Many of the limestone fragments

Figure 3 East Raised Beach

contain marine borings. Fine sands, shell grit, broken and intact shells are compacted between the local limestone debris. More exotic pebbles are also evident, derived from erosion of the west raised beach. This boulder beach deposit is cemented by calcium carbonate through percolation of groundwater and possibly by the leaching out of some carbonate minerals from the shells.

This is also the most fossiliferous area of the east raised beach. It contains dozens of recorded molluscs with gastropods being dominant but bivalves tend to be fragmentary being easily damaged in transportation by wave action on to a boulder shore. A large number of the recorded species are very small and not easily recognisable with the naked eye. Some shells still have colour markings. The majority of shells can still be found today on the modern boulder beach though with some exceptions only being found in Arctic waters. The deposits also contain foraminifera, bryozoans, barnacles, crustacean remains and echinoid fragments. The consensus, based on the molluscan fauna, is that sea temperatures were probably similar to today.

Note: On an extended walk outside this itinerary, the east Raised Beach can be traced *(with difficulty)*, north along the coast to Butts and Longstone Ope Quarries and terminates around Sandhole.

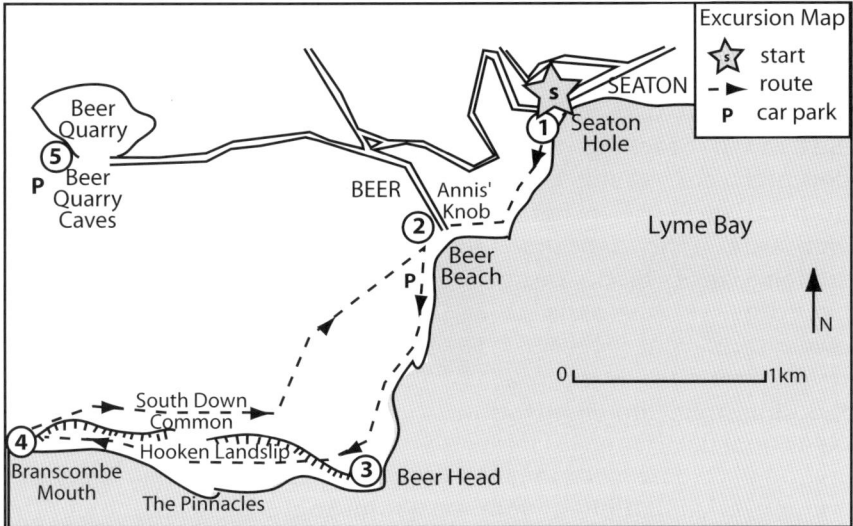

PURPOSE: To examine the Triassic and Cretaceous rocks exposed between Seaton and Branscombe Mouth and to study the nature and causes of landslides at Hooken Cliff. To visit Beer Quarry Caves and/or Beer Quarry *(intermittently worked).*

PRACTICAL DETAILS: Although the whole of the coastal section from Seaton to Branscombe Mouth can be walked in four to five hours allowing time for stops, a car is necessary if a visit is to be made to Beer Quarry Caves. Parking is available in central Seaton at SY 247902 or, if the walk along the beach west of Seaton *(cliffs of Mercia Mudstones)* is omitted, limited car parking is available at the top of the cliffs above Seaton Hole *(SY 235897).* There is a large car park at Beer *(SY 228888)* and parking at Beer Quarry Caves *(SY 214894).* Refreshments *(in season)* and toilets are available at Seaton Hole, in Beer itself and at Branscombe Mouth. Most of the cliff walks are easily graded apart from the return from Branscombe Mouth where there is a steep climb to the top of East Cliff or to Hooken Cliff after traversing the landslip *(Under Hooken).*

GEOLOGICAL SETTING: The geology of this coastal area is relatively simple. The oldest rocks exposed are the Triassic Mercia Mudstones that are exposed in the base of the cliffs on either side of Branscombe Mouth. The Mercia Mudstones reappear east along the coast where they are brought up by a **fault**, just to the east of Seaton Hole. They are overlain **unconformably** by the Upper Greensand of Lower Cretaceous age which is succeeded by the Upper Cretaceous Chalk. Beer Stone, from the Middle Chalk, has been mined since Roman times. Mantling the surface of much of the Chalk is a deposit of 'Clay-with-Flints' which varies widely in character but is essentially a weathering product.

EXCURSION DETAILS

Location 1 *(SY 235895)* Seaton Hole

Seaton Hole can be reached by walking along the beach from Seaton at low tide or by parking on the road above *(SY 235897)*. After descending to beach level, the Mercia Mudstones may be seen to the east where they are exposed as a result of the Seaton Hole Fault. This fault is a major structure which can be traced northwards as far as the Quantock Hills in Somerset where it joins another major fault. The Seaton Hole fault, which has a downthrow of 60 metres to the west, brings the older Mercia Mudstones against the younger, Lower Cretaceous rocks exposed in Seaton Hole. The Mercia Mudstones are mostly siltstones and mudstones which weather out into a series of small blocks. On exposure the blocks are reduced to small sub-spherical lumps. There are two greenish bands running through the Mercia Mudstones which are the result of **reducing conditions**. They may be original or they may be from the reduction of hematite around plant debris within the original muds from which the mudstones have been consolidated. Slight flexures in the mudstones indicate that they have been gently folded. The cliffs immediately west of the fault are formed of Upper Greensand, capped by Chalk *(Figure 1)*. Three main divisions within the Upper Greensand may be recognised within the cliff.

At the base there are pale green sandstones known as the 'Foxmould'

Figure 1

whose green colour results from the mineral glauconite. The lowest part of the 'Foxmould' is referred to as the Cowstones *(obscured by debris)* which are calcareously cemented sandstone doggers. Succeeding the 'Foxmould' is a series of sandstones, known as the Whitecliff Chert Beds, that have been toughened as a result of several included chert bands. The Upper Greensand succession is completed by the Bindon Sandstones. At the top of the cliff the Upper Greensand is overlain by the thin band of Beer Head Limestone *(see Location 2)* and the Middle Chalk.

Location 2 *(SY 229890)* Beer Beach

Beer Beach can be reached by following the footpath over the top of the cliffs from Seaton Hole or by driving to one of the car parks in Beer and then descending to the beach. At the northern end of the beach the main cliffs are cut in the Middle Chalk. At a higher level an exposure of white chalk can be seen in the uppermost part of the cliff. This is Annis' Knob which is mostly Upper Chalk with well-developed flint bands within it. The flint has been deposited from silica-rich water percolating down through the Chalk. At the southern end of Beer Beach a cliff section exposes the Upper Greensand at the base with the thin band of Beer Head Limestone *(of Cenomanian age, the oldest part of the Upper Cretaceous)* immediately above it. Above the Beer Head Limestone the Middle Chalk forms most of the remainder of the cliff. If the tide allows the base of the cliff may be followed so that a comprehensive view of Beer Beach may be obtained. It will be noticed that the bedding dips in different directions on either side of the beach. It dips gently westwards on the far side of the beach but in the foreground the beds are dipping gently towards the east. This indicates a syncline or downfold in the rocks.

Location 3 *(SY 227878)* Beer Head

This is best reached by following the footpath from Beer Beach along the cliffs to the south. Following the path southwards towards Beer Head there are magnificent views to the east. To the east of the mouth of the River Axe, Triassic rocks appear in the lower slopes below Haven Cliff and beyond is the beginning of the Undercliff landslips. On a clear day the whole of the west Dorset coast, as far as the Isle of Portland, can be seen. At Beer Head there is a magnificent view westwards over the

Figure 2

Hooken Landslip and further west to Branscombe Mouth. The instability in the cliffs here is the result of slippage on a thin band of clay at the base of the Upper Greensand. In the eighteenth century South Common, at the top of the present cliffs, extended much further towards the south. Huge cracks began to appear in the cliff top and, in March 1790, a vast landslide occurred which created an undercliff of broken blocks of Upper Greensand capped with Chalk, known as the Pinnacles *(figure 2)*. It slid down slowly and is still largely intact. The flint bands in the Chalk are still horizontal and can be matched up with the parts of Hooken Cliff from which the Pinnacles have become detached.

It is possible to descend the footpath that leads down from Beer Head to Branscombe Mouth, through the Hooken undercliff, to a vantage point where there is a small bench seat *(SY 223881)*. From this point the view embraces the cliff on the landward side of the landslip and the Pinnacles to seaward. The sequence in the main cliffs is best examined with the aid of binoculars. The best marker point on the cliff is the horizon formed by the adit along which the Beer Stone was formerly mined. This marks the approximate base of the lowest zone in the Middle Chalk. Below are the beds of Cenomanian Limestone *(thicker here than at Beer Beach-three beds instead of one)*. Above the adit a prominent line of flints can be traced, representing the base of the higher part of the Middle Chalk.

The path runs through the Landslip to Branscombe Mouth, providing very good views of the Upper Greensand and the lower part of the Chalk, although the cliffs are nowhere accessible for examination.

Location 4 *(SY 207881)* Branscombe Mouth

At Branscombe Mouth a diversion on to the beach and a short walk eastwards takes you to below the Pinnacles where the Upper Greensand and Chalk can be examined in the fallen blocks. A return to Beer may be made via the cliff path, leading eastwards from Branscombe Mouth to South Down Common.

Location 5 *(SY 214894)* Beer Stone Quarries

The quarries are reached by following the minor road that leaves the B3174 at SY 227894. Ample parking is available at the entrance to the Stone Quarries. The Beer Stone is locally developed hard chalk, some five metres in thickness, occurring in the lowest part of the Middle Chalk. The unusual texture of the Beer Stone probably results from finely comminuted organic debris.

Beer Stone appears to have been worked since Roman times and was used locally in Roman villas and other public buildings. The builders of Exeter Cathedral in Devon used Beer Stone widely in its construction. During the fifteenth century, when there was a great resurgence in the building and extension of parish churches in East Devon, Beer Stone was again almost ubiquitous in its use. The position of the quarries near the coast meant that the stone could be shipped to many locations in southern England and its use is recorded in Westminster Hall and Abbey, the Tower of London and Winchester Cathedral. After the middle of the sixteenth century the stone was mainly quarried for secular buildings. For the next 300 years the quarries were worked periodically, mainly for the building of houses. In Victorian and Edwardian times church building and restoration once again increased demand. However, in 1883, a change in management resulted in the gradual phasing out of the old workings largely because of increasing geological difficulties. The last removal of stone from the quarries on the south side of the road was in 1920. The Old Quarry Caves are open to the public and can be contacted on 01297 680282. They are, however, closed during the winter as the caves are used as hibernation chambers by several species of bats.

Beer Stone is still quarried intermittently on the northern side of the road opposite to the entrance to the old Quarry Caves. For further information on organised visits to the working quarry, contact 01297 680214.

---

an excerpt from the Guide Book to the Old Quarry Caves

Out of the Darkness
a brief history and description of the
Old Quarry, Beer
(John Scott and Gladys Gray)

Beer Stone: crystalline, granular limestone, the upper 8ft thick bedded, the lower 5ft harder and thinner bedded: mainly composed of the comminuted shells of *Inoceramus;* identifiable fossils are scarce, with *Inoceramus mytiloides, Orbirhynchia cuvieri, Gibbithyris semiglobosa, Conulus castanea, Hemiaster minimus, Nautilus, Ptychodus mammilaris, Lamna appendiculata*

Inoceramus

Recent research indicates that the comminuted material may be echinoid rather than bivalve

---

Thanks are due to Ramues Gallois for helpful information and comments on this chapter.

Dorset's Important Geological/Geomorphological Sites (DIGS)
Further information on all of the Dorset RIGS is available on
www.dorsetrigs.com and also from the

Dorset Wildlife Trust

8m

Hardown, Love's Lane
Morcombelake
SY 404944
National Trust
Upper Greensand

4m

Symondsbury
SY 445935
a walk round
the sandstones
of West Dorset

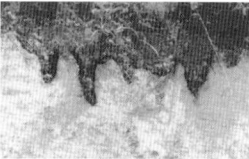

2m

Kingston Maurward Pit
Dorchester SY 718916
Upper Chalk and
Tertiary pipes

Poxwell Quarry
and a walk round
the Pericline
SY 743835
Portland Stone

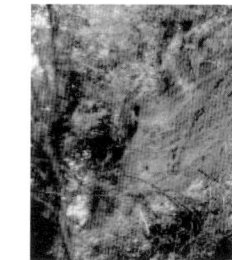

6m

5m

Red Lane Abbotsbury
SY 577854
Abbotsbury Ironstone

Redcliff, Arne
near Wareham
SY 932867
Eocene
Poole Formation
Agglestone Grits
and Corfe Member

7m

The Agglestone
Godlingston Heath
SZ 028827
Eocene
Poole Formation
Agglestone Grits

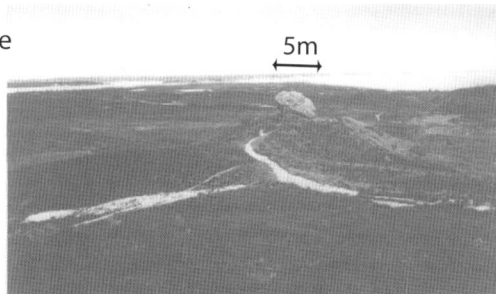

5m

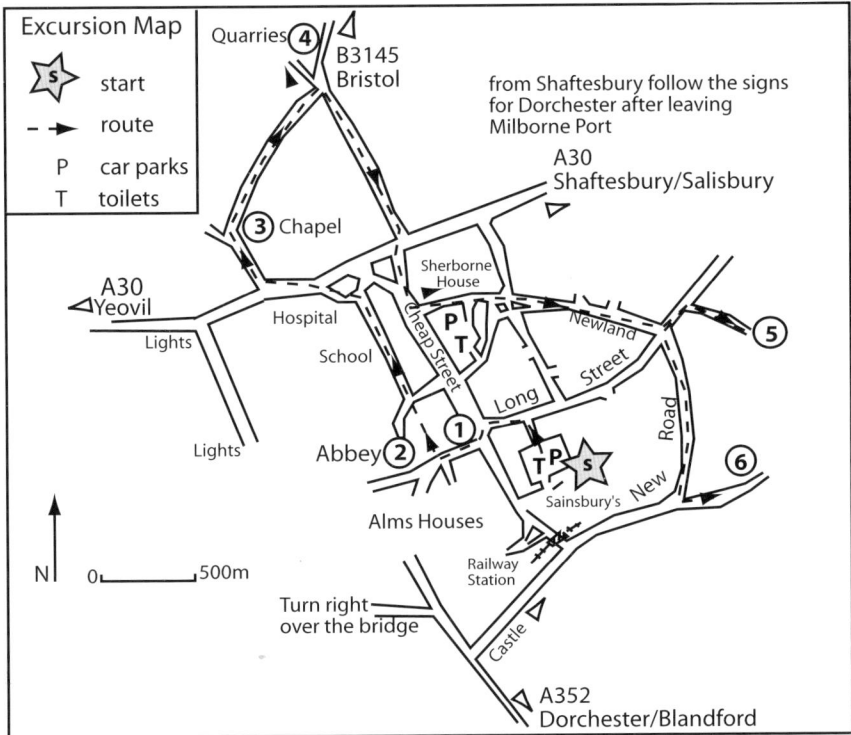

PURPOSE: To show that the distinctiveness of the buildings in Sherborne is governed by the local geology.

PRACTICAL DETAILS: Parking   ST 640164, OS map Landranger 183, Yeovil and Frome.

Entering Sherborne from the south on the A352, take the right turn signposted to the Castles, turn left (Gas House Hill) over the level crossing, then right and immediately right again to 'Culverhouse car park' opposite Sainsbury's. From the A30 *(Yeovil)* take the Dorchester road, then left after the town into the road towards the Castles. From the A30 *(Shaftesbury)* take a left turn towards the Castles and then right (Gas House Hill) and follow directions from the south.

Public transport: Buses from Dorchester and Yeovil and trains from Exeter, Yeovil Pen Mill and Waterloo.

Refreshments: Numerous pubs, restaurants and cafes.

Toilets: In the car park and in the shopping area.

Distance: Walk of about 4km within Sherborne. Two hours, or longer to look at more buildings.

Access: The main walk is through the town. One quarry is locked and requires permission and a key from Sherborne Castle Estates Office in Cheap Street, Tel: 01935 813182. Both Castles charge entrance fees.

GEOLOGICAL SETTING: *(Figure 1)* From British Geological Survey map, sheet 312, Yeovil. Sherborne straddles the Yeo valley with Inferior Oolite on the northern slope. The original part of the town has been built on a terrace of the valley gravels on the northern side of the river. On the southern bank the Lower Fuller's Earth Clay forms the lower slope with an outcrop of Fuller's Earth Rock forming a terrace above. This outcrop runs from east of Court House Dairy and through Sherborne Park. Above the Upper Fuller's Earth Clay the Forest Marble has been quarried on the hill to the south of the town. Near the top of this hill, on the eastern side of the cutting on the Dorchester road, is an outcrop of sandstone in the Forest Marble Formation. This sandstone was used for cobblestones on the pathway next to the Abbey.

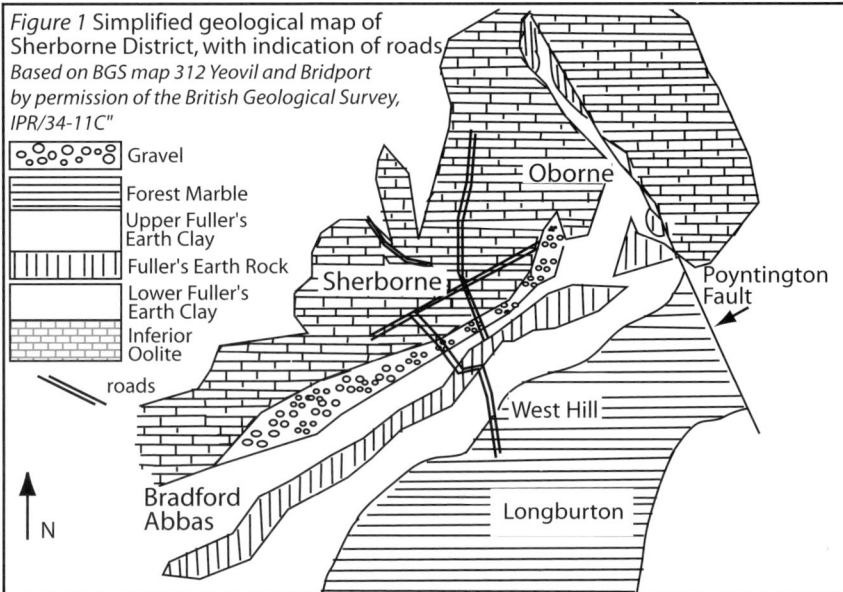

Figure 1 Simplified geological map of Sherborne District, with indication of roads. *Based on BGS map 312 Yeovil and Bridport by permission of the British Geological Survey, IPR/34-11C"*

Gravel
Forest Marble
Upper Fuller's Earth Clay
Fuller's Earth Rock
Lower Fuller's Earth Clay
Inferior Oolite
roads

There were over a hundred small quarries in the Inferior Oolite between Bradford Abbas and Oborne. The Forest Marble has been cut by many **faults** and in places is overlain by Cornbrash. There were at least six Forest Marble quarries either side of West Hill and in Longburton producing either shelly limestone or fine sandstone. The Poyntington Fault has displaced the outcrop of the Inferior Oolite and Fuller's Earth Clay on the eastern side of the map.

The quarries to the west of Sherborne, towards Bradford Abbas, are in the thinner Inferior Oolite but the remainder, from Sandford Lane eastwards, are in the thicker oolite, known as the Sherborne Building Stone. Two quarries are designated as Regionally Important Geological Sites (RIGS) and others are Sites of Special Scientific Interest (SSSI). The valley gravels, of limestone washed from the Inferior Oolite, have also been quarried.

EXCURSION DETAILS:

Take the northern exit from the car park and turn left along Long Street towards the Abbey. Most of the buildings are of Inferior Oolite from the quarries north of the town.

Location 1 The Conduit

On reaching the shopping centre in Cheap Street the 16th century Conduit facing you has been built of Ham Hill Stone from Montacute near Yeovil. Ham Hill Stone is an orange/brown limestone in which broken shell material has been deposited with all the fragments horizontally arranged. It is strongly cemented with iron-rich calcite and contains some oolitic material.

Location 2 The Abbey

Walk through to the Abbey *(Figure 2)* and, as you reach the Green, note the paving which is a mixture of stone with fine sandstone from the Forest Marble predominating. This has also been used for roof tiles, derived from some of the thinner beds.

Figure 2

Two colours are obvious on the southern walls of the Abbey. The darker colour is the Ham Hill Stone and the lighter is the Sherborne Building Stone which also has a very different texture to the Ham Hill Stone. It is a fine powdery limestone, coloured a light orange/cream by iron oxide mineral limonite, with a few fossils which are not usually present in the stone used for building. At the western end the much rougher appearance of the wall, also built of Sherborne Building Stone but in simply dressed blocks, shows that it was originally an interior wall.

Once inside the Abbey the following extract, from The Stones of Sherborne Abbey J Fowler (1938), can be useful:

Tufa *(Recent)*	Vaulting of nave and choir roofs (possibly local or brought from Caen)	1450
Purbeck Marble	Shaft in Lady Chapel	13th c.
	Abbots' tombs	13th c.
	Lower part of old font	15th c.
Forest Marble	Window shafts in Bishop Roger's chapel	13th c.
	Steps to altar	19th c.
	Shafts in restored Lady Chapel	20th c.
Inferior Oolite	Exterior walls and buttresses	15th c. & from
(Sherborne Building Stone)		16th c.onwards
Ham Hill Stone	All Norman and Perpendicular work	12th & 15th c.
	Upper part of old font and stone coffin	
	St. Aldhelm's doorway	10th or11th c.
	(Bottom bed of Ham Hill, a grey limestone 8' thick)	
	Conduit	16th c.
Keinton Stone	Floor in ambulatory	19th c.
(Lower Lias,	Steps at south & west entrances	19th c.
K. Mandeville)	Floors in Lady Chapel and Bow Chapel	20th c.

Purbeck Marble is found in many churches all over England and was also used for monuments and columns, especially in the 13th and 14th centuries. Look carefully at the Abbots' tombs and note that the Marble consists of masses of tiny round gastropods *(Viviparus)* all set in black or grey calcite. It is a fresh-water limestone but called a marble because it takes a polish. It can only really be used indoors - out of doors the iron content oxidises in time and the stone crumbles. There is only one pillar of Purbeck Marble in the Lady Chapel; the others have been replaced with Forest Marble, again so called because it takes a polish. Green and red Purbeck 'marbles', coloured by different iron minerals, are used in other churches in Dorset, *Viviparus* is always the defining characteristic.

Forest Marble is also a limestone consisting of fragments of shell laid down and neatly arranged in a horizontal fashion - like the Ham Hill Stone but in this instance it is grey. Very occasionally the beds are thick enough to be cut as ashlar but not from the Sherborne area. The deposits of Forest Marble limestone are not consistent, nor are they traceable from place to place, as it is most likely that the shells were deposited in occasional banks on an otherwise clay sea floor. The siltstone sequences are equally variable.

The Keinton Stone from the Lower Lias is a blue/grey limestone used in large flat slabs for flooring over much of West Dorset - particularly in the 19th century. Keinton Mandeville is in Somerset - a visit for another day.

The Sherborne Almshouses were built between 1430 and 1444, on the southern side of the Green, using stone from a quarry on the hospital site or possibly at Nethercombe Farm which was north of the A30 road. The 15th century records still exist in the Dorset County Records Office.

To find the quarries, leave the Abbey churchyard by the north gate up Hospital Lane. Take the left turn into Back Lane curving right to reach the A30. TAKE CARE crossing and, just to the left, turn north up Marston Road. Fork right up Coombe Road and on the right is an unnamed and neglected chapel.

Location 3 St Emerenciana's Chapel

The 13th century chapel of St. Emerenciana is next to the road. It is also built of Sherborne Building Stone although the window frame may be Ham Hill Stone *(covered in a "preservative")*.

Continue north up the road until you reach an H plan road layout beside the former Mermaid Inn. A kissing gate, on the left just beyond the building, leads into a public 'Open Space' which was one of the 19th century quarries recently used as a rubbish tip, now filled and covered.

Figure 3 Quarr Lane Open Space

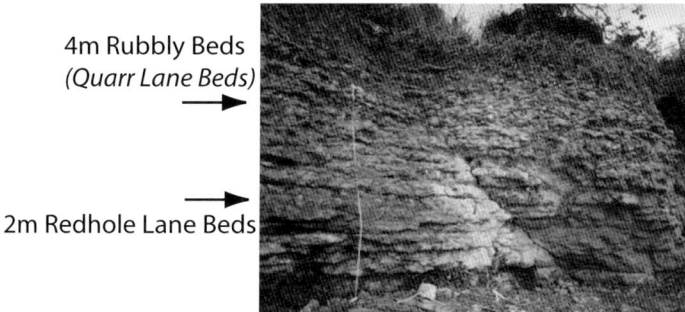

4m Rubbly Beds
(Quarr Lane Beds)
→

→
2m Redhole Lane Beds

Location 4 *(ST 636177)* On the western edge the Town Council have cleared a face of the Rubbly Beds *(Figure 3)*. These are above the Building Stone and were used for lime production. There are very few fossils in these beds, mostly belemnites and brachiopods, but please don't hammer at the face which would spoil it for the next visitor and possibly make it dangerous if undermined. Return to the road and go further up the lane alongside the mobile homes. As the track starts to rise there is a gate on the right. Here it is possible to see into the more recent of the 19th century quarries although the gate is usually kept locked to prevent fly tipping. To visit this quarry prior permission must be obtained from Sherborne Estates *(see page 157)*.

Return south and turn right at the A30 then left, after the traffic lights, back towards the town centre. Note the different style of houses, all built of the same Sherborne Building Stone. The shopping area has several opportunities for refreshments.

Walk eastward along Newland past Sherborne House to reach the Old Castle. Sherborne House was originally built for a member of the Digby family *(and recently occupied as a girls' school)*. The Old Castle belongs to English Heritage *(entrance fee)*.

Location 5 *(ST 648168)* The Old Castle

Bishop Roger of Caen, Abbot of Sherborne, built the castle in the first part of the 12th century. Fuller's Earth Rock, which is a pale cream powdery limestone with some blue tones, has been dug both from the moat and a quarry north of the castle and used for the interior walls. The exterior ashlar is Sherborne Building Stone and Ham Hill Stone. The latter, seen in an interior column, was used in 1299 and is the earliest recorded use. Some thin slats of Forest Marble limestone appear in a herringbone pattern on an interior wall. The stone in the undercroft has been identified as coming from Combe - near Nethercombe Farm.

Return to the crossroads and take New Road, first left and over the railway bridge, which leads past the wall of the New Castle, built by Sir Walter Raleigh in about 1594.

Location 6 The Stables

If the Castle grounds are open *(Thursday, Saturday & Sunday afternoons, entrance fee)* the stables are interesting, as the 18th century courtyard face is of Ham Hill Stone while the oldest rear wall is Inferior Oolite and the later side walls are of Forest Marble.

Returning to the road keep walking west with the stream and railway to your right. The car park is over the railway crossing.

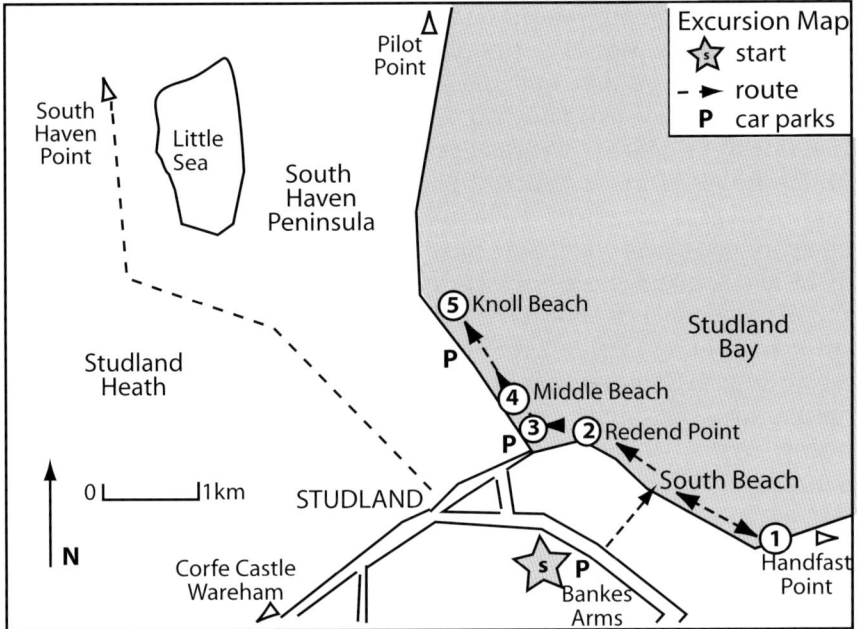

PURPOSE: To examine the Tertiary succession on South Beach Studland and Redend Point: to study the problems of coastal erosion and coastal management at Middle and Knoll Beaches: and to study the present pattern of the dune complex on the South Haven Peninsula.

PRACTICAL DETAILS: The walk from the southern end of South Beach to the northern side of Redend Point should take about one hour. It can only done at low tide as Redend Point is not passable otherwise and some important exposures along the northern cliff cannot be visited. The walk from Middle Beach to the sand dune complex and back should take about an hour and a half. Parking is available at the National Trust car park, next to the Bankes Arms *(SZ 037825)* and access to South Beach is via a footpath opposite the car park. Suitable clothing and footwear should be worn as there are often large accumulations of seaweed, which can be very slippery, at the southern end of South Beach and at Redend Point. Toilets are available at the bottom of the hill south of the Bankes Arms, at Middle Beach and at Knoll Beach. In summer there are refreshment facilities at South Beach, Middle Beach and Knoll Beach. In winter the café at Middle Beach is only open at weekends although the café and shop at Knoll Beach are open throughout the year.

GEOLOGICAL SETTING: The Studland Coast lies along the eastern side of the Isle of Purbeck where the Mesozoic and Tertiary strata are affected by the Purbeck **Monocline**. This resulted in the vertical inclination of the Chalk and the lower northerly **dips** in Swanage Bay to the south and Studland Bay to the north. The monocline forms the middle limb joining the Frome Syncline to the north with the Purbeck **Anticline** to the south. The Ballard Down **Fault** is exposed in the cliffs at the seaward end of Ballard Down where it disrupts vertical Upper Chalk strata and then curves away to the north. Here the dips in the Chalk correspondingly decline so that the Upper Chalk, at the southern end of Studland Bay, is seen dipping at low angles to the north. The succeeding Tertiary Eocene Beds *(West Park Farm Member, London Clay and Poole Formation)* also dip gently towards the north although they are soon masked at Middle Beach by blown sand at the southern end of the Studland dune complex.

The western part of the South Haven Peninsula is underlain by rocks of the Poole Formation. They are again masked by superficial **head** deposits and the blown sand of the dune complex to the east of the old north-south cliff line. The eastern part of the peninsula has grown steadily by accretion of sand dunes over the last few hundred years.

EXCURSION DETAILS

Walk down the path opposite the National Trust car park and descend the wooden steps to the foreshore of South Beach, Studland. Follow the beach southwards until the cliffs turn through a right angle and the Upper Chalk first appears at the base of a much-slipped cliff.

Location 1 *(SZ 043823)* South Beach

The Upper Chalk is exposed here to a height of two metres in the cliff with the basal bed of the overlying Eocene West Park Farm Member *(formerly Reading Beds)* seen to a thickness of 30cm. Above this the cliffs are much-slipped and carry a mass of often disrupted vegetation. After the Chalk had been laid down, as a fine white mud, it was uplifted and eroded before the West Park Farm Member was laid down on the eroded hummocky surface. Within the Chalk bands of flint *(made up of finely crystalline silica)* are visible which, unlike the rest of the Chalk, will survive long periods of erosion. Rolled flint fragments are found in the basal bed of the West Park Farm Member, indicating that the flints survived through the period of time that the Chalk was being eroded. They were then redeposited in the lowermost parts of the overlying rocks. The surface separating the West Park Farm Member and the Chalk is known as an unconformity which represents the long time gap between the deposition and uplift of the Chalk and the laying down of the West Park Farm Member. This is an important unconformity since it represents the junction between the Chalk of the Mesozoic Era below and the overlying West Park Farm Member of the Cainozoic Era *(Figures 1 and 1a)*. At low tide the unconformity may be traced along the beach.

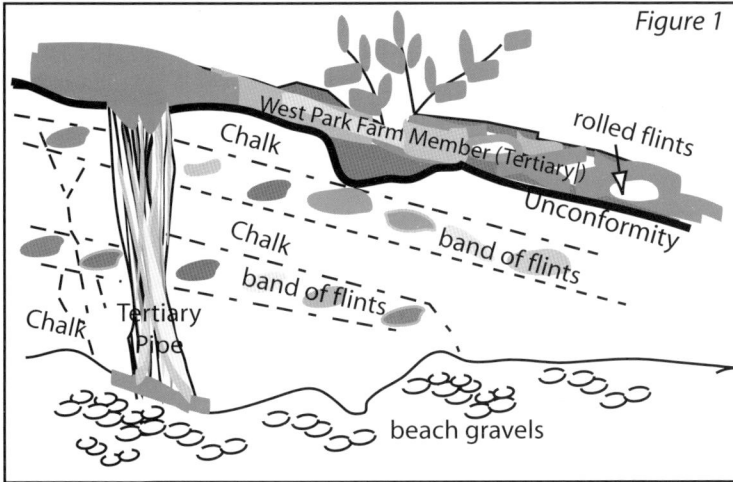

Figure 1

Figure 1a

Towards the Foreland and Old Harry Rocks, just beyond the first exposure of the Chalk/West Park Farm Member unconformity, there are several examples of solution pipes within the Chalk. These have been filled with material washed down from the overlying Tertiary Beds. It is thought that they developed because of solution of the alkaline Chalk by acidic water which percolated along vertical fissures or joints within the rock.

Location 2 *(SZ 038827)* Walk northwards along the beach, passing the steps used to descend to the beach. About 50m to the north there is a fallen sea stack in the Eocene Broadstone Sand *(formerly the Redend Sandstone)* now remaining as a series of large boulders on the beach. Beyond, the Broadstone Sand is exposed in a cliff some 10m high. The yellow-orange sand is stained red in a number of places and displays remarkable examples of **cross-bedding** *(Figure 2)* indicating deposition under changing current directions. In each sequence part of the older sediment is eroded away before new deposition takes place. Cross-bedding here most probably represents deposition in river channels, with the main flow being from the west. In some places the layers show quite unusual deformation *(Figure 2)*, known as convolute bedding, which results from the slumping of watery sediments after they have been deposited.

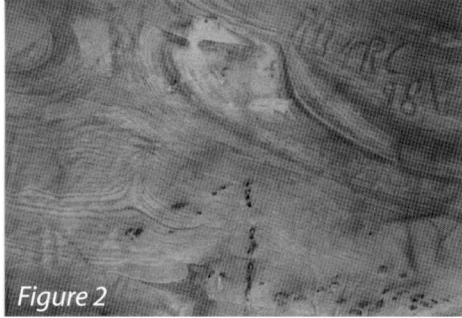

Figure 2

Location 3 *(SZ 037828)* On the northern side of Redend Point there are two main features of geological interest. Within the Broadstone Sand there are a number of small diameter *(a few centimetres)* cylindrical pipes within the rock which appear to cut across the cross-bedding. The pipes are often interconnected and are heavily iron-stained around their margins. Their origin is uncertain although they may be the result of organisms that have burrowed downwards into the sand. They appear to be tilted with the sand and therefore will have been formed before the rocks were folded.

The sandstone forms a wave-eroded shore platform, in which a number of potholes are present, which may initially have been formed by chemical action and later enlarged by the **corrasive** action of pebbles. Westwards, towards the shore of Middle Beach, the platform decreases in height as the sandstone dips below sea level. In the upper part of the cliffs up to 6m of grey, sandy clay and sand *(the Broadstone Clay)* are exposed. The clay is particularly rich in carbonaceous plant remains, including both leaves and stems, brought into the area by the rivers that at one time flowed in from the west.

Location 4 *(SZ 037830)* Middle Beach, Studland begins beyond the wave-cut platform which fringes Redend Point on its northern side. It marks the beginning of a long sandy beach, backed by sand dunes, that extends all the way to the entrance of Poole Harbour at South Haven Point. At Middle Beach the dunes are relatively narrow and are backed by the old sea cliff that can now be traced north-north-west to the western shores of Little Sea. Throughout the section of the beach between the slipway at Middle Beach and the beach frontage of the National Trust buildings at Knoll Beach, the dunes are now under attack from the sea and are retreating quite rapidly *(up to about a metre a year)*. In some places they are protected by gabion cages *(on either side of the* *slipway at Middle Beach and in front of some of the beach huts)* but this measure seems to have met with varying success. Seaward collapse of the cages is evident in places.

The National Trust has now adopted a policy of strategic retreat at Studland. Beach huts have been withdrawn up to 25m from their previous position and no further defence works are envisaged along this section of the coast. Erosion is thus likely to proceed unchecked and this will mean the eventual abandonment of the National Trust toilets, shop and café at Knoll Beach. In time the sea will have eroded westwards to the line of the old sea-cliff, some 60-70m west of the inner edge of the present beach. The sand, removed by erosion from the dunes, is drifting northwards and although there are still signs of accretion of the beach farther northwards in Studland Bay near Pilot Point, growth there is likely to be less than in the past.

Location 5 *(SZ 035840)* The sand dune complex of the South Haven Peninsula can best be seen from the beginning of the Heather Walk, five hundred metres north of the Knoll Beach Car park and just before the fenced-off section of the front dunes. Since the late 16th century old maps reveal that there has been a steady growth of the sand dunes seawards. Early maps, drawn about 1600, reveal that the South Haven Peninsula was then only a narrow strip of land corresponding to what is now known as Plateau Heath. Since that time four successive dune ridges have been built on the seaward side. The most landward ridge appeared on the 1721 map. The body of now enclosed water known as Little Sea also appeared on that map and has progressively become isolated from the sea. Zero Ridge, the most seaward of the ridges, has been growing over the last forty years. In the last few years, there were signs of an embryonic new ridge beginning to grow on the seaward side of Zero Ridge near Pilot Point. New dune growth is also apparent in Shell Bay beyond Pilot Point. However, during the last few winters, strong easterly winds have generated waves that have eroded this new ridge near Pilot Point. The winds have also been responsible for Zero Ridge suffering significant erosion on its seaward face. This damage is usually repaired naturally in the summer but, with rising sea levels, it is possible that the loss of dune frontage may become more permanent. However the summer of 2002 saw the new ridge begin to reappear near Pilot Point.

Ecologically the sand dune complex shows several points of interest. The seaward dunes are colonised by a range of grasses, such as Sand Couch, Sea Lyme and Marram Grass. The silica sand of the dunes encourages the invasion of heather from Studland Heath to the west. The heather has colonised all of the older dune ridges and has now reached the landward side of Zero Ridge. Gorse scrub has colonised much of First Ridge and oak/birch scrub has invaded the older ridges. Sallow-birch carr has developed in the wetter hollows (*'slacks'*) between the older ridges and has recently begun to appear in Zero Slack behind Zero Ridge.

Management of the sand dune complex is largely but not solely the responsibility of English Nature. Within the dune system there is a range of habitats that need to be protected so that wildlife is encouraged and suffers minimal disturbance. Several programmes of dune restoration are currently in progress. Further inland pine-cutting controls the advance of Scots Pine into the complex and the areas of Sallow-birch Carr are cut from time to time to encourage the growth of other aquatic plants.

Way-marked nature trails encourage the visitor to learn more about the landforms and ecology of the area.

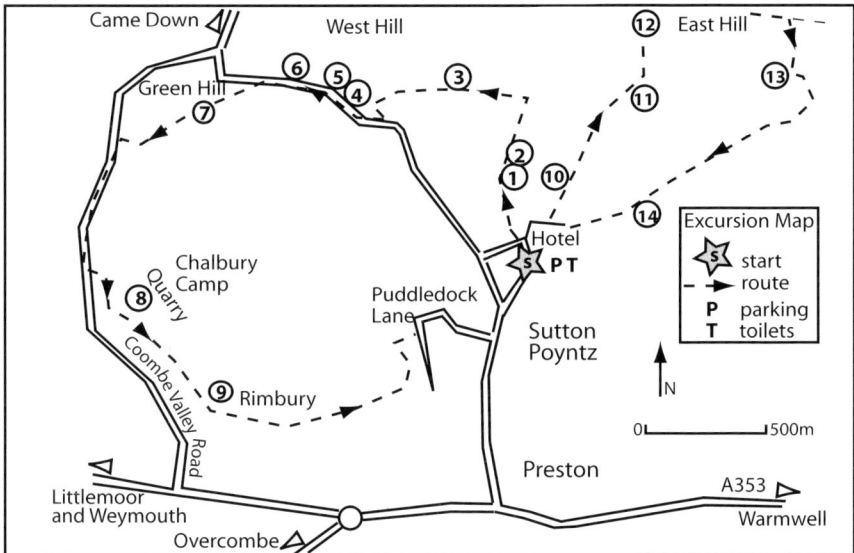

PURPOSE: The excursion aims to show the Jurassic and Cretaceous sequence of the Sutton Poyntz and Chalbury area and the complicated **faulting** of the Sutton Poyntz **Tectonic Inlier.**

PRACTICAL DETAILS: Sutton Poyntz is a spring line village, taking advantage of the powerful Spring Bottom source at the foot of the downs which now also partly supplies Weymouth. The Pumping Station, of fine true Portland Freestone, can be seen by walking north 70m from the duckpond. It is open on occasions Tel. 0345 300600 to check. The excursion is approximately 4.5km Locations 1-9; possible addition of 3km with Locations 10-13. Parking is on the road by the duckpond and the Spring Head Hotel, Sutton Poyntz at SY 706836

GEOLOGICAL SETTING: The Sutton Poyntz valley is sheltered from the north by the Chalk downs of West Hill and East Hill. The valley has been eroded in the Kimmeridge Clay by the River Jordan which cuts to the sea through a gap between the hills to the south of Winslow and Rimbury. They are formed by Portland and Purbeck Beds as is Chalbury, with its Iron Age fort, to the west. The use of local materials is seen in most of the cottages round the duckpond. Mainly local Portland Stone is used (*inferior to that from the Isle of Portland*) and brick from former brickpits in the Weymouth Lowland. Lower Kimmeridge Clay is exposed when trenches are dug in the village. The axis of the Sutton Poyntz **Anticline** passes through here.

Figure 1 The rock succession in this area is as follows:-

Chalk	CHALK
Gault and Greensand	
Unconformity	
Purbeck Beds	Pu
Portland Beds	
Kimmeridge Clay	
Corallian	
Oxford Clay	
Cornbrash	Cb
Forest Marble	FM

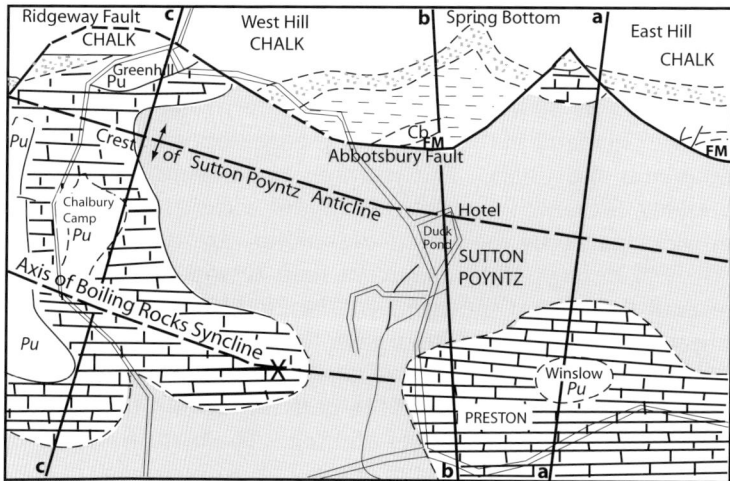

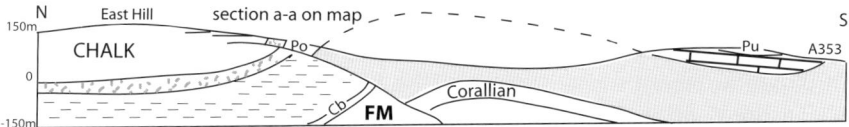

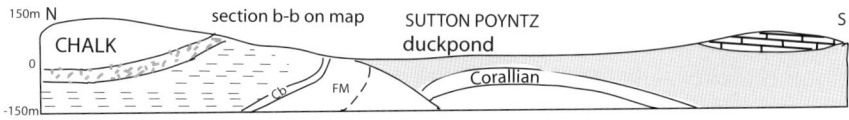

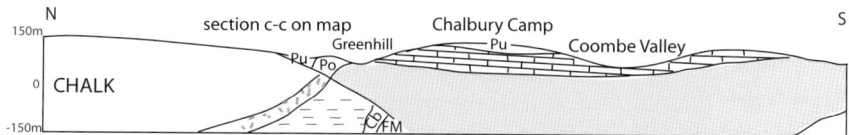

Ridgeway Fault   c   West Hill   b   Spring Bottom   a

CHALK   West Hill CHALK   East Hill CHALK

Greenhill Pu

Pu

Crest of Sutton Poyntz Anticline

Cb FM

FM

Chalbury Camp Pu

Abbotsbury Fault

Hotel

Duck Pond

SUTTON POYNTZ

Axis of Boiling Rocks Syncline

Pu

X

Winslow Pu

PRESTON

c   b   a

N   section a-a on map   S
150m   East Hill
CHALK   Po   Pu   A353
0
Corallian
Cb   FM
-150m

150m N   section b-b on map   SUTTON POYNTZ   S
CHALK   duckpond
0
Cb   FM   Corallian
-150m

N   section c-c on map   Chalbury Camp   S
150m   Greenhill   Pu   Coombe Valley
Pu Po
0   CHALK
Cb FM
-150m

EXCURSION DETAILS:

The walk commences at the duckpond, opposite the Spring Head Hotel *(SY 706838)*. Turn left beyond the pond *(west)* and then take a short lane to the right to the field where the platforms of former cottages are seen. Keep to the hedge and right of way.

Location 1 Before the field gate is reached, west of the waterworks property, there is a a shallow pit where the stream bends. The pit was a nineteenth century prospect working for the Middle Kimmeridge Oil Shale unit *(or Blackstone)*. The exposure showed that the Kimmeridge Clay is **younging** north along the route.

Location 2 Pass through the gate and access is possible to outcrops of flaggy limestones of the Middle Jurassic Forest Marble in the west bank of the stream. This indicates there has to be a major fault dislocation against the Kimmeridge Clay to the south with the fault downthrowing south probably over 300m *(named the Abbotsbury Fault because it can be traced so far)*. This fault is thought to pre-date deposition of the Gault, Greensand and the Chalk. The younger beds found here form the Sutton Poyntz Tectonic Inlier in which older rocks are surrounded by younger rocks, partly by the effects of faulting. Spreads of fossiliferous Cornbrash will be seen if the adjacent field is under plough. Former trenches near the stream showed **septarian nodules** of the Oxford Clay. The footpath continues north to a gate. To the left, beyond the gate, is Spring Bottom and the water-settling lake for the Pumping Station.

Location 3 *(SY 708845)* Turn left at the gate and follow the footpath to an eminence with a telegraph pole and seat. The feature is formed by the Upper Greensand. The Gault below is interpreted as resting **unconformabe** on Oxford Clay, the erosion down to this level being of mid-Cretaceous age following the movement on the Abbotsbury Fault. There are adjacent old workings in the Lower Chalk and the top grit of the Upper Greensand breaks through the turf and **dips** 40° north *(the opposite direction to the earlier beds below the unconformity)*. The few centimetres above the top grit is the level, rich in ammonites, of the Cenomanian Basement Bed. These can often be spotted without digging. Follow this level west to the corner of the hedge at the foot of the slopes and pass through the stile then south by the right of way to Plaister's Lane. Continue up hill over concealed Oxford Clay.

Location 4 *(SY 702843)* A good cutting exposes the Upper Greensand on the east side of Plaister's Lane. Outside Dell Cottage are some typical large rounded "cowstones" from the lower Upper Greensand. Crags of chert and glauconitic gritstone of the higher beds of the Upper Greensand, are seen dipping 30° north-west opposite Timber Lane.

Location 5 Behind garages further up the road, there is an old quarry in the Lower and nodular Middle Chalk dipping 30° north.

Location 6 (SY 697844) Yet further up the road on the north side, just beyond South Ridge, a small valley marks the site of a fault which maps in continuity with the Abbotsbury Fault seen near Location 1. Here the fault cuts the Chalk and, therefore, must be post-Cretaceous in age. From here it is termed the Ridgeway Fault. It has a downthrow to the north and is thought to represent a reactivation of the Abbotsbury Fault. Blocks of Upper Greensand can be traced along the fault in the small valley. Portland Beds crop out in the **footwall** of the fault beside the road and continue beyond the fault. These are the Exogyra Bed, with the Scar Cementstone above it, which is taken as the top of the Portland Sand; they dip 50-90° north *(steepest close to the fault)*.

Up the hill, beside the road, higher beds of the Portland and Purbeck Beds crop out. Before the crest of the hill cross the stile to the west. Note that on the north side of the Abbotsbury Fault, the Kimmeridge Clay, the Portland and the Purbeck Beds are preserved beneath the Cretaceous.

Location 7 (SY 694842) A footpath east of the road leads to the Coombe Valley road south of Green Hill. It passes an outcrop of olive-grey coloured sands of the Portland Sand. Approaching the road the **dolomitic** Scar Cementstone is dipping 36° north. North along the road it is followed by an old working *(Figure 2)* in the Portland Limestone (dip 56° N); the northern slopes of Green Hill are in the Purbeck Beds. Coombe Valley is a dry valley and, it is thought, its watertable was captured by the Sutton Poyntz valley at the col south of the footpath.

Figure 2 View of Chalbury Quarry (Location 8) from the west showing the units

Location 8 (SY 694837) To the south on the west side of the Coombe Valley, at the base of the Purbeck Formation, a scar of the **tufa** dips c. 7° south and is marked by a small fault. Thus the axis of the Sutton Poyntz Anticline has been passed. The Chalbury quarry shows almost the whole of the Portland Limestone. The tufa, at the base of the Purbeck

Beds shows the hollows of collapsed fossil tree trunks. The track, leading to the reservoir on Rimbury Hill, gives an overview of Boiling Rocks *(one of the earliest sources of water for Weymouth)*. To the south the rocks now dip north indicating the Boiling Rocks **Syncline**. Chalbury is an Iron Age 'A' contour hill-fort.

Location 9 *(SY 698835)* Return to Sutton Poyntz following the Rimbury Hill ridge to the east. Funeral urns of the Beaker Folk Rimbury-Deverel culture were found when the Reservoir was being excavated; the collection is mostly in the Dorchester Museum. The basal tufa crops out on the south side of the nearby wall. To the south is a view across the Kimmeridge Clay vale and the *(northward dipping)* Corallian Beds of the ridge of Jordan Hill just before Weymouth Bay is reached. In the distance the Portland and Purbeck Beds, on the Isle of Portland, should be seen dipping south, indicating that the axis of the Weymouth Anticline crosses Weymouth Bay.

Continue to the end of the ridge, bear left and come down into Puddledock Lane, now on Kimmeridge Clay and continue east to the main road leading back to the duckpond. A break may be appropriate here. The excursion can terminate here but the following localities allow the eastern side of the Sutton Poyntz Tectonic Inlier to be examined.

Location 10 *(SY 708842)* Go north from the duckpond, past the Pumping Station, then follow the lane to the right. Near the end of the lane and through Hunts Timber Yard, the right of way passes diagonally across a field. The lower part of this field is in Kimmeridge Clay and spoil, from footings for the first electricity pole on the right, yielded an ammonite aptychus of the lower Kimmeridge Clay. Reeds also mark Kimmeridge Clay below the second electricity pole. Spoil from the next pole in the field was of Oxford Clay indicating that the Abbotsbury Fault has been crossed. Noteworthy is the absence of the Forest Marble and Cornbrash seen on the west side of the inlier.

Location 11 *(SY 714845)* Pass through the stile and cross to the lane going up the west side of East Hill. The track has a long section of the Upper Greensand and, at the junction with the Lower Chalk, the Cenomanian Basement Bed. This has yielded good ammonite faunas including **heteromorphic** ammonites of the Lower Cenomanian. The east track side shows evidence of spectacular overthrusting of Upper Greensand over Chalk *(Figure 3 page 173)*. The thrusts appear to be horizontal and the Upper Greensand grit steeply dipping to vertical. The Upper Greensand and Gault to the west rest on Oxford Clay but, to the east, they rest on Portland Beds which form the lower spur of East Hill.

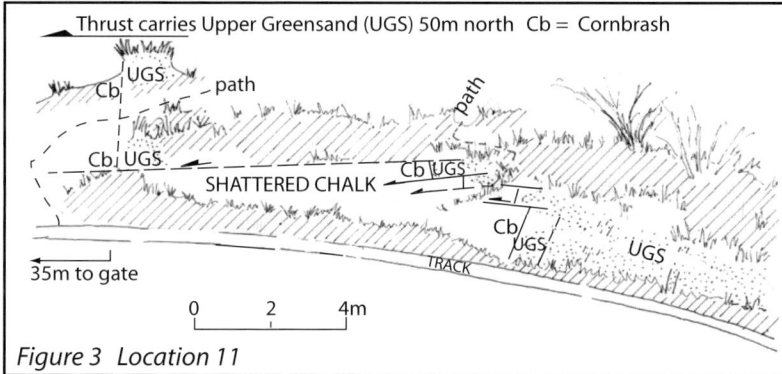

Figure 3 Location 11

Location 12 Up East Hill to the north-west through the gate and about 18m north of the wall, there is an outcrop of Upper Greensand grit, another 7.3m higher and another 3m higher and progressively to the east. These outcrops were proved in 1937 by the removal of the turf. Only one is clear at present. If the thrusts are still horizontal, as indicated in the track below, this means they must become lost in the Chalk of East Hill. The association of faulting, affecting the Chalk and therefore post-Cretaceous, along the line of the intra-Cretaceous Abbotsbury Fault, both here and at the western end of the inlier, indicates that the pre-Albian fault has been reactivated during later faulting and thrusting of the mid-Tertiary.

Location 13 *(SY 716845)* A climb to the east, diagonally up through the gorse, leads to the White Horse. The recommended route follows the right of way up the track on the east side of East Hill and then joins the South-West Coast Path to the east. The White Horse was carved in 1815 by removing turf from the underlying Chalk. It represents George III on horseback. Foolishly *(for a TV programme)* it was covered with aggregate of Portland Limestone and so can no longer be white. A return can be made to Sutton Poyntz either by the outward route or there is a right of way, crossing the White Horse and the field below, which joins the lane with the timber yard.

Location 14 *(SY 708840)* The hedge ditch, before the lane is reached, often exposes Kimmeridge Clay. A pit near by, dug during the 1918 survey, proved the Mutabilis Zone of the Kimmeridge Clay. Continue to the lane past the timber yard to return to the Pumping Station and duckpond.

Chapter 26 Jake Hancock **THE CHALK north and south of SHAFTESBURY**

Excursion Maps

Shillingstone chalk-pit

Charnage Down

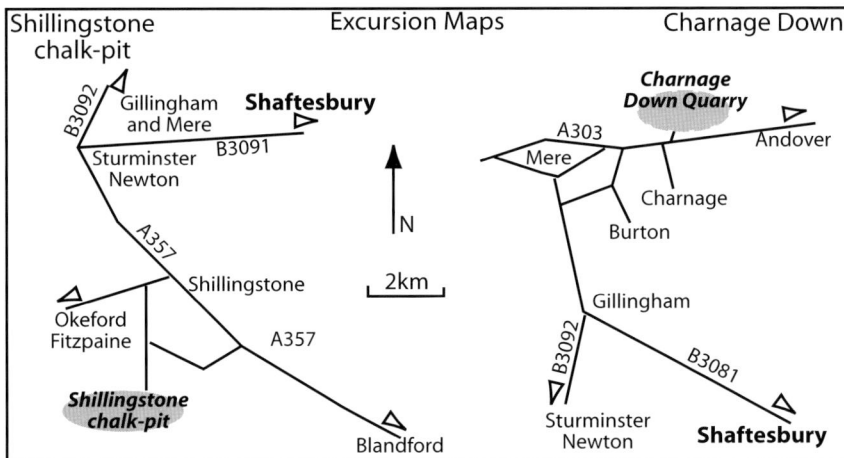

PURPOSE: To compare two facies in the Chalk: normal soft **white-chalk** and the **diagenetic hardground-chalk**; and to see the different developments of the Chalk Rock north and south of Shaftesbury.

PRACTICAL DETAILS: 100 years ago, when 'marling' the fields was a common practice, there were many small chalk pits. Working quarries in the Chalk today, are mostly for making cement and are fewer and larger. Within 15km of Shaftesbury there are only 3 or 4 good exposures. Shillingstone Pit ST 823099 is 1km south of Shillingstone village and some 7km north-west of Blandford. It is no longer worked but is a Site of Special Scientific Interest (SSSI) and should therefore be available for geological visitors. Entry is from the north.

Charnage Down ST 837329 is a working quarry and permission should be obtained from the office. There is room to park in the entrance area of the quarry which is just off the A303 about 3km east of Mere. It is easy to overshoot if approaching from the west, but the small turning to Charnage, on the south side of the road, is a signal to be ready to turn off the main road.

GEOLOGICAL SETTING: Chalk is a sediment formed from the skeletal fragments of the **phylum Haptophyta**. These fragments have been secreted as low magnesian calcite inside the organism. When they are released from their **cytoplasmic envelope**, the fragments are already a mineral species which is stable at surface temperatures and pressures. They are small, typically tablet-shaped laths or platelets, with a maximum diameter of only about 1μm. In life many of them are arranged in rings, known as coccoliths, mostly about 4-10µm across. Most of these coccolith rings are broken into their component platelets before incorporation into the initial chalk-ooze.

There are small amounts of other calcitic components, typically less than 10% of the rock, such as **benthic** foraminifera in white chalk, but non-calcareous material, such as clay minerals, seldom makes up more than 4% of the bulk composition.

Thus chalk is a special sort of limestone. Most limestones also start as biogenic material, but the initial composition is aragonite or high magnesian calcite. Both these forms of calcium carbonate are unstable at normal temperatures and surface pressures. Aragonite is **orthorhombic** and, if water is present, slowly reverts to calcite which being **trigonal**, has a more ordered lattice. High magnesian calcite is a convenient mineral concept used by sedimentologists. Under inorganic conditions, not more than 2% magnesium can substitute for calcium in the calcite lattice, because magnesium has a different **co-ordination** from calcium. However, many organisms, particularly at depths of less than 30m and temperatures of up to 30° C, can substitute much greater amounts of Mg^{2+} for Ca^{2+}, up to 17.7% in the **alveolinid** foraminifera. The lattice of such high magnesian calcite is distorted and even less ordered than aragonite; hence it has involved the organism in less energy to build it. The resultant mineral is less stable than aragonite at ordinary temperatures and pressures, and its inversion to low magnesian calcite is even faster, except in the deep sea.

Ordinary limestones have all recrystallised. This process has produced a hard rock with the calcite crystals interlocked. The calcite crystals in chalk are largely held together by no more than electrostatic attraction, and so chalk, free from diagenesis, is a friable, powdery rock. Chalks are mostly formed in relatively deep water, more than 100m. Such sediment of open seas is formed by a rain of coccoliths deposited as faecal pellets of larger organisms, mostly **copepods**, a group of crustacea only a few mm long.

Superimposed on this simple picture, there are two common variations in southern England. One of these, alternations of beds of chalk with marly chalk or marly clay, best seen in the Chalk Marl, is only weakly developed in north-east Dorset, and is not now clearly exposed near Shaftesbury. A second variation is both well-developed and well-exposed in the Shaftesbury district and needs some rather detailed discussion. This is the development of nodular and hardground-chalk.

At the time of accumulation, the surface of chalk-ooze was extremely watery, had a porosity of around 70-80% and was well oxidised.

Between about 0.35 and 1m beneath the surface, the interstitial water was already **anoxic** from the activities of nitrate-reducing and sulphate-reducing bacteria. The more important sulphate-reducing bacteria transformed sulphate ions to H_2S, which normally escaped into the overlying **aerobic** zones, where it was reoxidised to sulphurous and sulphuric acids:

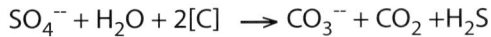

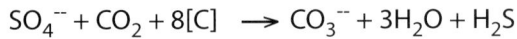

$$SO_4^{--} + H_2O + 2[C] \longrightarrow CO_3^{--} + CO_2 + H_2S$$

$$SO_4^{--} + CO_2 + 8[C] \longrightarrow CO_3^{--} + 3H_2O + H_2S$$

The new carbonate ions combined with available calcium and were precipitated as calcite, which formed a binding framework of crystals. If the process lasted long enough, a nearly continuous bed of lithified chalk formed, which, followed by sea-bed erosion, resulted in a rocky hardground or conglomerate on the sea-floor.

Why does such lithification of chalk occur only at select levels and has not affected all chalk-ooze? There are two major controls.

(1) chalk which accumulated in relatively deep water, certainly greater than 300m, but possibly even at depths between 100 and 300m where there is a low bacterial content and where the bacteria grow very slowly, and their activity is inhibited by a high hydrostatic pressure.

(2) normal chalk accumulation is too fast to provide sufficient organic food for the bacteria. All the indications are that nodular chalk and **hardgrounds** reflect a slower accumulation of ooze, a situation which normally results from a shallowing of the sea. This increases bottom currents and can increase the number of aragonite shells, which can provide further reactive $CaCO_3$, for the precipitation of a calcite mosaic-framework. If nodular chalks and hardgrounds reflect shallowing, widespread developments of them will represent **eustatic** falls in sea-level.

Another lithology found in the Chalk is flint. This is a mosaic of very small crystals, mostly only a few μm across, of quartz. Holes in the mosaic contain water vapour. The density is 2.57-2.64 compared with 2.65 for pure quartz.

Study of present day pelagic chalks show that the silica comes from organisms which secrete SiO_2, not as quartz but as hydrous and amorphous opal. Shortly after the death of the organism and the breakdown of any organic sheath of the opal, the opal crystallises as cristobalite in spherical crystal aggregates known as lepispheres, of the order of 3-10μm in diameter, composed of bladed crystal 30-50nm thick. Cristobalite is normally thought of as a high temperature mineral of SiO_2, stable above about 1475°C. However, in the same way that some calcitic organisms secrete the relatively disordered high magnesian calcite because it needs less energy, so cristobalite can crystallise at low temperatures because it needs less energy than is needed to crystallise quartz. To make it even easier, this is a completely disordered low-cristobalite, known as opal-CT.

The first stage in the process of forming flints has the effect of concentrating the Si in sea-water from only 0.02mg/kg to discrete crystals of SiO_2. Low cristobalite can invert directly to low quartz but there is no evidence that this has ever happened in the Chalk. Instead the disordered cristobalite, under certain unknown conditions, can be redissolved and transfer to nearby new centres of crystallisation as low quartz. Sometimes calcite crystals are enveloped, but more commonly the calcitic coccoliths actually speed their own replacement by quartz. The effect is a particle by particle replacement so that the flint faithfully mimics all existing micro-structures. Although details of the controls are controversial (and therefore would involve too much space to discuss here), it is clear that animal activity and organic material help the concentration and crystallisation e.g. burrows of crustacea, such as Thalassinoides and deposit-feeding worms such as Zoophycos. Their form may be preserved but the new flint acted as a centre for further quartz formation which often continued beyond the original organic burrow, the form of which may be completely lost.

The growth of the flint occurs some metres below the sediment-water interface and the hard flints are not available for organisms which like to encrust hard surfaces, e.g. many cyclostome bryozoa. Tabular flints parallel to the bedding have formed at levels where there were high concentrations of organic material. Flints not only preserve structures in the original chalk: when they are hollow the internal 'flint-meal' preserves some fossils, e.g. **planktic** foraminifera, which have been lost by later solution in the surrounding chalk.

EXCURSION DETAILS

Location 1 (ST 823099) Shillingstone Pit *(Figure 1)*

This is a rambling pit which goes through some 80m of the Chalk in a series of separate exposures, the lower ones being difficult to piece together. The higher part, from which there are magnificent views eastwards of the Chalk scarp, is still reasonably clear and is important for the development of nodular chalks and hardgrounds. The Ogbourne Hardground is obvious in the main upper face of the quarry. Some 5.5m above this is the Hitch Wood Hardground. These are the lowest and the highest of the complex of hardgrounds known as the Chalk Rock.

Figure 1 upper part of chalk-pit, Shillingstone

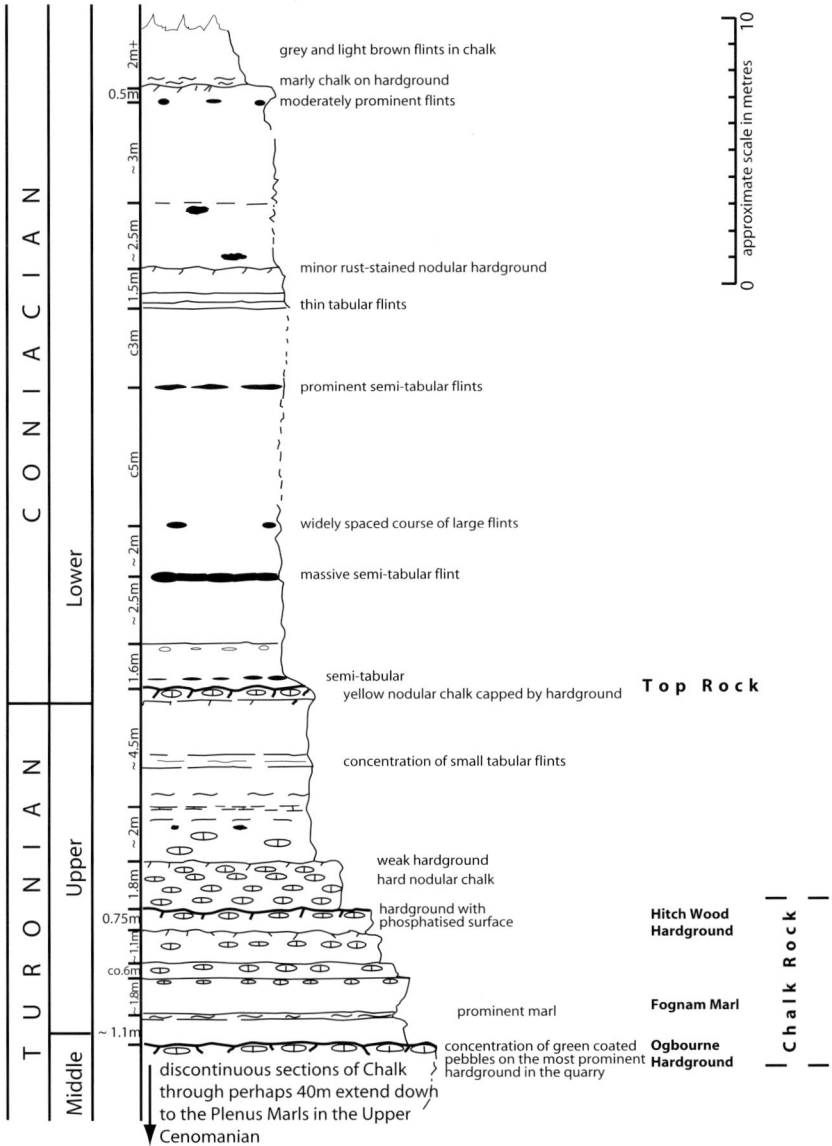

approximate scale in metres

10

0

CONIACIAN

TURONIAN

Lower

Upper

Middle

grey and light brown flints in chalk

marly chalk on hardground
moderately prominent flints

2m+
0.5m
~3m
~2.5m
1.5m
c3m
c5m
~2m
~2.5m
1.6m

minor rust-stained nodular hardground

thin tabular flints

prominent semi-tabular flints

widely spaced course of large flints

massive semi-tabular flint

semi-tabular
yellow nodular chalk capped by hardground

Top Rock

~4.5m

concentration of small tabular flints

~2m
1.8m
0.75m
~1.1m
co.6m
~1.8m
~1.1m

weak hardground
hard nodular chalk

hardground with
phosphatised surface

**Hitch Wood
Hardground**

prominent marl

Fognam Marl

concentration of green coated
pebbles on the most prominent
hardground in the quarry

**Ogbourne
Hardground**

Chalk Rock

discontinuous sections of Chalk
through perhaps 40m extend down
to the Plenus Marls in the Upper
Cenomanian

Figure 2 chalk-pit, Charnage Down

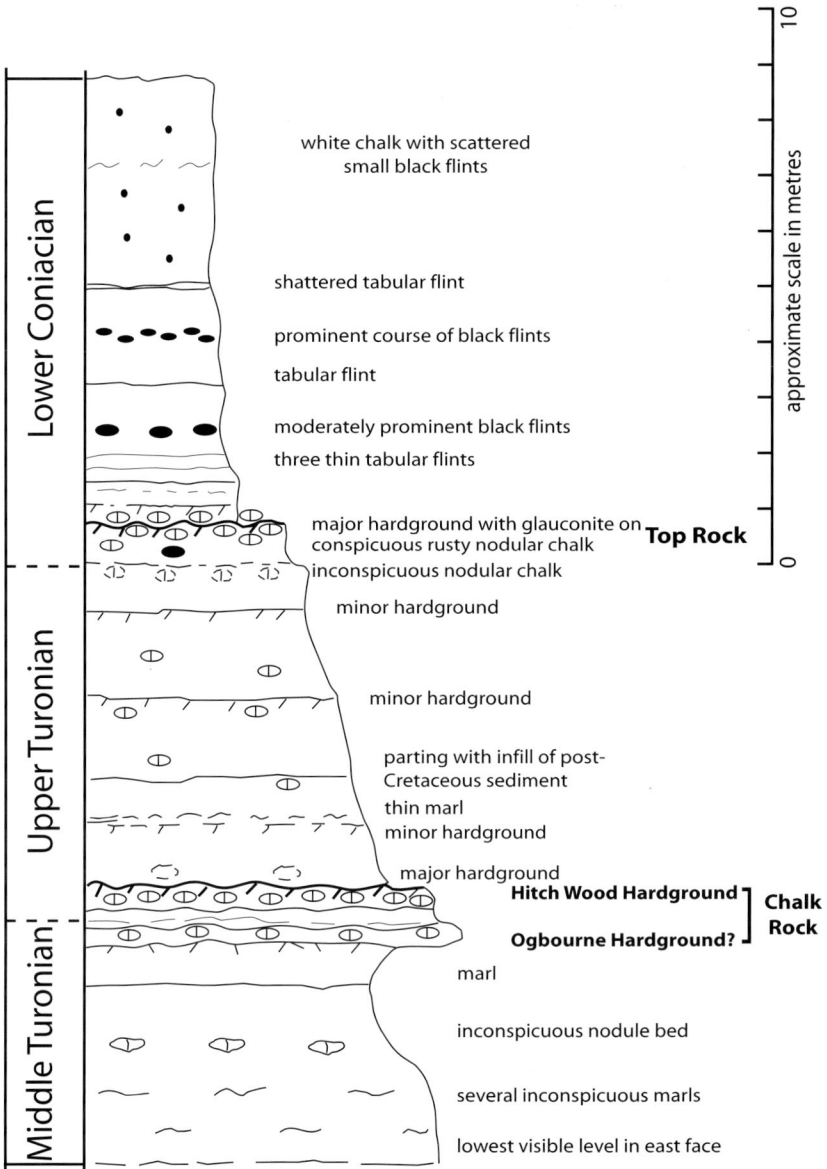

white chalk with scattered
small black flints

shattered tabular flint

prominent course of black flints

tabular flint

moderately prominent black flints

three thin tabular flints

major hardground with glauconite on **Top Rock**
conspicuous rusty nodular chalk

inconspicuous nodular chalk

minor hardground

minor hardground

parting with infill of post-
Cretaceous sediment

thin marl

minor hardground

major hardground

Hitch Wood Hardground ⎤ **Chalk**
                          ⎥ **Rock**
Ogbourne Hardground? ⎦

marl

inconspicuous nodule bed

several inconspicuous marls

lowest visible level in east face

Lower Coniacian

Upper Turonian

Middle Turonian;

approximate scale in metres

10

0

The Chalk Rock represents a close-set succession of troughs in sea-level that can be recognised, not only in north-west Europe, but which affected the Rocky Mountain region in the Western Interior of the U.S.A. The degree of condensation is amazing: the 5.5m of Chalk Rock here is equivalent to about 60m of chalk *(and that is still somewhat condensed)* in Kent and Sussex, about half the total thickness of the Turonian stage there. It has been shown that, on top of the Ogbourne Hardground alone, there is a **non-sequence** which is represented by 20-40m of chalk in basinal successions. There is also considerable erosion beneath the Ogbourne Hardground.

Fossils are not common. In any case, no zones are suggested because the zones in this part of the Cretaceous are in a state of flux at present. The stage and sub-stage boundaries are based on the known ages for the hardgrounds elsewhere. The base of the Upper Turonian is fixed by the lowest *Inoceramus perplexus* Whitfield, and the base of the Coniacian, by the base of the Zone of *Cremnoceramus deformis erectus* (Meek).

Location 2 *(ST 837329)* Charnage Down *(Figure 2)*

The most striking feature here is the strong condensation of the Chalk Rock, which is only a little over a metre thick. It seems that **penecontemporaneous** erosion removed all softer chalk down to each preceding hardground in turn, but the exposures are now rather poor. A more clearly developed triple hardground, less than a metre thick, used to be visible in a small pit in Warminster Plantation, north-east of East Knoyle *(ST 887310)*.

Fossils are more common here than at Shillingstone. Inoceramids can be found above the Top Rock. Abundant *Cremnoceramus crassus* (Petrascheck) of the Lower Coniacian has been recorded. The Top Rock contains *Concinnithyris?*, *Holaster (Sternotaxis)* and sponges. Around a metre below the Top Rock are *Micraster* gr *normanniae* Bucaille, *Sternotaxis placenta* (Agassiz) and inoceramids. Interestingly, the Hitch Wood Hardground is poorly fossiliferous, whereas further east in Buckinghamshire and Hertfordshire, it is this hardground which has yielded most of the fossils classically regarded as the Chalk Rock fauna.

In the platform towards the north-east corner of the quarry are deep cracks in the floor of the Chalk. These are 'gulls' formed by the lateral movement to the south known as 'cambering', where the whole hillside has started to move sideways and downwards.

Thanks are due to Jim Kennedy for a number of helpful suggestions.

Rudist Bivalves - Dorset

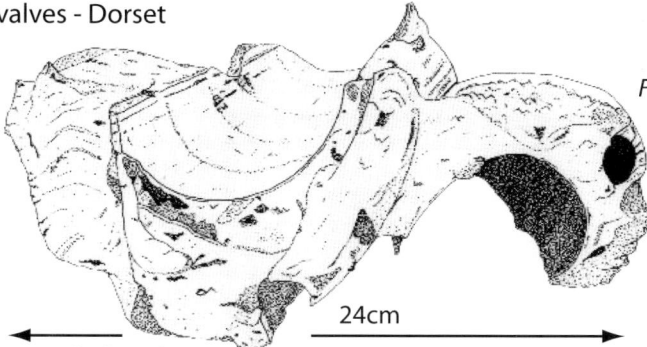

Figure 1a

24cm

©RJC

These unusual fossils come from the Chalk-Greensand boundary near Melcombe Bingham. They were found during a field walk by the DGAG. The first fragment *(Figures 1a/1b)* was found by Mr Tony Holmes, the second *(Figure 2)* by Colonel J M Woodhouse. Rudists were a reef-building bivalve which flourished around 100**Ma** in the Tethys Ocean which was once approximately in the area of what is now the Mediterranean.

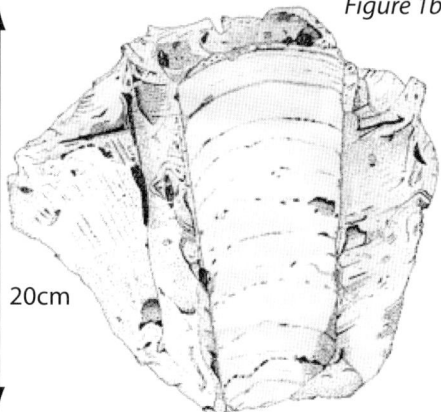

Figure 1b

20cm

'Dorset' then was located on a continental shelf at the northern edge of the Tethys Ocean. Fossil Rudists are common along what is now the North African coast. As far as we know these are the only two of this type to be found in Dorset. There are more details of the fossils on the DGAG web site: www.dorsetgeologistsassociation.com

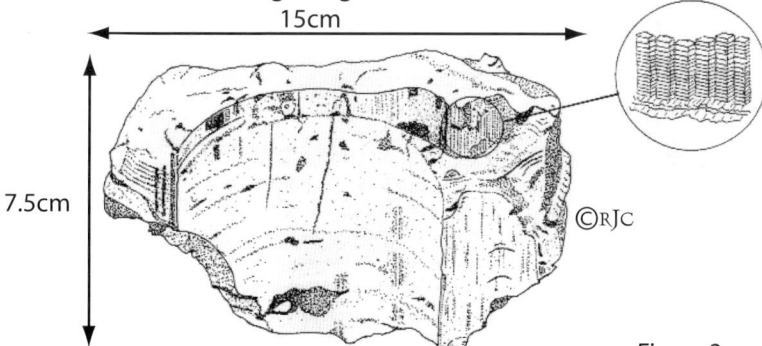

15cm

7.5cm

©RJC

Figure 2

Chapter 27 Adrian Brokenshire

**TOUT QUARRY and WEST WEARES
ISLE of PORTLAND**

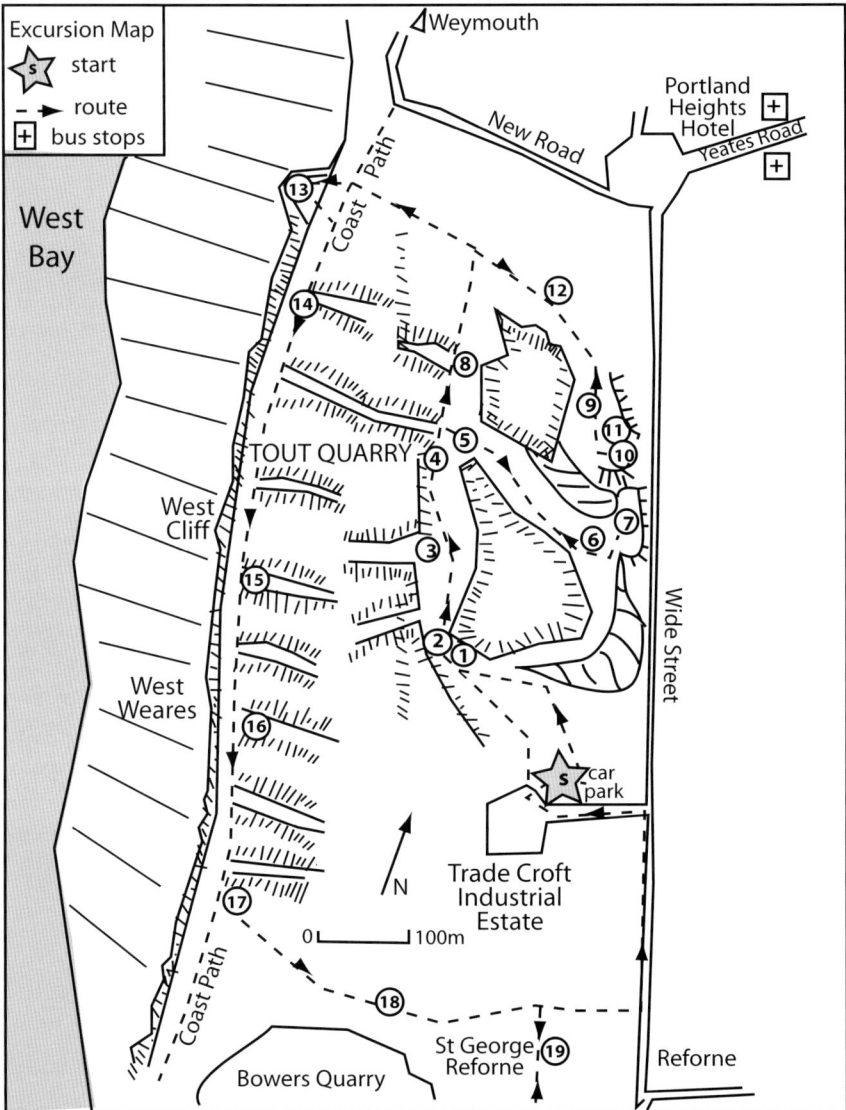

Excursion Map
- ⭐ s start
- – – ▸ route
- ⊞ bus stops

West Bay

Weymouth

New Road

Portland Heights Hotel ⊞

Yeates Road ⊞

⑬

⑭

West Cliff

TOUT QUARRY

⑧

⑫

⑨

⑪
⑩

⑤

④

③

⑥ ⑦

②①

⑮

Wide Street

West Weares

⑯

⑰

N

0 ⊢——⊣ 100m

⭐ s car park

Trade Croft Industrial Estate

⑱

Coast Path

Bowers Quarry

St George Reforne ⑲

Reforne

PURPOSE: To see and study various aspects of Portland's geology and associated industrial history by exploring a long redundant quarry. A short cliff top walk to view the West Weares and Cliff. To point out small areas of geological interest that are accessible, easy to explain and to view rather than attempt to explain all the geology of Portland.

PRACTICAL DETAILS: Tout Quarry *(SY 684725)* is an area of national, geological and ecological interest. The quarry is also a sculpture park in which the sculptures can be viewed at the same time as the geological setting. Leaflets on Tout Quarry and other Portland walks are available from Tourist Information Centres. Information panels are mounted within the quarry featuring walks, sculptures, some geology and ecological interest. Free car parking is off the road from Trade Croft Industrial Estate and the access is well marked. The nearest toilets are at the rear of the Portland Heights Hotel. Buses on and off the Island also stop near the hotel. Please remember that, although Tout is no longer a working quarry, rock piles and scree slopes can be unstable. The map shows the route and locations visited on this excursion. With time allowed for stops the visit should take about 2.5 hours.

GEOLOGICAL SETTING: The rocks exposed in the quarry and in the cliffs are of late Jurassic age, Portlandian Stage. The oldest rocks, exposed at the base of the cliffs, are the Portland Sands. The bulk of the exposure is in the Portland Limestone Series with a thinner capping of the lower part of the Purbeck Beds.

The brown/buff, grey/blue massive Portland Sands composed of dolomite grains rather than quartz, and the varying beds of the Portland Limestone Series on the Island, are fully marine. The fossils within them, such as ammonites, are testament to this. The thinner capping of the Lower Purbeck Beds is non-marine, laid down in lagoonal conditions, often hyper-saline. Flooding of the low lying margins is indicated by the Dirt Bed and its famous fossil trees. Shallowing conditions produced the Marl and Slatt Beds, thin bedded and containing small freshwater molluscs and minute crustaceans *(ostracods)*.

The capping of the Lower Purbeck Beds is at its greatest on the north of the Island and thins considerably to the south. When Tout was a working quarry a considerable amount of overburden had to be removed to extract the best stone, the Freestone and the Whit Bed. With its lack of distinct bedding the Freestone could be cut in any direction while the Whit Bed *(a corruption of 'white')* was prized for its pure white colour.

Modern quarries on the Island produce a much larger hole in the ground than at Tout due to the size of machinery used and quantity of stone removed. However there is less waste and overburden removed as much more of the stone is used. The Freestone and the Whit Bed are still the prized stone but others, such as the Top Cap, Skull Cap and Chert Beds *(similar to flint)* are crushed for road metal and, in the past, were used for concrete blocks. Often these beds, including some of the Roach, are used in coastal defence schemes. The Roach is sometimes also used as an ornamental stone.

EXCURSION DETAILS

Location 1 *(SY 685723)* A small grassed area beside the access path gives a superb overview of the quarry, its narrow gullies, large blocks of stacked waste stone used as retaining walls, and the removed overburden. A vast amount of time and effort was used to quarry in this manner and the whole process was very labour-intensive. Unlike modern quarries on the Island there is little to see above the natural soil profile against the skyline. All 'worked out' space within the quarry was utilised and the environment left by these activities is a superb haven for wildlife with its scree slopes, grassy glades and sheltered gullies.

Location 2 A large block on the left of the path is of Lower Purbeck Cap rock with **tufa** *(flow stone)*, coloured brown by iron salts, on its surface. The deposit of calcite is formed by water running down the rock face when it is *in situ*, the same process by which stalactites are formed in caves. Water, with dissolved ions from the natural stone, runs down through any fissure or jointing in the rocks. The flow stone is a good indicator of which 'way-up' a now-loose block was originally in the rock face. There is a thickening on the down side where water drips off and flows over the uneven surface. This block is lying on its rear face and the water flow, at the time of deposition, appears on the block as a deposit now running south to north.

Location 3 Several blocks in this area are of the Lower Purbeck Cap, with deep single holes surrounding a well defined, porous-like structure. These are not drill holes but cavities left by tree branches which were dissolved away, leaving the cavity. The surrounding structure is of algal origin. The algae grew around the branch in a lagoon, trapping sediment within its structure as it grew. The soft algae have disappeared but the sediment, trapped within, is still visible.

Location 4 Several blocks are of interest here. Some have 'flow stone' on their surfaces *(try to work out the original 'way-up' of the rock face).* Another has a tree branch hole with surrounding algal mat but this one is worth a closer examination. The surfaces of the sediments are **mamillated** and covered with minute off-white calcite crystals. Yet another block has a series of drill holes, this time a product of modern extraction of the stone using pneumatic drills and explosive. Envisage a gang of men, on a bench of stone, drilling the holes in unison with hand tools then prising the blocks from the face with metal wedges; back breaking work.

Location 5 Lano's Arch *(Figure 1)*

Note the date above the key stone. This is a superb structure with not a bit of mortar in sight. The fact that it has stood so long, virtually intact, is a credit to the building skills of the men who made it. It was built to allow two way traffic of stone to the cliff top and overhead to the merchants' railway to the north. Go just through the arch and there is a typical 'workman's hut' built into the retaining wall. If you wanted somewhere to make a brew, why import materials when you could create a shelter whilst stacking the blocks which retain the overburden?

Location 6 The stacked blocks here are mainly of Portland Limestone, the Chert Beds and the Roach. Lenses and bands of silica-rich chert stand out in blues and grey against the lighter limestones. The Roach can be examined for its fossil content, moulds and casts of marine molluscs; the bivalves *Laevitrigonia gibbosa* and *Trigonia incurva*, locally called 'osses 'ead' *(Figure 2a)* supposed to look like horses' heads and the gastropod *Aptyxiella portlandica,* the 'Portland Screw' *(Figure 2b).*

Figure 2a

Trigonia
©RJC *incurva* x 0.25%

Figure 2b

Aptyxiella
portlandica x 0.50%

Location 7 This is an original rock face in the Lower Purbeck Beds with the Portland Beds buried by waste material. The bench you are standing on is also made-up ground, from stacked waste stone and overburden. Note the very small working area to extract the stone, compared to a modern quarry. Use *Figure 3* to work out the rock sequence: Caps, Dirt Beds, Marls and Slatt *(corruption of slate)* are very distinct.

Figure 3
A typical
Portland Quarry

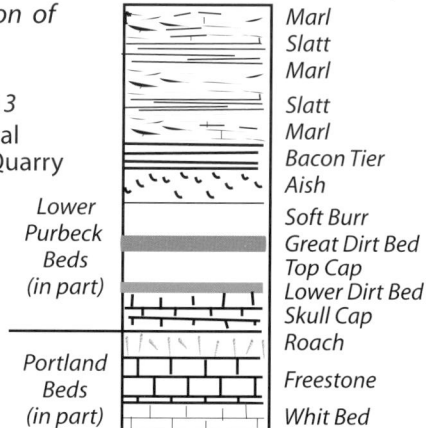

Lower
Purbeck
Beds
(in part)

Portland
Beds
(in part)

Marl
Slatt
Marl
Slatt
Marl
Bacon Tier
Aish
Soft Burr
Great Dirt Bed
Top Cap
Lower Dirt Bed
Skull Cap
Roach
Freestone
Whit Bed

Location 8 This is the workshop area for the Portland Sculpture Trust and an opportunity to examine small pieces of the Freestone, and the Whit Bed, which are scattered around the entrance. Several large slabs of Lower Purbeck Limestone, with ripple marks, lie to the side of the entrance, evidence of shallow marine, lagoonal conditions with wave action. You might be lucky enough to find a sculpture course working on site and, with permission, be able to view some of the fine stone work carried out here.

Location 9 Another natural rock face in the Lower Purbeck Beds, note the 'flow stone' down the natural joint. Early quarrymen often exploited these joints when extracting stone. On the accessible faces try to find one of the dirt beds, a dirty grey/brown friable material with rolled, grey limestone pebbles, bedded horizontally. Partway up the face is an area of fissure fill, thin bedded Slatt cemented by 'flow stone', very prominent against the more massive limestone. The fill material remained cemented to the face after the adjoining rock had been quarried away. Some fissure-fill sites, on the north of the Island, were the source of many late Pleistocene mammal remains at the turn of the 19th century.

Location 10 This is a natural Lower Purbeck rock face with the holes of dissolved out tree branches surrounded by their algal deposits. *Figure 3* is useful here for working out the stratigraphy.

Location 11 Low on the corner of the huge natural block, between locations 9 and 10, is a section of Portland Limestone full of oyster fragments. Note the differential weathering, with the harder oysters standing proud against the softer limestone.

Location 12 This was part of the Merchants' railway used to take stone to the cliff edge, and onto other lines, to remove it from the Island. Note the very narrow gauge, as the carts were horse-drawn. There were no rail sleepers but separate blocks on each side of the track, holding the rails in place, left the centre clear to prevent the horses slipping or tripping. Some blocks still have the original iron peg, which held the rail, sealed in by lead. The grooves in the blocks are not from wear but levelling off of the blocks to get an even track.

Location 13 This promontory, of made up ground from quarry waste, was used to dump waste stone over the cliff. It gives fine views along the West Cliff and into the West Weares coastal slope. The chert bands in the Portland Limestone form a very prominent feature of the cliff face. Taking care of the edge look down into the Weares and see if you can differentiate between naturally fallen stone from the cliff face and the dumped material. The natural falls are all of uneven blocks in mixed sizes, with small scree and debris. The dumped stone is more evenly sized, and roughly square, due to the methods of extraction. Look down closer to the water's edge where a large area of stone appears to be of a smaller and more uniform size. This is where stone used to be selected and squared on site before being moved out by sea.

Location 14 Several large blocks are leaning out from the cliff edge in a rather precarious position. They look as if they will collapse over the cliff edge at any moment. They have been like this for many years but will eventually end up in the rock debris that forms the coastal slope. As you walk the coast path you will notice more fissures in the path surface. These are opening up as the leaning blocks slowly move seaward, allowing natural north-south jointing to widen as pressure is released from them.

Location 15 Here a large slab of Portland Limestone set in the cliff edge, with only a single rail line to the cliff edge showing, was part of the system to dump waste material over the cliff. Note the gullies leading to the cliffs, used for the same purpose. You can also see the retaining walls which make use of the Slatt as well as block stone.

Location 16 These are the remains of a set of bridges built to allow stone movement along the cliff top track while still being able to dump waste stone and overburden over the cliff.

Location 17 This point, once again, gives good views along the cliff and the Portland Sands can be seen more clearly.

Location 18 The path passes close to the huge workings of Bowyer's Quarry. You might be able to see some of the massive machinery used to extract stone from a modern quarry. Large amounts of reserve stone are stacked against the skyline.

Figure 4a
St George's
Church

Location 19 On the return route to the car park it is worth a slight detour, into the grounds of the redundant St George's Church, to view some of the gravestones and the church itself *(Figures 4a and 4b)*. They are both monuments to the superb craftsmanship of past stonemasons working with their local Portland Stone.

Figure 4b
Gravestone 1898
Portland Stone

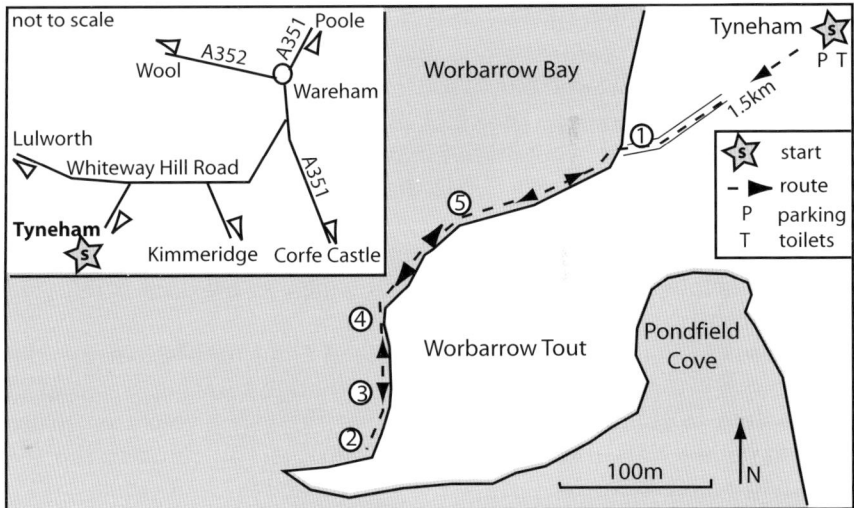

PURPOSE: To examine the upper Jurassic-lower Cretaceous Purbeck Limestone Group exposed at Worbarrow Tout.

PRACTICAL DETAILS: Caution: Access to the site is only possible when the Lulworth Range Walks are open. This excursion involves scrambling over large, and sometimes unstable, boulders and cobbles. Tides and/or high winds can severely limit the accessibility of this section. It is best viewed on a falling tide on a calm day! Tide timetables should be consulted. Algal growths over the rocks, especially during the winter months, can make them very slippery. Falling rocks are a hazard and hard hats are essential. Stout footwear is recommended. Please do not hammer in case you damage something of importance. To check when the Ranges are open telephone 01929 404819 *(recorded message)*. Coaches are not allowed under any circumstances. Any unexploded shells should reported at the earliest opportunity to a Range Warden.

Access: Worbarrow Tout is situated at the west end of Gad Cliff on the east side of Worbarrow Bay. Turn south off the Whiteways Hill road which runs across the Lulworth Gunnery School Ranges *(SY 895815)*. Follow this narrow road which runs diagonally down the Chalk escarpment before flattening out to run along the Tyneham Valley *(Wealden Group)*. Park in the large car-park at SY 882802 *(contribution of £1.00 requested)*. Just below the car park and over the bridge on the left are the only available toilets. Follow the footpath signs to Worbarrow Bay *(about 1.5km)* with the the wooded Tyneham Valley on your right.

Nightingales *(in season)* and occasionally buzzards, may be heard and/or seen. Bring your own refreshments!

GEOLOGICAL SETTING: Worbarrow Tout lies 17km west of Durlston Bay which provides the reference section for the Purbeck Limestone Group, henceforth referred to as the PLG, and south of the axis of the Purbeck **Monocline** delineated by the Chalk ridgeway. The strata at Worbarrow lie close to the axis of the Purbeck Monocline which imparts a steep **dip**. This has the advantage of providing a very compact strike section through the late Jurassic and early Cretaceous strata. The Purbeck Limestone Group (PLG) is 77.5m thick and has been logged and a section published in the Proceedings of the Dorset Natural History and Archaeology Society.

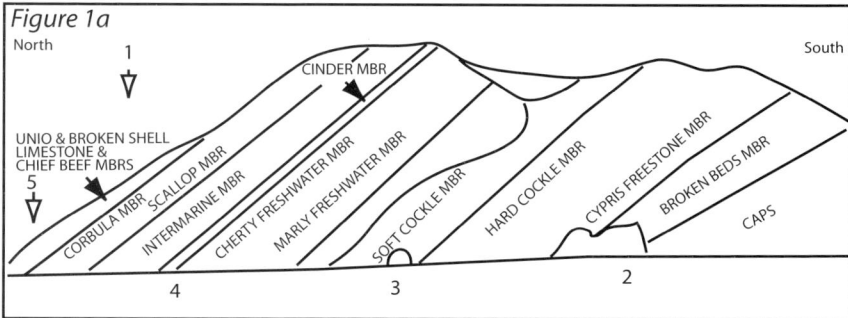

Figure 1a

North · 1 ▽ · CINDER MBR · South

UNIO & BROKEN SHELL LIMESTONE & CHIEF BEEF MBRS · 5 ▽ · CORBULA MBR · SCALLOP MBR · INTERMARINE MBR · CHERTY FRESHWATER MBR · MARLY FRESHWATER MBR · SOFT COCKLE MBR · HARD COCKLE MBR · CYPRIS FREESTONE MBR · BROKEN BEDS MBR · CAPS

4 · 3 · 2

Figure 1b

Figures 1a/b are a sketch section and photograph of Worbarrow Tout viewed from the west. The numbers relate to those on the excursion map of the Tout.

Note that it is easier to see the different beds from this distance. It can be difficult to work out exactly which bed you are looking at when close up.

EXCURSION DETAILS

Location 1 *(SY 871797)* Before descending to Worbarrow Bay, stand above the small grassy viewing platform above Worbarrow Bay. To the east is Pondfield Cove with the cliff rising to the western end of Gad Cliff. The Portland Stone Group *(marine limestones)* which forms the protective toe of the Tout rises up Gad Cliff and, with the underlying Portland Sand Group, forms the precipitous buttress capped by a thin veneer of Purbeck strata. The Portland strata are underlain by the dark blue-black, black and grey clays and shales of the marine Kimmeridge

Clay Group. Turn and look to the west and the thick sequence of clays, sands and grits of the fluviatile Wealden Group, which overlies the PLG, forms the multicoloured cliff of the bulk of the bay. A thin Lower Greensand Group *(transgressive marine sequence)* and the fully marine Gault overlie the Wealden. The Gault is overlain by the more resistant Upper Greensand and Chalk, both deposited in marine conditions. The latter forms the high cliff upon which is perched Flower's Barrow, an Iron Age hill fort. The bay is cut in the considerably softer clays of the Wealden Group, the only resistance being offered by one of the coarse iron-cemented grits. These were deposited in channels by swiftly flowing water presumed to be draining eroding uplands to the west or northwest. Descend into Worbarrow Bay and then make your way along the foot of the steeply dipping slab *(Unio Member)* of Upper Purbeck strata. Carry on around the foot of the Tout, now crossing tilted ledges of limestone. Ideally the section is rapidly traversed to reach the lowest strata before retracing one's steps. Tides often dictate otherwise so this itinerary may need to be read in reverse order!

Location 2 *(SY 869795)* The Portland Stone Group at the tip of the Tout is composed of the Shrimp Bed, a massive white **micritic** limestone which contains marine bivalves. The basal part of the PLG are the Caps, Broken and Dirt Beds Members. The steeply dipping and undulating surface is composed of the Caps. The Caps are algal limestones composed of fine calcareous muds produced and trapped by **stromatolites**. These were deposited in hypersaline conditions along a Purbeck shoreline. Depressions on the surface may be dinosaur footprints; previously considered unlikely, discoveries within the last 10 years have confirmed their presence in the Slatt and Hard Cockle Beds on the Isle of Portland; an horizon which is certainly worth watching. This bed is overlain by finely laminated brown-black shales with white laminae, deposits which were laid down in very shallow water. The laminae represent a series of events which may be seasonal. The remains of conchostraceans *(small bivalved arthropods)* are occasionally found flattened on the laminae. Their presence supports the hypothesis that they were able to develop and breed very rapidly when there was freshwater; perhaps seasonal influxes produced during a rainy season were responsible for both the laminae and the conchostraceans' rapid **ontogenesis**. The Broken Beds are superbly exposed and named after the shattered and jumbled strata which appear in two principal layers. Theories proposed to explain this phenomenon include the rotting of buried vegetation *(the horizons are temptingly close to those where the remains of the fossil forest occurs at Lulworth Cove)*, the removal of evaporite minerals and the folding of the strata providing an opportunity for the thinner beds of limestone to become **brecciated**. A combination of the latter two are considered the most likely causes. Abundant evidence for the previous presence of evaporite minerals has been demonstrated, including gypsum in the Caps, Broken Beds and Dirt Beds Member. A layer of calcitised evaporites separates the two brecciated units. The Great Dirt Bed *(of Portland and Lulworth Cove)* is represented by a darker band at the base of the lower and thinner of the brecciated limestone layers. Leaving this small cove at the foot of the Tout, walk around the more massive limestones of the Cypris Freestones Member which pass upwards into increasingly flaggy limestones, alternating with laminated sandy shales, of the Hard Cockle Member. Watch for **ripple marks**, halite pseudomorphs *(fossilised cubic salt crystals with hopper-shaped faces)* which are sometimes of considerable size and even scattered vertebrate remains. The halite pseudomorphs show a range of preservational modes. They may be flattened or three-dimensional and have calcite or other sediment-filled casts.   One horizon has yielded tiny pseudomorphs in **intraclasts** of a calcite mud.

Location 3 The Soft Cockle Member is easily recognised as the harder ledges are suddenly replaced by a series of softer micrites and clays. These are interspersed with sandy layers of altered evaporites. In the lower part of this member is a deposit of massive gypsum. Wave-washed blocks of this are normally present on the foreshore or just above. This represents a **sabkha** deposit where gypsum and nodular anhydrite forms just below the surface in an arid coastal environment, as in parts of the modern Persian Gulf. Tightly folded *(ptygmatic)* bands of gypsum demonstrate that the original anhydrite was hughly expanded during rehydration to form the gypsum. *Figure 2* is a fallen and wave washed block of gypsum from the Soft Cockle Member showing ptygmatic folding of the gypsum. Veins of fibrous Satin Spar run through these blocks and represent a much later phase

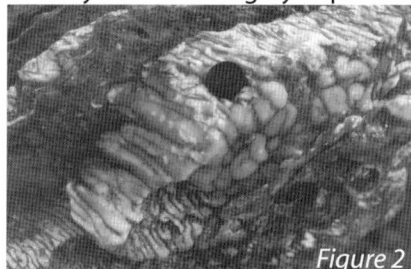
Figure 2

of gypsum formation which occurred during the folding of these strata. The axis of the crystals would have been normal to the direction of the pressure during formation. This member becomes increasingly dominated by **micrites**, often with halite moulds and psuedomorphs and some thin algal limestones. A prominent intraclast limestone, probably the result of a flood event, is present near the top.

The Marly Freshwater Member comprises shales/clays with occasional micrites. During the 1980s a narrow fissure of ostracod-rich sparry limestone was found cutting down through both the clays above and below a **micrite**. With careful observation it could still be seen in late 2001. This was interpreted as a tectonic fissure created during local earth movements. This unit at Durlston Bay has the famous Beckles Mammal Bed present; no evidence of this horizon has been found here.

In 1985, I took the base of a distinctive cherty ostracod-microsparite overlying a thin brown shale as the base of the Cherty Freshwater Member. Above this is a sequence of argillaceous micrites. Chert is well developed in the upper 3m where the micrites become especially massive and interbedded with shales and clays. The thickest of the massive cherty limestones, fallen blocks of which can be examined on the foreshore, contains silicified gastropods and the remains of the calcareous algae *Chara*; the latter are abundant on the base of the freshwater micrite below the Cinder Member which is also covered with the branching burrows of an arthropod, cf. *Thalassinoides*. This fauna and flora are equated with freshwater environments. However careful scrutiny of fallen and *in-situ* blocks of the cherty micrite reveals the presence of halite pseudomorphs. Strong seasonality with winter rains and summer evaporation is suggested as a mechanism for this paradoxical juxtaposition. The casts of the footprints of dinosaurs *(the tracks were made in the muds which now underlie the limestones)* are sometimes to be seen on fallen blocks or on the overhanging limestones *(binoculars are useful!)*.

Tridactyl footprints *(Figure 3)* left by bipedal dinosaurs are not unusual, the evidence for quadrupedal dinosaurs much less common. The uppermost limestone is present with a similar trace fossil fauna in Durlston Bay.

Figure 3
cast of a truncated tridactyl dinosaur
footprint on the base of one of the
Cherty Freshwater Member's limestones

The Jurassic-Cretaceous boundary has long been the subject of debate. The 'Purbeck Beds' were once regarded as belonging entirely to the Jurassic. It has been suggested that the base of the Cinder Bed should be regarded as the boundary between the Jurassic and the Cretaceous though, in recent years, mounting evidence placed the boundary close to the base of the Purbeck Limestone Group. Others use a North Sea borehole sequence to correlate between marine ammonite faunas and micropalaeontological data which is represented in both marine and terrestrial sequences. They place the boundary within the Cherty Freshwater Member. Whatever the boundary's position, the Cinder Member remains an easily recognisable rough oyster-rich biomicrite which forms two quite distinct parts. A lower more calcareous Hard Cinder is overlain by a Soft Cinder which is more marly.

Location 4 Numerous blocks of the Cinder Member litter the toe of the Tout and a close examination of them is often rewarding. In addition to the profusion of disarticulated *Praeexogyra distorta*, barnacle plates are occasionally found along with the spines of the echinoid *Hemicidaris purbeckensis*. Fish remains are also present. An horizon of imbricated *(vertical or nearly vertically stacked)* oysters has been recorded pointing to quite powerful water flow across the oyster-rich sediment. The Cinder Member, representing for whatever reasons a more normally marine environment, really does mark a significant change in lithology here at Worbarrow Tout. Above it, the limestones are predominantly bivalve **biosparrudites**, a less common lithology in the strata seen so far where latterly micritic limestones have dominated. The Intermarine Member, so called because it lies between the Cinder and Scallop Members with their marine or quasi-marine faunas, is rich in bivalve biosparrudites and is the unit which is predominantly quarried further east around Langton Matravers and towards Swanage. The dominant bivalve is *Neomiodon* while other invertebrates include gastropods. Dinosaur tracks are relatively common and six producing horizons have been identified though spotting them may be more to do with the luck of having the sunlight raking the bedding planes. They occur as both internal and external moulds. Primarily they are **tridactyl** and tentatively associated with iguanodontids and theropods. Throughout the strata above the Cinder Member, bedding planes are occasionally scattered with small pebbles and/or algal intraclasts; derived ostracods from lower in the Purbeck beds have also been recovered. These same horizons are often quite rich in the disarticulated remains of fish and reptiles including turtle bones and crocodile teeth. Amongst the fish remains, the button-like teeth of *Lepidotus* and pycnodontids are the most common but the higher crowned hybodontid shark teeth are also met with.

Sandy limestones, often heavily **bioturbated**, are a hall-mark of the relatively thin Scallop Member. The lower of the bioturbated sandstones is especially fossiliferous. The pecten *Chlamys* is common; a Lucinid bivalve and an example of the bryozoan *Pyriporopsis portlandensis* have also been collected from blocks identified as coming from this horizon. The upper bed has especially prominent oblique burrows on its surface. The overlying Corbula Member is devoid of the sand which was so abundant in the Scallop Member. The shales and clays between the limestones are often crowded with crushed shells. Small crystals of the variety of gypsum called selenite are frequent and suggest the mobilisation of corrosive acids derived from the decay of iron pyrites. Reacting with the carbonate in the shells, calcium sulphate has been produced and formed the gypsum. The limestones show an increasingly high proportion of micritic sediment. Algal growths are observed and pseudomorphs-after-gypsum have been described. These fine-grained sediments are occasionally plant-rich and insect remains have been recorded. Beautifully preserved bivalves and gastropods are present on the surfaces of many of the limestones. Dinosaur tracks have been recorded from one horizon within this member. An extensive slab with scattered pebbles and generally rolled vertebrate remains marks the top of this member. Rare phosphatised remains of Kimmeridgian fossils have been found amongst the pebbles. They may point to the contemporaneous erosion of Kimmeridgian strata not too far from here but drifting tree roots and a more distant source is not impossible. However they may have arrived, this is unequivocal evidence that somewhere, the not-long deposited Kimmeridge Clay was already exposed and being eroded. Food for thought!

The overlying Chief Beef Member is characterised by the presence of black shales and bivalve biosparrudites which are predominantly composed of the bivalve *Neomiodon*. Rare dinosaur footprints have been observed preserved as casts on the underside of the limestones. The recognition of the base of the Broken Shell Limestone Member (BSLM) is not easy. The continuation of the succession of biosparrudites and shales lacks any clear marker horizon; in Durlston Bay the BSLM is a very substantial limestone and readily recognisable.

Location 5 *(SY 870797)* At this point you start to follow the steeply dipping limestones that run back towards Worbarrow Bay. These limestones tend to have irregular surfaces. A bioclastic limestone, resting on a pale grey-green micritic limestone with poorly preserved bivalves and gastropods, contains concentrations of iron pyrites which are breaking down leaving iron stained patches and associated rotten limestone. The surface of this bed has frequent examples of the freshwater bivalve *Unio* scattered over its surface along with pebble to cobble-sized clasts of limestone of a different lithology. Patches of pale grey-green micrite similar to that underlying the bed are developed on the surface and may be remnants of algal stromatolites. These limestones belong to the Unio Member.

Above them are the Upper Cypris Clays and Shales Member. These strata are best observed on the foreshore where they form seaweed-covered reefs. Biomicrites *(cf. Purbeck Marble)* composed of the small freshwater snail *Viviparus* are also present. Characteristic sections through the larger bivalved Unios can be seen and scattered vertebrate remains are not uncommon. The transition from the predominantly limestone/shale intercalations of the Purbeck strata to the clastics of the overlying Wealden, which are devoid of carbonates, is not exposed in the foreshore or cliff.

Aerial view of Worbarrow Tout
from Dorset. a Photographic Atlas
© Dorset County Council 2000

Subscribers

The Book Committee would like to thank all the subscribers whose financial backing gave much moral support to this project

ANTHONY GANNON

DAVID A. LLOYD BSc. FGS

PETER & EDNA FOOKES

MICHAEL Le BAS

ALF TINGEY

STEVE GAYLER

DOREEN SMITH

SHEILA ALDERMAN

MARGARET DYOS

HEATHER J RAGGETT

GEORGE RAGGETT

PAUL CLASBY

RON HAMMOCK

ADRIAN SMITH

YVONNE FARRELL

MICHAEL P KING

JILLIAN BROWN

G D SWANN

DR AND MRS J A LARKIN

MAUREEN KEATS

PETE GREEN

ADRIAN BROKENSHIRE

PETER & JOYCE AUSTEN

MICHAEL HOUSE

TONY & LARISSA SHEEHAN

TONY HANNAH

PETER J BATH

M. BRAY

JOY VOOGHT

PAUL C ENSOM

TERRI PIERCE-BUTLER

DORSET Natural History & Archaeological Society

ROBERT CHRISTIAN

HUGH MANNALL

MALCOLM HOWELL

PIP O'NEILL

ALASTAIR McDONALD

MIKE & ROSEMARY BROADEY

MICK RIMMINGTON

GINNY & REG APPLEBY

DUNCAN COLVILLE

MARY & GEORGE SUDBURY

DR M P FRYATT

DR MIKE COSGROVE

PAT STRAW

MRS E STEPHENS

C R WISEMAN

ROY MUSGROVE

JOHN CHAFFEY

RUTH CHAFFEY

LINDA MORLEY

JOHN AND JILL PATRICK

NIGEL GRAHAM

BRIAN STEBBINGS

BRIAN ROWED

GEOFFREY S DEARN

OLIVE & KEITH HOPPER

EILEEN WHEELER

BARBARA DARRALL

IAIN & HELEN DAVEY-SMITH

HARRY & HELEN GRENVILLE

DONALD AND SUE SMITH

PETER MARTIN

SYLVIA AND LAWRIE BUBB

ALAN HOLIDAY

JEANNE STARK

STEVE ETCHES

TONY HOLMES

JAN FREEBORN

DEREK CLIFT

JOHN DAVIS

MALCOLM & FRANCES BILLINGE

CHRIS WILSON

MICHAEL GROVER

BOB GIBSON

ROB DEAN

PAULINE PEIRCE

JANET& EDWARD GRIFFITHS

CHRIS PHILLIPS

MIKE BOWLER

CHARLES JACKSON

GWENDA BREWER

JOHN BOLTON

ANNE WOOD

As well as the book committee and those acknowledged at the end of chapters, there are a number of people who have been directly involved in the preparation of this book

Iain Davey-Smith provided vital back-up, invaluable computer expertise and programming material

Jake Hancock reviewed Michael House's contributions and made valuable comments on the whole book. Martin Vine and Tony Sheehan read and commented on various chapters

Doreen Smith drew computer representations of the sketch on page 164 and of all maps, tables, cross sections and logs except for pages 178-9

Sheila Alderman, John and Jill Patrick, Roy Musgrove, Nigel Graham, Margaret Dyos, Maureen Keats, Cathy Race, Mike King, Alf Tingey, Mike Steele, Bob Christian, Ray Chapman, Ron Hammock, Tony Sheehan, Doreen Smith, Richard Edmonds and George Raggett walked the Dorset countryside, sometimes in very inclement weather, to check various chapters. Comments by many people, on the chapters and the book in general, when the book has been set out at meetings or when the excursions have been used for field trips, have been invaluable

Visitor/Heritage Centres and Museums with geology and other relevant displays which could be incorporated with these excursions include: Budleigh Salterton Museum; Sidmouth Museum; Lyme Regis: Philpot Museum and Dinosaurland; Charmouth Heritage Coast Centre; Harbour Life West Bay; Bridport Museum; Portland Museum; Chesil Beach Centre; Weymouth Museum and Nothe Fort; Sherborne Museum; Dorchester Museum and Dinosaur Museum; Blandford Museum; Shaftesbury Abbey; Gillingham Museum; Lulworth Heritage Centre; Wareham Museum; Kimmeridge Bay Visitor Centre; Square and Compass, Worth Matravers; Coach House Langton Matravers; Corfe Castle Museum and National Trust Visitor Centre; Tithe Barn Swanage; Studland National Trust (Knoll Beach); Red House Museum, Christchurch; Gillingham Museum (geology display set up by the DGAG in 1996)

Health and Safety Guidelines

Safety on all these walks is mostly a matter of common sense. However, much of the Dorset coast is somewhat unstable and emergency situations can arise quite unexpectedly. Standard precautions follow for those who might be unaware of the particular difficulties

1. On all walks, stout ankle supporting footwear is recommended. Inland, footpaths are rough and occasionally boggy, not only after wet weather. On the coast the same applies of course with the added specialities of boulder beaches, slippery seaweed and algae and wet sand. Wellingtons might be advisable in some cases

2. Gravel beaches can also have their hazards. Sometimes a rock bed is covered in a layer of rounded gravel. Step on such and it becomes a bed of 'marbles'. Sprained ankles and damaged ligaments can be the result.

3. Some of the walks are in isolated places though none are far from 'civilisation'. It would be advisable to let someone know where you are going especially if you are unfamiliar with the territory. Take the relevant OS map with you. A grid reference will make it easier for help to find you should you need it. Grid references are read west to east, then south to north. Mobile phones can be useful but are not always operative in undulating countryside or under cliffs

4. On the shoreline it is advisable to start all walks on a falling tide. Even if there seems plenty of time to complete an expedition, finding something of particular interest can considerably lengthen your journey time. Many of the cliffs are unscalable should the tide find you still at the foot of them

5. Some of the cliffs are very unstable. They are hazardous whether you are at the foot or walking along the top of them. Keep clear of the edges. Not only might you fall, you may dislodge material onto others at the foot. Keep clear of the foot for the same reason and also because rock falls are common without human triggering. Landslides are also common in places. Rock and mud can move very rapidly indeed. Always keep one eye on the cliff and listen for falling material. Cliff falls are most common after weeks of prolonged rain especially if the rain follows a drought. People have been killed on the Dorset coast under these conditions and many have found themselves in difficulty

6. Grass slopes can be slippery. If you begin to slide at the top of a slope above a cliff, there is often little to stop you going over the edge and, sometimes, nothing at all to break your fall once over the edge. Many Dorset cliffs have stony beaches at the base which are likely to cause injury even if the drop is only a few feet

7. Mud can be a dangerous trap as once dried it looks like solid material. Often it is only a crust which will break easily especially as feet concentrate weight on a small area. Abandoned wellingtons and boots are a common sight in some areas. Walkers have had to be hauled out of deep mud by the rescue services before now

8. Preferably collect fossils and rock samples from loose material. *In situ* collecting can result in damaged specimens and the spoiling of a visual aid for future visitors

9. Quarries and pits can have many of the same hazards as cliffs. Take care always. Even small pieces of rock can cause considerable damage when falling from a height. Hard hats are advisable in rock quarries, working quarries will require them and safety jackets also. Always obey any instructions from the quarry staff. Any other action may make such places off bounds to all

10. Undergrowth can make areas deceptive. Climb through, if you must, with great care. It is easy to become disorientated in thick scrub. Where the scrub is growing on unstable ground deep fissures are common. Sprained ankles are a frequent result. Much of the material is gorse and blackthorn both of which are well covered in sharp thorns. Undergrowth can also conceal adders, the UK's only poisonous snake. Adders are likely to avoid well-used pathways but do like to sun themselves on grassy banks. They are harmless if left undisturbed and are likely to rapidly disappear if they hear you approach

11. Keep to designated footpaths or ask permission to look further afield. Surrounding land usually belongs to somebody who may take offence at unauthorised wandering

12. Always keep dogs under control. Farm animals and wildlife are easily disturbed. Dogs have needed rescuing or been killed chasing rabbits off cliffs

13. Leave gates as you find them

14. Do not climb through fences, their particular purpose is easily destroyed by stretching the strands of wire

15. Take particular note of hazards mentioned in individual chapters. The expeditions are written by members who are familiar with the territory. Their advice is worth taking

16. If you do get into trouble, please do not be too embarrassed to call the rescue services. They will do all they can to extricate you. Call 999 and, with an reasonably accurate location (see number 3), they will be on their way within minutes

Bibliography

Chapter 1 Bowleaze Cove
Leaflet published by Dorset's Important Geological/Geomorphological Sites Group (DIGS)
Trace Fossils available from the Dorset Wildlife Trust

Chapter 4 Burton Bradstock
Callomon J H and Cope J C W 1993 *The Jurassic Geology of Dorset, guide to excursions* 14-20 September 1993 University College London.
Callomon J H and Cope J C W 1995 *The Jurassic Geology of Dorset.* In (Taylor, P. D. (Ed.) *Field Geology of the British Jurassic* Geological Society London pp51-103.
Chandler R B (1982) *The first record of Staufenia (Staufenia) sehndensis (Hoffmann) in Britain.* Proceedings of the Geologists' Assocociation 93, pp301- 4.
Callomon J H and Chandler R B 1990 *A review of the ammonite horizons of the Aalenian-Lower Bajocian stages in the Middle Jurassic of Southern England.* In (Cresta S. & Pavia G.; eds) *Atti del meeting sulla stratigrafia del Baiociano.* Memorie descrittive della carta geologica d' Italia. 40, pp85-111.
Callomon J H and Chandler R B 1994 *Some early M. Jurassic ammonites of Tethyan affinities from the Aalenian of southern England.* Palaeopelagos Special Publication 1, pp17-40 8 pls.
Chandler R B & Sole D T C 1996 *The Inferior Oolite at East Hill Quarry, Bradford Abbas, Dorset.* Dorset Proceedings 117 pp101-108.
Dietze V. & Chandler R B 1997 *S. S. Buckman und der Inferior Oolite.* Fossilien 1997/4: 207-214 10 figs. Korb.
Dietze V. & Chandler R B 1998 *New Ammonites from the Zigzag Bed of Dorset.* Dorset Proceedings 119 pp109-116.
Chandler R B, Glover L and Smith D 1999 *A temporary section in the Inferior Oolite (Middle Jurassic) at Coldharbour Business Park, Dodge Cross, Sherborne.* Dorset Proceedings 120 pp69-72.
Sandoval J & Chandler R B 2000 *The sonniniid ammonite Euhoploceras from the Middle Jurassic of south-west England and southern Spain.* Palaeontology 43, part 3 pp 495-532 13 pls.
Chandler R B, Dietze V, Sommer V and Gauthier H 2001 *Remarks on the Astarte Bed (Upper Bajocian, Middle Jurassic) of Burton Bradstock (Dorset, Southern England).* Hantkeniana 3 pp 5-23, Budapest.

Chapter 9 Frampton to Compton Valence
Wilson V et al *Geology of the Country round Bridport and Yeovil* Mem. Geo. Survey of GB 1958
Putnam B 1998 *The Prehistoric Age* (Discover Dorset Series) Dovecot Press
Putnam B 2000 *The Romans* (Discover Dorset Series) Dovecot Press

Chapter 10 Hardy Monument
Leaflet published by Dorset's Important Geological/Geomorphological Sites Group (DIGS)
A Traverse across the Weymouth Anticline available from the Dorset Wildlife Trust

Chapter 12 Highcliffe to Barton
Burton E St J 1933. *Faunal horizons of the Barton Beds in Hampshire.* Proc. Geol. Assoc., Vol. 44, Pt. 2, pp.131-167
Melville R V and Freshney E C 4th Edn. 1982 *The Hampshire Basin and adjoining areas.* British Regional Geology Institute of Geological Sciences ISBN 0 11 884203X
British Caenozoic Fossils. (Tertiary and Quaternary) 5th Edn. 1975 The Natural History Museum. ISBN 0 11 310024 8

Chapter 14 Kimmeridge Bay
Cox B M and Gallois R W 1981 *The stratigraphy of the Kimmeridge Clay of the Dorset type area and its correlation with some other Kimmeridge sequences.* Rep.Inst.Geol.Sci. London 80/4 pp1-44

Chapter 17 Lyme Regis
Hallam A 1960 *A sedimentary and faunal study of the Blue Lias of Dorset.* Philosophical Transactions of the Royal Society vB243, pp1-44

Hallam A 1986 *Origin of limestone-shale cycles:climatically induced or diagenetic?* Geology v14, pp 609-612

House M R 1987 *Are Jurassic sedimentary microrhythms due to orbital forcing?* Proceedings of the Ussher Society v6 pp 299-311

Weedon G P 1985 *Hemipelagicshelf sedimentation and climatic cycles: the basal Jurassic (Blue Lias) of south Britain.* Earth and Planetary Science Letters v76 pp321-335

Weedon G P, Jenkyns H C, Coe A L & Hesselbo S P 1999 *Astronomical calibration of the Jurassic time-scale from cyclostratigraphy in British mudrock formations.* Philosophical Transactions of the Royal Society v A357 pp1787-1813

Chapter 18 Nether Compton

Bristow C R et al 1995 *Geology of the country around Shaftesbury.* Memoir for the 1:50,000 sheet 313 (England and Wales)

Fowler J 1936. *Sherborne behind the seen.* Reprinted 1986 Sherton Press ISBN 0-949002-61-5

Chapter 21 Raised Beaches of Portland Bill

D H Keen *Late Pleistocene deposits and mollusca from Portland, Dorset.* Geology Magazine 122(2) 1985 pp181/186

Chapter 26 The Chalk north and south of Shaftesbury

Bathurst R G C 1971 *Carbonate sediments and their diagenisis.* Amsterdam. Elsevier 620pp

Bromley R G and Gale A S 1982 *The lithostratigraphy of the English Chalk Rock.* Cretaceous Research 3, 273-306

Gale A S 1996 *Turonian correlation and sequence stratigraphy of the Chalk in southern England.* In (Hesselbo S P and Parkinson D N; eds.) *Sequence stratigraphy in British geology.* Special Publications of the Geological Society of London 103, 177-195

Hancock J M 1990 *Sea-level changes in the British region during the Late Cretaceous.* Proceedings of the Geologists' Association 100 (for 1989) 565-594

Hancock J M 1993 *The formation and diagenesis of chalk.* In (Downing R A, Price M and Jones G P; eds) *The Hydrology of the Chalk of north-west Europe.* Clarendon Press Oxford 14-34

Mortimore R N, Wood C J and Gallois R W 2001 *British Upper Cretaceous Stratigraphy.* Joint Nature Conservation Committee Peterborough 558pp

Walaszczyk I and Cobban W A 2000 *Inoceramid faunas and biostratigraphy of the Upper Turonian - Lower Coniacian of the Western Interior of the United States.* Special Papers in Palaeontology 64, 118pp 32pls

Chapter 27 Tout Quarry, Portland

Townsend W G 1975 *Lithostratigraphy and deposition of the type Portlandian.* Journal of the Geological Society of London v131 pp619-638

Chapter 28 Worbarrow Tout

Abbink O A, Calloman J H, Riding J B, Williams P D B and Wolfard A. 2001 *Biostratigraphy of Jurassic-Cretaceous boundary strata in the Terschelling Basin, The Netherlands.* Proceedings of the Yorkshire Geological Society 53, pp275-302

Casey R 1963 *The Dawn of the Cretaceous Period in Britain.* Bulletin of the Southeastern Union of Scientific Societies, pp115

Ensom P C 1985 *An annotated section of the Purbeck Limestone Formation Worbarrow Tout, Dorset.* Proceedings of the Dorset Natural History and Archaeological Society 106, pp. 791.

Ensom P C *Derived fossils in the Purbeck Limestone Formation, Worbarrow Tout, Dorset.* Proceedings of the Dorset Natural History and Archaeological Society 106, p66

Milner A R and Batten D J (eds.) 2002 *Life and environments in Purbeck times.* Special Papers in Palaeontology 68 268pp

West I M 1975 *Evaporites and associated sediments of the basal Purbeck Formation (Upper Jurassic) of Dorset.* Proceedings of the Geologists' Association 6, pp205-225

Index

Glossary

aerobic	aerated: strictly means containing free oxygen
alluvial fan	sediments deposited by stream/river system on reaching flatter land
Alpine Orogeny	a mountain building episode which formed the present day Alps
Alveolinidae	Family of **benthic** foraminifera
anhydrite	the anhydrous form of gypsum (=calcium sulphate)
anoxic	without oxygen
anticline	an upward fold in rock strata
argillaceous	sedimentary rock with silt to clay size particles 0.06 -<0.004mm
benthic	living on the surface of, or in, the sediment on the sea floor
biomicrite	limestone rock of tiny crystals of calcite which contains large numbers of the fossilised remains of animals or plants
biosparrudite	coarse shelly limestone with visible crystals of calcite (sparry calcite)
bioturbated	sediment which has been disturbed by the actions of animals, sometimes plants
braided	many wandering channels in a river/stream system
brickearth	fine-grained deposit from reworking of windblown material
brecciated	used to describe a rock broken into angular fragments
calcarenites	calcareous sediment in which a large proportion of the clasts are sand sized
calcitised evaporite	evaporites, in this case gypsum, which have been replaced by calcite
calcrete	limestone precipitated as surface/near surface deposit by evaporation in semi-arid climates
clast	a rock or mineral particle derived by weathering/erosion
coccoliths	calcareous plates formed by a microscopic **planktonic** plant
colluvium	unconsolidated material at the bootom of a cliff or slope
competent	a strong, well cemented rock
Conchostracans	(Clam shrimps), small shrimp-like crustaceans in a bivalved shell
concordant coastline	a coast parallel to the dominant structural trend of the area
convolute bedding	a structure where the sedimentary laminae are heavily contorted
co-ordination number	the number of negative ions round any one cation in a mineral lattice
copepods	small marine crustacea of great variety and huge numbers in all seas
corrasive	erosion by rock fragments drawn persistently across a surface
cross-bedded	structures produced by migration of bed forms with inclined surfaces
crush breccias	fault rock with angular fragments >2mm
cryoturbation	folding of sediments caused by expansion due to ice activity
current-bedding	showing where rock has been deposited by water movements
cytoplasm	the part of the cell outside of the nucleus but inside the cell wall
debris fans	sediments deposited by landslips
dedolomitisation	replacement of the Mg atoms in dolomite by Ca atoms. The Ca atoms are larger than the Mg atoms, so expansion occurs
dextral displacement	rock movement to the right, looking across the fault-plane
diagenesis	chemical, physical & biological changes in sediment after initial deposition
dinoflagellates	microscopic unicellular organisms
dip	angle of slope of beds from horizontal at 90° to the **strike**
dogger	hard, rounded well-cemented block of sediment
doline	a hollow in limestone formed by solution/subsidence of the surface
dolomitic	magnesium replacing calcite in limestone
dolomitised	replacement of calcium atoms in limestone by magnesium atoms. As the Mg atoms are smaller than the Ca atoms, shrinkage occurs
eustatic	a change of sea-level over majority of the earth
evolute	outer whorl of ammonite shell not overlapping inner whorls

fault (normal) movement in rock where the lower inclined surface has moved upward in relation to the upper inclined surface

ferruginous containing iron

fetch the extent of open water over which a wave-building wind blows, determining height/energy, thus depositional/erosional capabilities

footwall the lower of the two faces in a fault

fluvial/fluviatile referring to a river or stream

graben a dropped block between two **faults**

gulls splits, often cambered, parallel to a rock face or valley slope

Haptophyta a **phylum** of microscopic organisms of the Kingdom Protista

hardground early diagenetic **lithification** which starts as nodular centres and can form a hard surface

head deposits poorly sorted rock debris, mantling hill slopes

Hercynian/Variscan mountain building episode which affected the older rocks deep beneath Dorset *(see Introduction, page 12)*

heteromorphic ammonoids which have unusual coiling to their shells

horst an uplifted block between two **faults**

hypersaline water with a salinity much greater than that of ordinary sea water

inlier older rock surrounded by younger rock because of erosion

interlocking spurs interdigitation of valley slopes from a meandering stream in a V-shaped valley

intraclast a usually angular or sub-rounded fragment of micrite, clay or shale torn up during flooding and redeposited soon after it was lain down

inverted relief areas of high relief which have become depressions due to high erosion rates

lignite fossil wood

lithification hardening of a soft sediment by compaction, dewatering and cementation

mamillated with a rounded surface

marine transgression sea flooding over land areas because of a long term rise in sea-level

micrite a limestone rock made of crystals of calcite/aragonite mud <0.004mm

monadnock a residual feature formed after a long period of sub-aerial erosion

monocline folded strata where the rocks on each side of the steep middle limb are horizontal or gently dipping

Mya million years ago

Nivation hollow hollow produced by frost action and **solifluction** in and around a large patch of snow

non-sequence a gap in the sedimentary record shown by the absence of part of the fossil succession

ontogenesis various stages of development of an organism

oolitic/ooliths small rounded grains with a sand/shell nucleus coated with calcareous or iron compounds

orogeny a mountain building episode

orthorhombic system of crystal symmetry with three axes of unequal length at right angles

outlier younger rocks completely surrounded by older rocks *cf* **inlier**

packstone clastic limestone supported by its own grains with some calcareous mud

pencontemporaneous almost at the same time

peneplain an almost level surface resulting from long time subaerial erosion

phosphatised original mineral replaced with phosphate

phragmocone the coiled chambered sections of an ammonite *cf* belemnite

phylum the largest category into which organisms can be fitted

pipe clay a fine-grained clay important in the ceramics industry

planation	a level surface produced by long continued erosion, usually marine
planktic	floating, *i.e.* not swimming, in surface waters
plunge	the direction and angle of **dip** of the beds on the axis of a fold
poorly sorted	a mix of rock particles of many different sizes and/or materials
psammosere	the succession of vegetation that develops on sand dunes
reducing	chemical change in the sediment, relating to oxygen content/shortage
reverse fault	a fault in which the movement along the inclined fault is up-**dip**
ripple marks/trains	patterns produced in sediments by movements of water or wind
sabkha	coastal flats bordering a lagoon in regions with a semi-arid climate
septarian nodules	rounded concretions with cracks, from dewatering of the sediment during **lithification,** which are then filled with crystalline calcite. The calcite filled cracks are called septa (partition) hence the name
shear plane	where rocks have moved during a phase of intense deformation
slickensides	grooves formed on a fault plane with movement of two rock faces
solifluction	down slope movement of rock debris most effective under periglacial conditions
solution pipe	cylindrical hollow in the Chalk, formed by solution of the Chalk and usually infilled with sandy material or gravel
sparry limestone	limestone which contains a large amount of coarse, *i.e.* sparry, calcite
strike	horizontal measurement along a rock surface at 90° to the **dip**
strike fault	a fault whose direction is parallel to the **strike** of the rocks
stromatolite	a laminated, often rounded, calcareous structure built up by algae over a long period of time
superimposed	a drainage system which appears unrelated to the underlying structure, probably inherited from a since eroded rock cover
syncline	a simple downfold in strata
tectonic inlier	an outcrop of older rock surrounded by younger rock due to earth movements (tectonics) and then erosion
teleost	bony fish similar to present species
terracettes	stepped slips on a steep incline where soil has moved downhill
thrust faults	where rock slides over and above other rock
tourmalinised	medium to high temperature mineralisation in which tourmaline replaces other minerals, often associated with alteration of granite
trace fossils	fossilised evidence of life processes of plants and animals including tracks, traces and burrows associated with feeding, movement and protection
transgressive	*see marine trangression*
transverse faults	rock movement oblique to the strike of the strata
tridactyl	three toed
trigonal	crystal system with three horizontal axes and a vertical three fold axis
tufa	calcium carbonate deposited by evaporation which includes stalagmites, stalactites abd flowstone deposits
unconformably	not following in sequence of age or strata
unconformity	a surface representing a major break in a sedimentary sequence
Unio	a freshwater mussel
valley bulge	upward arching of strata, caused by frost action, along the axis of a valley
valley-in-valley	an inner valley incised within an outer valley usually because of renewed downcutting
wackestone	limestone of carbonate particles in a mud-matrix supporting texture
white chalk	very pure white **micritic** limestone mainly formed of coccoliths and Haptophyta
wrench faults	faults with lateral/horizontal displacement, with no vertical components
younging	becoming stratigraphically younger in a particular direction